the
resource
room
primer

the
resource
room
primer

Natalie Madorsky Elman

with
Janet H. Ginsberg

Prentice-Hall, Inc.
Englewood Cliffs, New Jersey 07632

Library of Congress Cataloging in Publication Data

Elman, Natalie Madorsky.
   The resource room primer.

   Bibliography: p.
   Includes index.
      1. Resource programs (Education)—Handbooks, manuals,
etc. I. Ginsberg, Janet H., joint author. II. Title.
LB1028.8.E43   371.6'21   80-20819
ISBN   0-13-774406-4

*Editorial/production supervision and interior
   design by Linda Schuman*
Cover design by Infield/D'Astolfo Associates
Manufacturing buyer: Edmund W. Leone

Printed in the United States of America

10 9 8 7 6 5 4 3 2 1

PRENTICE-HALL INTERNATIONAL, INC., *London*
PRENTICE-HALL OF AUSTRALIA PTY. LIMITED, *Sydney*
PRENTICE-HALL OF CANADA, LTD., *Toronto*
PRENTICE-HALL OF INDIA PRIVATE LIMITED, *New Delhi*
PRENTICE-HALL OF JAPAN, INC., *Tokyo*
PRENTICE-HALL OF SOUTHEAST ASIA PTE. LTD., *Singapore*
WHITEHALL BOOKS LIMITED, *Wellington, New Zealand*

*This book is dedicated to the memory of my father
who never knew how much he inspired
the writing and completion of this work
and to his grandchildren,
Susan, Michael, and Elisabeth*

contents

2

identifying children for the resource room   10

3

planning an IEP, due process, and parents' rights   39

4

setting up a resource room   67

5

getting off to a good start   78

6

planning what to teach   83

7

choosing materials and equipment for the resource room   116

8

sharing a day in the life of a resource room teacher   146

9

developing good public relations   156

10

supporting the classroom teacher   *166*

11

solving problems in the resource room   *176*

12

including the gifted and talented   *183*

13

implementing a secondary level resource room   *204*

14

administrating a resource room *228*

appendix **A**

special education state agencies and addresses *245*

appendix **B**

PL 94-142 *250*

appendix **C**

resources for teachers *270*

appendix **D**

in-service materials *280*

appendix **E**

national special education agencies and addresses *287*

index *291*

figures

forms

tables

preface

The Resource Room Primer is written to respond to a growing need in the special education field. School districts across the nation have been motivated by new federal legislation to provide new programs for handicapped children. Many districts have had special education programming for years but may find their programs in need of updating. This book responds to that need.

Although the Public Law 94-142 (PL 94-142) does not state specific guidelines, the resource room concept complies with all the criteria of the law, including providing the least restrictive environment. Much more important than just "complying" with the law, the resource room concept has been used successfully by school districts across the country. It is an excellent answer for the education of all types of handicapped and exceptional learners, from the gifted to the multiply handicapped.

The resource room concept enables handicapped children to remain in the regular classroom for most of the school day. The regular classroom teachers are able to help these children with the support they receive from the resource room teacher. The parents of the child enrolled in the program are able to feel secure knowing that their child will be educated with the mainstream of the school population while receiving additional help.

Here is a practical guide for students of special education, professors of special education, administrators, and teachers of the handicapped. Not only are practical suggestions offered on how to set up and implement a successful resource room program, but the book is filled with helpful teaching techniques and problem-solving devices that are the result of years of teaching experience. It has been designed to be a helpful, practical, easy to use book with many actual worksheets and forms ready to adapt to any resource room program. Rather than expounding upon educational theory, this book shows how to put already accepted theories into practice. The author has made a concerted effort to keep the language simple and to the point. It is written for those students and practitioners who have a special education background and are aware of the rationale for the practices and procedures needed to educate handicapped youngsters.

This book could not have been completed without the cooperation and help of many people. The photographs were taken by Brian Edgerton, and Chapter 2 was contributed by Nancy A. Tomevi, Ed.D. To the Warren Township Board of Education, Dr. Angelo Tomaso, Superintendent; Arnold Gundersen, principal of Central School where this resource room model was developed; the Warren Township Child Study Team, Lois Israel, Director; Catherine Bebbington who drew the picture of a resource room; Hadassah Horn who hand printed the learning center worksheets; Jean Rappaport who shared her editing expertise; and to all those loyal friends and relatives who gave help, encouragement, and support, a warm and sincere THANK YOU!

Above all, I extend heartfelt thanks and appreciation to Stanley Elman, whose love, encouragement, and support were always there.

the
resource
room
primer

all about
resource rooms

1

WHAT IS A RESOURCE ROOM?

"A resource room is any setting in the school to which a child comes to receive specific instruction on a regularly scheduled basis, while receiving the major part of his/her education elsewhere (usually in a regular or special class program)" (Weiderholt, p. 4).

The new federal legislation called PL 94-142 mandates under least restrictive environment 121a.500 that

> . . . to the maximum extent appropriate, handicapped children, including children in public or private institutions or other care facilities, are educated with children who are not handicapped, and that special classes, separate schooling, or other removal of handicapped children from the regular educational environment occurs only when the nature or severity of the handicap is such that education in regular classes with the use of supplementary aids and services cannot be achieved satisfactorily. . .

Section 121a.5 defines *handicapped* as follows:

> . . . those children evaluated . . . as being mentally retarded, hard of hearing, deaf, speech impaired, visually handicapped, seriously emotionally disturbed, orthopedically impaired, deaf-blind, multi-handicapped, or as having specific learning disabilities, who because of those impairments need special education and related services.

The terms used within this definition are further defined in the regulations. (See Appendix B.)

Thus, a child who is enrolled in a resource room program will be mainstreamed into the regular school program in response to PL 94-142. The terms *mainstreaming* and *resource room* go hand in hand. A handicapped child who is enrolled in a regular classroom but goes out for resource room instruction is mainstreamed. This instruction is varied and individualized for each child. It may consist of the child's reading program which cannot be carried out in the regular classroom or reinforcement of the reading instruction that takes place in the classroom. Skills like auditory memory, auditory discrimination, spelling, handwriting, self-expression, improved self-image, language usage, visual discrimination, and visual memory are just some of the things taught in the resource room. The kinds of skills that can be taught or reinforced in a resource room program are varied and geared toward each individual's problems and abilities.

The important thing is that handicapped children who are able to handle a regular classroom program with resource room backup are kept in the mainstream of school life. It must be emphatically stated that *not all* handicapped children can gain the maximum benefit from a mainstreamed situation. There are handicapped youngsters who learn best in a smaller group with fewer distractions, and these children would not be candidates for a resource room program. The structure that a well-planned self-contained special education class can provide is essential to the learning process for some handicapped children. This, then, would be the "least restrictive environment" for those children.

Each child's own unique learning style, handicap, and personality must be considered before the best program can be chosen. The resource room is designed to benefit a wide variety of handicapped students and can include those with specific learning disabilities, emotional difficulties, slow functioning, physical handicaps, and visual or auditory impairments.

Mainstreaming with a resource room program is one good solution to educating some handicapped children. If mainstreaming will produce a successful learning situation, then that is the best alternative for that child.

Some parents fear placement into special education because of an implied stigma. They often fear that their child will not receive a quality education, which means "like everyone else," or that their child will be shunned by others and never "get out" of special education.

The resource room program answers this problem in many ways. The most reassuring aspect for parents is the continuation of the regular classroom assignment. Parents are assured that their children will continue to enjoy their peer group and participate in a regular curriculum that has been tailored to meet each child's needs. There is no opportunity for parents to think their child will be ostracized, labeled, or hidden away.

The resource room teacher, in contrast to a self-contained special education classroom teacher, is able to concentrate on each child's deficits. He/she does not have to juggle lessons in social studies, science, health, and so on with a classroom of children who have a variety of learning problems. The resource room teacher's schedule allows time to meet with other teachers, visit classrooms, and keep records. Not only does the resource room teacher benefit from a more efficient use of pupil/teacher time, but the child benefits greatly from this concentrated effort.

The classroom teacher also benefits from the support, both moral and educational, received from the resource room teacher. The classroom teacher no longer has to feel total responsibility for the progress of the learning disabled student. This is now shared. The resource room provides both program backup and actual materials to be used in the classroom. If necessary the resource room teacher can spend planning periods in a particular classroom to help a child adjust. The help that a good resource room program can offer is limitless.

There are no specific guidelines in PL 94-142 governing a resource room program. This allows each school district flexibility in determining which type of program best fits the needs of its handicapped population. Each district must refer to its own state's special education legislation for guidelines.

The resource room program described in this book provides services in such a way that many handicapped children can stay in a regular class-room with resource room help and derive maximum benefit from their education. Adaptations can also be made to modify this program to many of the types of resource rooms that will be discussed in this chapter.

A resource room program may have different titles. It may be called a learning lab, a workshop, a remediation center, an instructional service center, a help room, a teaching room, a resource room, or many other similar names. These programs all have one common element. They provide support services for children enrolled in a regular school program. This support can be offered in a number of ways, as discussed below.

WHAT ARE THE DIFFERENT TYPES OF RESOURCE ROOMS?

Traveling Resource Room

This program provides a resource room teacher for two or more schools. The program may be elaborate enough to have a special room set up at each school for the resource room teacher to use or as spartan as a briefcase of materials that the resource room teacher carries from school to school. Financially, this type of system may be the most efficient in school districts with few handicapped children.

There are many drawbacks to the traveling resource room. Because there is no permanent staff member, the carry-over or continued support to the classroom teacher is limited. There is also a disadvantage in not having the room and teacher available for crisis intervention or a "time-out" room for problem children. In a traveling resource room setup, the teacher is not available to help with ongoing problems. This is not advantageous for the child or the regular classroom teacher. A stationary room, attractively set up with a full-time teacher has more impact than a drop-in teacher. Because we are dealing with the attitudes of the staff and the children, an itinerant program, though better than no program at all, is far from ideal.

Materials and Methods Type

This is a program set up strictly as a resource for teachers. The materials are checked out for use with the children in the regular classroom. In some resource rooms of this type, the resource room teacher also helps the regular classroom teacher with programming and monitoring of the children's progress. In this model the resource room teacher does not do remedial work with the children on an ongoing basis although he/she may do short-term tutoring as the need arises. Often this type of program is shared by several schools, and its services are limited.

⋇Combination Classroom Program

In this program a full-time teacher runs a self-contained classroom for learning disabled children and a "drop-in" center for mainstreamed students. In other words, some children are assigned to this classroom for a full day, and some are assigned for short blocks of time either daily or several times a week. This type of program is an ambitious one and must be planned accordingly. It is a taxing program for the resource room teacher and can be distracting for the children. Often a program of this type does not afford the time necessary for efficient programming.

⌣ Full-Time Resource Room Program

The full-time, permanently established resource room is the model that is most preferred. It incorporates the materials and methods type into a full-time resource room program. It is a program that offers direct remedial, new skill, and reinforcement teaching for the learning disabled. It also serves as a resource to the rest of the school because it provides materials and programming ideas to the regular staff for the children enrolled in the program. It can also serve as a time-out room for problem children, a parent educating center, an ongoing conference center, and, when needed, a "gripe" center. When properly established and implemented the full-time resource room can aid in destigmatizing special education programs.

There are many different types of full-time resource rooms.

Resource Room for One-Type Handicap.   These resource rooms are set up to serve one specific handicap, for instance, a resource room for the emotionally disturbed or for the physically handicapped. They are sometimes utilized in larger school districts or in multidistrict cooperative programs which enroll many handicapped children. The children are able to be enrolled in regular classes and utilize the resource room on a part-time basis. Special self-contained classes are set up for those handicapped children who cannot benefit from this program.

The advantage of this type of program is the ability to concentrate programming. Program planning and grouping children become more individualized. Smaller districts often cannot support such a specialized resource room program. They have neither the funds nor the population to justify this approach. Furthermore, there is the belief that sometimes a more diverse group of children working together provides a more enriched environment for the child.

Resource Room for a Variety of Handicapped Children. This program includes those handicapped students who can function in a regular classroom but need additional support for a variety of reasons. This type of resource room does not provide for handicapped children requiring a self-contained program. The children served by this type of resource room might include those physically handicapped, emotionally disturbed, perceptually handicapped, communication handicapped, visual and hearing impaired, learning disabled, mentally retarded, and so on.

Limited Focus Resource Room. This resource room concentrates on a specific subject area. It might focus on language arts, or math, or science, or any one subject area. The decision to provide this type of resource room is based on the following:

1. The needs of all the children being served
2. The existence of other funded programs in the schools that are available to handicapped children (that is, Title I programs, state compensatory programs, and so on)
3. The size of the entire school population
4. The scheduling problems unique to each school.

The advantages of this type of program include being able to concentrate the planning and activities for one learning area. This can make teaching more efficient and concentrated for specific deficits.

The main disadvantage is that a child who needs remediation for more than one subject area may have to leave the regular classroom frequently to accommodate scheduling problems for more than one program. For example, the child might have resource room for language arts from 10:00 to 10:30 and Title I for math from 1:00 to 1:30. This approach also necessitates the child's adjusting to the personality of an additional teacher.

Multifocus Resource Room. Rather than focusing on one learning area such as language arts or math, a multifocus resource room accommodates all subject areas that need to be reinforced or remediated. This means the child can be remediated in several subject areas in one program. By careful scheduling and good planning of group time and independent activities, this type of room can work most effectively.

The disadvantages are: Increased planning time is needed for classroom teacher conferences and for the resource room teacher to plan lessons on a wider variety of subject areas. Also, the resource room teacher must be skilled in teaching each additional subject.

Dividing the time for children who need more than one area of remediation can be handled in several ways. One way is to teach reading or language arts on Monday, Wednesday, and Friday and math and science on Tuesday and Thursday. You would then schedule accordingly. Another way is to split your lesson time. This is only effective if all the children in the group are deficit in the same areas and are on basically the same levels.

Chapter 4 on setting up a resource room gives some important points about scheduling. Also, having a variety of learning centers set up in this type of room to accommodate both subject areas and different skill levels will help students use their time productively.

Group Instruction Approach. Children are scheduled in groups for resource room instruction based upon the similarity of their needs. This type of program often does not have children working independently. This means that reinforcement of learned skills must be taken care of either at home or in the regular classroom. The children usually attend the resource room in short blocks of time for instruction only, and in this situation the resource room teacher will often have to vary the activities in one session to allow for the short attention spans of some children.

One-to-One Approach. In the one-to-one approach, the child and the teacher work for a given period of time to remediate or to learn new skills. This approach would not be efficient for a large resource room population. There are some children who learn best in a one-to-one situation, but just as often, children are well served in small groups, where the input of the others can be a positive reinforcement. Members of a small group can also give valuable feedback to the child on his/her behavior, which can serve as further reinforcement.

Learning Center Approach. Learning centers may be used to reinforce the skills of some while others are working in a group with the teacher. The best learning centers are self-directing. That is, the student can understand what to do without much teacher assistance. The centers are assigned to the children either on a weekly plan or on a daily plan. By evaluating the center work done each day, the teacher and the child can assess whether a skill has been mastered. This type of programming affords good flexibility in scheduling and activity design. More children can be accommodated at one time, and a wider variety of skills can be learned simultaneously.

Dual Track Resource Room. This program is primarily for handicapped children but also includes services for the gifted and talented. A dual track program can utilize any of the types mentioned earlier. The inclusion of gifted and talented students for even a small amount of time encourages acceptance of a resource room program. Often, children who looked down on special programming are eager to be included in the gifted and talented program. It also gives the resource room teacher a good opportunity to broaden his/her teaching experience. In addition, the gifted and talented students are involved in a worthwhile program giving them an opportunity to share their talents with others. Though there may be more work in planning and implementing this type of program, the benefits are many. Chapter 12, "Including the Gifted and Talented," contains more information about implementing this type of program.

WHO TEACHES A RESOURCE ROOM?

In most states a certified teacher of the handicapped is required to teach a resource room, but this varies according to state law. Some states require individual certification for each handicap taught. However, there are other states which are not as demanding about special requirements for teachers of the handicapped in a resource room. Each state's special education legislation must be analyzed so that the resource room teacher's certification is in compliance with state law. Specific requirements for resource room teacher certification are not included in PL 94-142. (See Appendix B—PL 94-142.)

WHAT AGE GROUPS USE A RESOURCE ROOM?

Resource rooms can be used in elementary schools, middle schools, high schools, and even colleges. The very concept of a resource room being a place to come to for special help can be utilized wherever people learn. This book describes a program to be utilized in an elementary school with modifications for secondary levels. These methods have been successfully used with kindergarten through high school students.

HOW EFFECTIVE IS THE RESOURCE ROOM APPROACH?

Wiederholt, Hammill, and Brown, in *The Resource Teacher: A Guide to Effective Practices,* succinctly stated the values associated with the resource room concept.

1. Students can benefit from specific resource support while remaining integrated with their friends and age-mates in the school.
2. The resource teacher has an opportunity to help more children than does a full-time special class teacher. This is especially true when the resource teacher provides indirect services to children with mild or moderate problems by consulting extensively with their teachers.
3. Resource programs are less expensive to operate than special self-contained classes.
4. Because young children with mild, though developing, problems can be accommodated, later severe disorders may be prevented.

5. Flexible scheduling means that remediation can be applied entirely in the classrooms by the regular teacher with some resource support or in another room by the resource program personnel when necessary; also, the schedule can be quickly altered to meet the children's changing situations and needs.

6. Since the resource program will absorb most of the handicapped children in the schools, the self-contained special education classes will increasingly become instructional settings for truly and relatively severely handicapped students, the children for whom the classes were originally developed.

7. Because of the resource teacher's broad experience with many children exhibiting different educational and behavioral problems, he/she may in time become an in-house consultant to the school.

8. Because the noncategorical approach avoids labeling and segregation, it minimizes the stigma that might be associated with receiving special help.

9. Since many elementary schools are large enough to accommodate one or more noncategorical resource teachers, most students can receive help in their neighborhood school; thus, the necessity of busing handicapped children across the town or county to a school that houses an appropriately labeled class or resource program is eliminated or at least reduced.

10. Because placement in the resource program is an individual school matter involving the principal, the teachers, and the parents, no appreciable time lapse need occur between the teacher's referral and the initiation of special services for the child.

11. In the noncategorical alternative, medical and psychological workups are done only at the school's specific request, rather than on a generalized screening-for-placement basis; thus, the school psychologist is freed to do the work that he/she was trained to do instead of being relegated to the role of psychometrist. [Note: This point is subject to regulations in each state's special education legislation.]

The support of the regular school staff is vital to the success of all the resource room programs described. Whenever possible, this should include the availability of backup materials to the regular classroom. In each one of the programs described, the resource room teacher should be available to the regular classroom teacher on a consultant basis.

The resource room program described further on in this book will be a full-time program servicing children with a variety of handicaps. It will be utilizing a learning center approach, and the subjects covered will be multifocused. The inclusion of a gifted and talented program (dual track) is recommended, and its implementation is shown in Chapter 12.

An attempt will be made to show step-by-step how a successful resource room can be set up and maintained. Modifications of the program can be easily adapted by the reader.

REFERENCES

Wiederholt, J. L., D. Hammill, and V. Brown, *The Resource Teacher: A Guide to Effective Practices*, pp. 10–11. Boston, Mass.: Allyn & Bacon, 1978.

Nancy A. Tomevi, Ed.D.

identifying children for the resource room

2

THE RESOURCE ROOM TEACHER'S ROLE
IN IDENTIFYING STUDENTS WHO ATTEND
THE RESOURCE ROOM

Th screening and identification of students who can profit from resource room instruction is an important first step. The role of the resource room teacher in this process varies. In some states, the resource room teacher is expected to screen and identify students who are possible referrals for resource room enrollment. In other states, certified educational evaluators are assigned to this task.

Regardless of the personnel used to implement this procedure, there are specific activities that can facilitate screening and identification. This chapter will describe procedures that can prepare classroom teachers, school staff, and parents to assist in the screening and identification that can lead to testing procedures and program placement.

In order to properly identify and place children in a resource room program, several important questions must be answered.

1. *What population will your resource room serve?* Will it serve learning disabled students, multihandicapped students, or a mixture of students with mild handicapping conditions? Usually, a resource room program will not be able to serve all handicapped students in a particular school or district effectively. (See Chapter 1.)
2. *What are the general characteristics of the particular students to be served?* What is their age range, disability group, cognitive ability level, academic achievement level, behavioral attributes, and so on?
3. *What are the criteria for a student to be enrolled in the resource room program?* For example,
    a. Two years below current grade level placement on standardized test
    b. Teacher recommendation
    c. Study team recommendation
    d. Parental request?

These questions may be answered in your state handbook of special education rules and regulations. Become familiar with the laws governing the resource room programs in your state.

It is a good idea to have written criteria of guidelines for the resource room program to be distributed to the teaching/administrative staff. These written guidelines should state the following in clear terms:

1. Who the resource room will serve
2. How the students will be selected
3. How the students will be scheduled
4. To whom the resource room teacher will report (the building principal, the special education director, members of the special service team, and so on).

STAFF INVOLVEMENT

Once the administrative details relating to the resource room program have been clearly defined, it is time for the resource room teacher to know the other teachers and staff members with whom he/she will be working. The development of positive staff–resource room teacher relationships is an important prerequisite for a successful screening and identification program. It is extremely important that the resource room teacher be able to describe clearly the objectives of the resource room program to classroom teachers. Once the classroom teachers are convinced that the resource room program can be of benefit to their students, the job of screening and identification for the resource room program has begun.

The classroom teacher is an excellent resource person to screen potential resource room students. The classroom teacher recommendation procedure can be done informally: Who is having difficulty in your room? What seems to be the student's problem? Why are you concerned? If the informal approach is used, it is a good idea to jot down a few notes concerning the teacher's comments about the student either during your conversation or when you return to the resource room. This will help you to organize the student's problem areas as well as the classroom teacher's areas of concern. Once the classroom teacher's list of children with problems is established, it is recommended that the resource room teacher review the student's school records (achievement tests, reading tests) and correlate the teacher's comments and concerns with the records available. A sample format for this procedure follows:

Student *John Smith*   Teacher *Jones*   Grade *4*   Date *9/79*

Teacher Comment	*Standardized Test Results*
1. reading is poor	2.3 (Iowa: 4/78)
2. disrupts class	none
3. incomplete homework	none
4. good math computations	5.5 (WRAT: 4/78)

Resource Room teacher comment: *individual reading assessment. Possible R.R. student for reading.*
Follow up: Tested 10/6/79—Spache. Needs comprehension remediation. Schedule for R.R. 4x per week; 1/2 hr. individual session. (Comprehension score—2.8)
Progress: Spache—5/20/80 Comprehension 3.6
Recommendation: Re-check comp. level 9/80.

This type of information can be placed on an index card and filed alphabetically by student. In this manner, the resource room teacher has a screening and identification instrument that is quick, easily referred to, and can provide a "waiting list" of those pupils who may profis from resource room instruction later on.

Another example of classroom teacher assistance in screening and identifying possible students for a resource room program is the classroom teacher checklist. (See Forms 2–1, 2–2, and 2–3.) If the checklist approach is used, it is vital that the classroom teacher understand how to use the checklist and what it is to accomplish. For example, informal screening in the form of checklists is only one step in the identification of a student's special needs.

It may help to think of the total process in the following sequence:

1. Screening
2. Identification of special needs
3. Diagnostic evaluation
4. Evaluation of program needs
5. Program placement

It is important that administrators, school staff, and parents be informed each step of the way.

It is the responsibility of the resource room teacher to outline the parameters of the resource room screening and identification program to a particular staff before distributing a checklist. (Do not place the checklist in teacher mailboxes and expect to get back usable information the next Monday morning!) Instead, plan an in-service program to explain the screening system to the staff. *Be sure the administrator in charge of the staff is aware of your plans.*

Regardless of the particular resource room model being implemented or the screening procedure used, some points should be constantly held in mind.

1. A screening program must be flexible and suit the particular needs of the district and/or school that the resource room will serve. For example, the screening procedure for a rural district, where the resource room will service a variety of children with special needs, will of necessity be a different screening procedure than the one used in a large suburban district with a variety of special education services. Tailor the resource room screening program to fit the needs of the local school setting.

2. The screening procedure for the resource room must be clearly stated and understood by the administrative staff, classroom teachers, and the parents. A screening is only the first step toward resource room enrollment. All students screened will not be enrolled in the resource room program.

3. It is important that the school staff understands that the screening process can be initiated at any time through a request or a referral. Do not assume that because a particular school population has been screened in September, the screening process is finished. Problems arise; new students enroll in school. It is a good idea to establish a procedure whereby the school secretary (or others involved in enrolling students) notifies the resource room teacher

CLASSROOM ADJUSTMENT RATING SCALE
IDENTIFICATION SCREENING

Child's Name_____Date_____

Section I: Please rate every item on the following scale:

    1 = not a problem   3 = moderate problem 5 = very serious problem
    2 = very mild problem 4 = serious problem

Child's Classroom Behavior:
____disruptive in class
____fidgety, hyperactive, can't stay in seat
____talks out of turn, disturbs others while they are working
____constantly seeks attention, "clowns around"
____overly aggressive to peers, (fights, is overbearing, belligerent)
____defiant, obstinate, stubborn
____impulsive, is unable to delay
____withdrawn
____shy, timid
____does not make friends
____over conforms to rules
____daydreams, is preoccupied, "off in another world"
____unable to express feelings
____anxious
____worried, frightened, tense
____depressed
____cries easily, pouts, sulks
____does not trust others
____shows signs of "nervousness" specify:_____
____specific fears specify:_____

Other Behaviors:
____lacks self-confidence
____overly sensitive to criticism
____reacts poorly to disappointment
____depends too much on others
____pretends to be ill
____poor grooming or personal hygiene
____other, specify:_____

Child's Academic Performance:
____underachieving (not working up to potential
____poorly motivated to achieve
____poor work habits
____difficulty following directions
____poor concentration, limited attention span
____motor coordination problem
____other, specify:_____

Child's Performance in Specific Academic Areas: (Please rate each item from 1 to 5 as above.)
____reading____math____numbers
____writing____colors____concepts
____language skills problems, specify:_____

Section II

From your experiences with this child, please check (√) any of the following which you believe relate to the problems you have reported:

____separation or divorce of parents
____illness or death of a family member
____lack of educational stimulation in the home

____economic difficulties
____under family pressure to succeed
____family difficulties

Section III

From your experiences with this child, please check (√) where he/she would lie on the following dimensions taking into account the direction of each item:

Know child well						Barely know child
1	2	3	4	5	6	7

Child seems easy to like				Child seems difficult to like		
1	2	3	4	5	6	7

Child has significant school adjustment problems				Child has no school adjustment problems		
1	2	3	4	5	6	7

FORM 2-1 (Developed by Raymond P. Lorion, Emory L. Cowen, Robert A. Caldwell, and the staff of the Primary Mental Health Project, Center for Community Study, University of Rochester, Rochester, New York.)

```
                          42 POINT LIST
           IDENTIFICATION OF PUPILS HAVING PROBLEMS THAT ADVERSELY
                      AFFECT THEIR LEARNING

Please identify any of your pupils who:

   1.  Wear glasses or have been identified as having a visual problem.
       a.  _____  Problem with glasses.
       b.  _____  Problem without glasses.

   2.  Seem nearsighted or farsighted beyond a slight deviation from what
       would be expected.

   3.  Have observable irregularities, such as crossed-eyes, running eyes,
       etc., that seem to interfere with their learning.

   4.  Appear to rub their eyes excessively.

   5.  Demonstrate abnormal or overstrained postures during reading or who
       read their materials by placing them too close to their eyes or who
       lose their place.

   6.  Have more than the expected amount of difficulty expected for
       his grade in words, sentences, or names.

   7.  Seem to have difficulty in recognizing colors expected for their
       age group.

   8.  Consistently use inappropriate grammatical construction with spoken
       or written communication.
       a.  _____  Difficulty due to bilingualism.
       b.  _____  Difficulty due to other factors.

   9.  Hear spoken language but appear to have more than an average amount
       of difficulty understanding what is said.
       a.  _____  Difficulty due to bilingualism.
       b.  _____  Difficulty due to other factors.

  10.  Consistently answer questions in awkward or incoherent ways.
       a.  _____  Difficulty due to bilingualism.
       b.  _____  Difficulty due to other factors.

  11.  Wear hearing aids or have been identified as having hearing problems
       that interfere with learning.

  12.  Usually turn their heads to one side when listening.

  13.  Have chronic soreness or running ears requiring more than average
       amount of medical attention.

  14.  Do not relate well to their peers, or who appear excessively quiet,
       withdrawn, nervous, or depressed.

  15.  Appear to have excessive amount of fear and anxiety.

  16.  Are consistently aggressive.

  17.  Are consistently more explosive than expected.
```

FORM 2-2   (1976 Handout, Teaching Children with Special Needs. [Original source unknown.])

18. Have been identified as having emotional or social problems that may affect their learning.

19. Appear to have a "flat" personality, a seeming inability to warmly respond.

20. Receive regularly prescribed medication for seizures or behavior control.

21. Appear to have an excessively short attention span for age group.

22. Are retarded in reading or arithmetic more than one year for their expected grade.

23. Are oversize or undersize more than one year for the average of your class.

24. Are overage or underage more than one year for the average of your class.

25. Have more than an average amount of difficulty in remembering things, or in their ability to solve problems.

26. Require more than an average amount of repetition and drill in acquiring new concepts, or who have less than an average amount of vocabulary.

27. Have been clinically identified as retarded individuals by one or more individual tests of intelligence.

28. Appear excessively inflexible to change of activities.

29. Seem way out or lost, or who learn at an abnormally much slower rate than expected.

30. Consistently appear not to want to learn.

31. Consistently appear not to live up to their potential.

32. Just cannot see the point.

33. Consistently cannot see the whole picture (concept, idea).

34. Have a physical or chronic health problem which consistently affects their learning.

35. Are receiving homebound instruction or regular private tutoring for learning problems.

36. Have speech problems with what they are saying and/or that produce some type of unacceptable behavior. (Disregard bilingualism.)

37. Have speech patterns that call more than an average amount of attention to them.

38. Have been or are currently enrolled in a speech therapy program.

FORM 2–2   (cont.)

39. Have greater than average problems with balance, coordination, or movement.

40. Are too easily frustrated, who give up too easily, or who are socially immature for their age.

41. Consistently appear to be highly distractable.

42. Have been identified by appropriate personnel who are awaiting special placement.

FORM 2–2 (cont.)

TEACHER'S CHECKLIST ON LEARNING DISABILITIES
For Regular Classroom Above Grade One

This is an observational checklist. Do not use those items above child's
developmental/grade level. If the preponderance of checks are in columns
3 and 4, refer the child to your school district psychologist for a thorough
educational/diagnostic evaluation.

Child's Name_____Date_____
Grade_____Age_____Teacher_____

	1 Never	2 Sometimes	3 Frequently	4 Always
Reads word-by-word				
Reads below grade level				
Mispronounces words				
Has difficulty in closing words vocally				
Gets mixed up on sound/symbol associations				
Cannot rhyme words				
Cannot remember words				
Reverses words in reading				
Leans forward when reading				
Loses place when reading				
Forgets what he has read				
Prefers to print				
Has poor eye tracking skills				
Slumps forward when writing				
Cannot copy from chalkboard to paper				
Prints from bottom to top of each letter/number				
Cannot draw basic geometric shapes				
Slants letters inconsistently				
Spaces poorly between letters/words				
Cocks head incorrectly when writing				
Forgets formation of letters				
Has difficulty staying on the line				
Grasps pencil improperly				
Reverses words/letters when writing				
Cannot tell time to the hour				
Cannot tell time to the minute				
Shows poor one-to-one correspondence				
Cannot recall basic math facts through 10				
Cannot recall basic math facts through 20				
Arithmetic skills below grade level				
Forgets specific arithmetic processes seemingly known				
Uses fingers or other devices to count				
Unable to draw a human figure in proportion				
Gets letters out of order when spelling				
Quickly forgets spelling words				
Spells same word two different ways in same report, essay, or letter				

FORM 2-3 (Academic Therapy Publications, 20 Commercial Boulevard, Novato, California
94947.)

	1 Never	2 Sometimes	3 Frequently	4 Always
Confuses sounds when spelling				
Cannot recall sequence of syllables				
Spells below grade level				
Has a speech problem (lisp, articulatory, substitution)				
Draws poorly				
Spells phonetically				
Uses bizarre spellings				
Is awkward				
Does unpresentable work				
"Blows up" easily				
Cries easily when upset				
Has poor peer relationships				
Gets confused when given a series of auditory directions				
Does not know left and right on himself				
Does not know left and right on others				
Shows poor coordination				
Is inattentive				
Disturbs others				
Is rigid physically				
Alternates use of hands for activities				

FORM 2–3 (cont.)

of new enrollments. In this way, the resource room teacher can quickly scan the student's previous records and reports to identify a need for immediate screening procedures.

Once you have completed a screening procedure and identified the students who appear to be in need of further diagnostic testing, plan to see these students in their classroom setting. If at all possible, observe the students in the classroom during the periods when the students demonstrate their greatest strengths as well as their greatest weaknesses. Here again, the resource room teacher needs to be a good observer. It will help to keep a checklist of student behaviors, class activities, and materials that seem to be difficult or easy for the students. (See Checklist Forms 2–4 and 2–5.) Review your observations and questions with the classroom teacher following the observation period. Perhaps the two of you can identify some changes in the classroom activities that will contribute to a better learning situation for the student within the classroom setting. (See Chapter 10.)

Following the classroom observation, it may be decided that diagnostic testing is needed. If so, arrange a testing schedule as soon as possible. In order to arrange individual evaluation of a student for possible resource room enrollment, parental permission for testing is necessary. Here is where your contact with classroom teachers, screening notes, and classroom observation notes are important.

REFERRAL PROCEDURE

At this point, it is necessary to understand the referral system in your particular school setting. Remember, before a child can become involved in testing for possible placement in the resource room program, parents or guardians must be notified of this action. This writer has found the following procedures to work effectively. (See Table 2–1—sample outline of the referral procedure [p. 25]. This outline should be clearly understood by teaching staff, administrators, and parents.)

1. Work with the classroom teacher to complete the formal referral form used in your school or district. (See Form 2–6, pp. 27–28.) The reason(s) for the referral must be clearly and objectively stated on the referral form (for example, John is reading below his current grade level placement as measured by the Iowa group test, or John's math scores in his current math series mastery tests are below expectancy for his grade and level placement).

2. After the referral form is completed by the classroom teacher and/or other staff members working with the student, the written referral should be sent to the school principal. It is imperative that the principal "know what's going on in the building." If this step is not included in your current referral procedures, ask that it be included.

INFORMAL OBSERVATION CHECKLIST

The following are some things you might observe during informal observations. Under each heading are just a few key behaviors which might indicate that a particular problem exists. What are some other behaviors which you have observed in each of those areas? Please list them under the appropriate heading.

Reading - Informal Observations

Visual Difficulties

1. Visual discrimination problems
   a. The child confuses letters or words which appear similar
   b. The child fails to note internal detail and confuses words such as beg for bog
   c. The child fails to see general configurations of words such as ship for snip

2. Rate of perception is slow
   a. The child is a word-by-word reader
   b. The child hesitates at each word
   c. The child fails to recognize pictures or words presented at a rapid rate

3. Difficulty following and retaining visual sequences
   a. The child fails to duplicate patterns from a model-- distortions of order occur
   b. The child may reproduce a sequence when a model is present but cannot revisualize the sequence from memory

4. Visual memory disorders
   a. The child fails to remember what he/she wore the previous day
   b. The child fails to remember words seen previously

5. Visual analysis and synthesis
   a. The child fails to divide words into syllables
   b. The child fails to put words back together which have been divided into syllables

6. Prefers auditory activities
   a. The child memorizes stories that have been heard but cannot read the story

Auditory Difficulties

1. Auditory discrimination
   a. The child fails to hear similarities in words which have the same beginning, medial, or ending sounds
   b. The child fails to hear the double sounds of consonant blends such as rust and reads and spells it as rut
   c. The child fails to discriminate short vowel sounds heard in isolation--the child recognizes the differences in the words pin, pen, pan when seen but not when heard in isolation
   d. The child cannot think of rhymming words
   e. The child cannot listen for prefixes and suffixes and think of other words with similar endings.

FORM 2-4 (Teaching Children with Special Needs; Maryland State Department of Education; Division of Instructional Television Seminar Program, State Department of Maine; David Stockford, Consultant, Department of Educational/Cultural Services, Augusta, Maine 04333.)

2. Auditory analysis and synthesis
   a. The child cannot break a word into syllables or blend individual sounds into whole words

3. Reauditorize sounds or words
   a. The child cannot remember the sounds that letters make
   b. The child may recognize a word visually but cannot remember how to say it
   c. The child substitutes words although meaning may be retained-- "The puppy is eating the food" for "The dog is eating his dinner."

4. Auditory sequencing
   a. The child cannot follow a rhythm pattern
   b. The child distorts pronunciation of multisyllable words such as emeny for enemy
   c. The child transposes letters when writing because he/she cannot retain a sequence of sounds

5. Prefers visual activities

Written Language

Handwriting

1. The child can speak and read but cannot execute the motor patterns necessary for forming letters, numbers, or words

2. The child can copy but cannot use written symbols for purposeful communication

3. The child forms the letters inaccurately

4. The child uses irregular spacing between letters and words

Language

1. The child makes frequent spelling errors

2. The child cannot properly select and organize words into sentences

3. The child omits words and/or word endings

4. The child uses improper verb tenses and pronouns

5. The child distorts the order of words within sentences

6. The child exhibits better language when writing than when speaking

7. The child exhibits better language when speaking than when writing

Auditory Language

Receptive Language

1. The child is unable to follow verbal directions

FORM 2-4 (cont.)

2. The child scores low on tests given orally

3. The child may understand nouns but not words that represent
    actions, qualities, feelings, or ideas

4. The child may attend to short sequences of verbal material but
    tunes out lengthy verbal instructions

Expressive Language

1. Reauditorization
    a. The child cannot remember words for spontaneous usage
    b. The child hesitates and pauses frequently during oral
        communication
    c. The child avoids oral communication and relates ideas
        through gesture
    d. The child communicates in short phrases
    e. The child fails to express abstract ideas

2. Defective syntax
    a. The child tends to omit words
    b. The child distorts the order of words
    c. The child uses incorrect verb tenses and makes other
        grammatical errors

FORM 2-4   (cont.)

Observation Sheet

Date	Name	Behavior	Time	Situation

FORM 2-5

3. Once the principal has reviewed the referral, the parents/guardians of the student referred must be notified. It is preferable that the teacher, principal, or resource room teacher contact the parents/guardians and arrange an appointment to "discuss John's school program" or "to review John's performance on a recent school screening procedure."

4. When the parents/guardians arrive for their appointment, be organized and prepared to present the screening results, an overview of classroom behaviors listed on the referral form, and recommendations as to the next step in the process: further identification procedures or diagnostic evaluations. If parents/guardians are involved in the initial identification process, they often are more supportive of the program. At this meeting, review screening records, standardized group scores, and any other relevant information with the student's parents/guardians and ask for their input regarding the observations you describe. This is a good time to obtain their written permission for individual testing of the student. Explain to them that this testing does not mean that their student will be enrolled in a special program, only that the student will be considered for enrollment based on the results of further observation and testing.

5. Give the parent/guardians a definite time span within which the student will be evaluated, and arrange a tentative appointment time for them to return to the school to review the student's test results. Stick to this schedule. Remember, once a possible problem has been identified, parents/guardians are anxious and concerned about the testing results. So are students. Do not increase their anxiety with unnecessary delay in this procedure.

Table 2-1   Student Referral Process*

The following is intended to serve as a guide to facilitate the student referral process.

Step I–Pre-referral stage

Process: Principal, teachers, and study team members meet at the building level on a regular basis to discuss possible referrals

Outcome: Classroom teacher knows what to do next with students under consideration

Step II–Referral stage

Process: Teacher completes referral form on student(s) recommended for referral in Step I and meets with parents

Outcome: Completed referral form has the signatures of parents, building principal, and classroom teacher and is forwarded to the study team by the building principal

Step III–Study Team stage

Process: Study team receives referral, notifies parents that referral has been received, and assigns responsibilities for diagnostic evaluation

Outcome: Diagnostic assessment of student under referral can begin

Table 2-1 (cont.)

Step IV–Diagnostic stage

    Process: All diagnostic assessments are conducted (formal and informal evaluations)

    Outcome: Recommendations based on diagnostic assessments are made by those conducting the assessments

Step V–Recommendation stage

V-A Process: Study team, principal, teachers and parents meet to discuss recommendations made as result of diagnostic assessments

    Outcome: 1. Recommendations for program are developed as result of group discussion

                2. Recommendations are sent to the Superintendent of Schools for approval

V-B Process: Study team or study team representative, and parents meet to discuss all approved recommendations for the student involved

    Outcome: Parents understand and support study team recommendations

Step VI–Implementation stage

VI-A Process: Appropriate staff personnel, study team members, teachers, etc., and parents meet to develop an I.E.P. (Individual Educational Plan) for the student

    Outcome: I.E.P. is completed

VI-B Process: I.E.P. is implemented by placing student in appropriate special program or making necessary adjustments in regular classroom routine

    Outcome: Recommendations for student program are implemented

Step VII–Program Review stage

    Process: Effectiveness of the I.E.P. and its implementation is reviewed at least annually by the study team, parents, principal, and teacher(s)

    Outcome: Effectiveness of I.E.P., special placement, regular classroom adjustments, etc. is determined and recommendations for continuing or revising the program/placement are made

*Functions of the Placement Committee in Special Education: A Resource Manual. National Association of State Directors of Special Education, Washington, D.C., 1976.

SCREENING AND TESTS THE RESOURCE ROOM TEACHER CAN ADMINISTER

As stated earlier, the resource room teacher may be required to participate in the formal testing procedures that can lead to a particular student's enrollment in a resource room program. Do not administer any tests unless

```
                        Referral Form

                                    Date of Referral _____

Name _____ Age _____ DOB _____
        Last          First      M.I.

School _____ Grade/Team _____ Teacher _____

Home Address _____ Home Phone _____

Father's Name _____ Occupation _____ Bus. Phone _____

Mother's Name _____ Occupation _____ Bus. Phone _____

Date of Parent Contact _____

TEST RESULTS (Standardized, Individual and/or group tests)

Date                 Name of Test                    Scores
_____
_____
_____
_____


In Speech Therapy?   Yes _____ No _____

In Remedial Reading? Yes _____ No _____

     (If "Yes," please note space for comments.)

MEDICAL INFORMATION  Is this child on medication?  Yes _____ No _____

     (If "Yes," please indicate what) _____

Hearing Screening Results _____ Date _____

Vision Screening Results _____ Date _____

Other Comments _____
_____
_____


BUILDING PRINCIPAL

Grade(s) Repeated _____ Date of Previous Referrals _____

Information pertinent to this Referral:


_____          _____
Principal's signature                  Date
```

FORM 2-6 (Referral Form, Department of Special Services, Warren Township Elementary Schools, Warren, New Jersey 07060.)

Reason for Referral (Please include any pertinent background information. Use additional page if needed.)

	Signature of Referring Person

Parent Comment

Parent Signature	Date

FORM 2–6   (cont.)

✱ 1. You hold appropriate certification/training to give the test.
✱ 2. You have read the test manual.
✱ 3. You have "practiced" the test administration format on several students informally (your children, children of friends, children in a practicum).
✱ 4. You have a basic understanding of what the test is to measure, as well as test norms and standardization procedures.
✱ 5. You know what information the specific test can contribute to a student's actual program in your resource room.

In other words, do not administer a test that assesses math abilities if your resource room only accommodates specific reading problems. Know the range of problems that you can handle in your resource room and become expert at dealing with those specific problems. (See Chapter 1.) Use a standard battery of tests that you, as a resource room teacher, feel comfortable in giving to prospective students.

Hammill (1971) points out that there are three reasons for school evaluations.

✱ 1. Classification of the learner
✱ 2. Placement justification
✱ 3. Planning an appropriate educational program for the student.

Identify the reason(s) for evaluating students for the resource room enrollment with these three points in mind. Why is this student being evaluated? Davis (1977) elaborates on this topic and suggests that there are two types of school evaluations.

✱ 1. Formal evaluation, or the administration and evaluation using standardized tests
✱ 2. Informal evaluation, or criterion referenced diagnostic measures.

Formal evaluations or standardized tests (that is, WISC-R; Stanford-Binet, Wide Range Achievement; Detroit Test of Learning Aptitudes) should be administered by a trained evaluator in a setting other than the classroom. These tests require a formal training period (usually a graduate study program) before the examiner is certified or qualified to administer the tests and report the results and implications.

Informal evaluation measures include the classroom teacher's administration of text mastery tests, criterion reference tests, classroom observations, and definition of specific educational tasks (Davis 1976).

Resource room teachers may identify students for their programs with either type of testing battery. (Again, know the laws governing the resource room teacher certification in your state—what type of testing are you trained and certified/qualified to administer to students?)

Identification of a particular student as learning disabled, emotionally disturbed, mentally retarded, or any other classification is a serious matter.

It is imperative that both formal and informal evaluation techniques are utilized before a student is identified and enrolled in a special education program. The following references may be helpful:

✶ Hammill, D., and N. Bartel, *Teaching Children with Learning and Behavior Problems*. Boston: Allyn & Bacon, 1975.

✶ Jahn, A., and J. Ysseldyke, *Assessment in Special and Remedial Education*. Boston: Houghton Mifflin, 1976.

✶ Johnson, R., and P. Magrah, *Developmental Disorders: Assessment, Treatment and Education*. Baltimore, Md.: University Park Press, 1978.

Table 2-2 lists formal tests that are commonly used as educational diagnostic instruments.

PLACEMENT

As a resource room teacher, you should know the rationale for each student's placement.

1. Why was the student suggested for placement in this program?
2. What is the student's measured level of achievement in his/her current program?
3. How can the resource room program enhance this student's achievement?
4. How will resource room placement help or hinder this student's progress?

In this writer's opinion, no student should be placed in a special education program unless this program is definitely needed! This calls for formal diagnostic evaluations as well as informal evaluation techniques and the input of the classroom teacher, the parents/guardians, and the student. Generally at the age of eight, or second and third grade level, the student is old enough to express his/her opinion of current academic problems. Often a student is best able to pinpoint specific difficulties—"I have trouble with math; I can't do addition and subtraction work." Whenever a student is being considered for resource room enrollment, ask these questions:

1. Is the student having difficulty achieving in the regular program?
2. Why is achievement in the regular classroom program difficult?
3. Can the resource room program help this student achieve more satisfactorily?

Keep in mind that to answer these questions there is a need for both formal and informal evaluation, resource room teacher observation of student performance in the classroom setting, parental input, and a specific program plan for each student before resource room placement is finalized.

Table 2-2 Formal Tests Which Are Commonly Used as Educational Diagnostic Instruments

Area of Concentration	Name	Company	Description
Intelligence	Peabody Picture Vocabulary Test	American Guidance Service, Inc.	K–adult. A wide-range individual picture vocabulary test using 150 plates containing four pictures each. Raw scores can be converted into mental age, standard I.Q., and percentiles. Quick and easy to administer. No verbal or written responses required.
	Stanford Binet Intelligence Scale	Houghton Mifflin Company	K–adult. Item classification system for reporting performance in six categories: general comprehension, visual-motor ability, arithmetic reasoning, memory and concentration, vocabulary and verbal fluency, judgement and reasoning.
	Weschler Intelligence Scale for Children Revised (WISC-R)	Psychological Corporation	Ages 5–15. Verbal (information, comprehension, arithmetic, similarities, vocabulary, digit span); performance (picture completion, picture arrangement, block design, object assembly, mazes, coding).
	Weschler Preschool and Primary Scale of Intelligence (WPPSI)	Psychological Corporation	Ages 4–6.5. Verbal (information, vocabulary, arithmetic, similarities, comprehension, sentences); performance (animal house, picture completion, mazes, geometric designs, block design). Eight of the eleven tests provide same measures as WISC.
	Goodenough-Harris Drawing Test	Harcourt Brace Jovanovich, Inc.	K–8. A nonverbal test of mental ability. Contains Draw-a-Man, the new Draw-a-Woman, and a Self-Drawing Scale. Separate standard scores for boys and girls. Scored for 73 characteristics.

Table 2-2 (cont.)

Area of Concentration	Name	Company	Description
	McCarthy Scale of Children's Abilities	Psychological Corporation	Ages 2.5–8.5 years. Six scores: verbal, perceptual-performance, quantitative, composite, memory, and motor.
	Minnesota Preschool Scale	Educational Test Bureau	Ages 1.5–6 years. Tests verbal, nonverbal, and total.
	Pictorial Test of Intelligence	Houghton Mifflin Company	Age 3–8 years. Tests seven areas: picture vocabulary, form discrimination, information and comprehension, similarities, size and number, immediate recall, and total.
	Slosson Intelligence Test	Slosson Educational Publications	Age: 2 weeks and over. Verbal responses. Above four years stresses mathematical reasoning, vocabulary, auditory memory, and information.
Visual Perception	Purdue Perceptual Motor Survey (PPMS) (Kephart Scale)	Charles E. Merrill Publishing Company	Ages 6–10. Purpose: to identify those children lacking perceptual motor abilities involved in academic success. Balance, posture, body image and differentiation, perceptual-motor match, rhythmic writing, ocular control, and form perception.
	Developmental Test of Visual Perception (DTVP) (Frostig)	Consulting Psychologists Press	Ages 3–8. Tests eye-motor coordination, figure-ground discrimination, form constancy, position in space, spatial relations, and total; with perceptual quotient.
Visual-Motor	Detroit Tests of Learning Aptitude	Bobbs-Merrill	Ages 3–6. Tests in 20 categories. Measures stimulus to response procedure. Designed to establish strengths and weaknesses in psychological constitution to help solve learning problems. Involves input and output both automatic and associational.

Category	Test	Publisher	Description
	Developmental Test of Visual Motor Integration (VMI)	Follett Publishing Company	Ages 2–15. Twenty-four geometric forms to be copied. A separate age equivalent form for each sex is provided.
	Bender Visual Motor Gestalt Test	Western Psychological Services	Ages 4 and over. Primary use in area of detecting neurological dysfunction. It also is used as a projective assessment tool.
	Harris Test of Lateral Dominance	Psychological Corporation	Ages 7 and up. Includes knowledge of right and left, hand dominance, eye dominance, and foot dominance.
Motor	Oseretsky Tests of Motor Proficiency	American Guidance Service, Inc.	Ages 4–16. Translated from the Portuguese edition.
	Lincoln-Oseretsky Motor Development Scale	C. H. Stoelting Company	Ages 6–14. A revision of Oseretsky tests of motor proficiency.
Auditory Perception	Wepman Auditory Discrimination Test	Western Psychological Services	Ages 5–8. Tests ability to discriminate differences in phonemes used in the English language.
	Kindergarten Auditory Screening Test	Follett Publishing Company	Grades K–1. Scores in three areas: speech in environmental noise, phonemic synthesis, same/different.
	Goldman-Fristoe-Woodcock Test of Auditory Discrimination	American Guidance Service, Inc.	Ages 4 and up. Tests speech-sound discrimination under both quiet conditions and background noise.

Table 2-2 (cont.)

Area of Concentration	Name	Company	Description
	Detroit Tests of Learning Aptitude	Bobbs-Merrill	*See visual-motor area.
Language	Detroit Tests of Learning Aptitude	Bobbs-Merrill	*See visual-motor area.
	Screening Tests for Identifying Children With Specific Language Disability (Slingerland)	Educational Publishing Service	Grades 1–4. Total of eight tests including visual coping for point, visual coping near point, visual perception-memory, visual discrimination, visual perception-memory in association with kinesthetic memory, auditory recall, auditory perception of beginning and ending sounds, and auditory associations.
	Illinois Test of Psycholinguistic Abilities	Illinois University Press	Ages 2–10. To determine difficulties in communication and mental-verbal processes. Tests input-output channels. Includes: auditory, reception, visual reception, visual sequential memory, auditory association, auditory sequential memory, visual association, visual closure, verbal expression, grammatic closure, manual expression, auditory closure, and sound blending.
	Templin-Darley Screening and Diagnostic Tests of Articulation	University of Iowa	Ages 3 and over. Includes screening test, consonant singles-initial and final, vowels, dipthongs and combination, and clusters.
	Assessment of Children's Language Comprehension	Consulting Psychologists Press	Ages 2–6. Includes four scores: vocabulary, two-word phrases, three-word phrases, four-word phrases.

Category	Test	Publisher	Description
	Goldman-Fristoe Test of Articulation	American Guidance Service, Inc.	Ages 2 and up. Tests sounds in words, sounds in sentences, and stimulatability.
	Myklebust Pupil Rating Scale	Grune & Stratton	Grades 3–4. Provides range of observations in following behavioral areas: auditory comprehension, spoken language, orientation, motor coordination, and personal-social behavior.
Social Behavioral	Mooney Problem Checklist	Psychological Corporation	Grades 7–9, 9–12, 13–16, adults. Grades 7–9 include health, school, home, family, money, work, boy-girl relationships, self, and so on. Grades 9–12 include health, finances, social-psychological relations, sex-marriage, vocational, and so on.
	Vineland Social Maturity Scale	American Guidance Service	Birth to maturity.
	Cain-Levine Social Competency Scale	Consulting Psychologists Press	Ages 5–13. The rating scale based on parental information including self-help, initiative, social skills, and communications.
	Devereaux Behavior Rating Scale	Devereaux Foundation Press	K–4. A teacher rating scale for use in screening emotional and behavior problems. Includes factors, such as classroom disturbance, impatience, disrespect, external blame, achievement, and external reliance.
	AAMD Adaptive Behavior Scales	American Association of Mental Deficiency	Ages 3–12 years. Contains two parts. Part 1 includes physical, language,and numerical development. Part 2 includes violent, antisocial, unacceptable, and inappropriate behavior.

Table 2-2 (cont.)

Area of Concentration	Name	Company	Description
	Behavior Problem Checklist (Quay-Peterson)	Children's Research Center	Grades K–8. Measures problem behavior in following areas: conduct disorder, personality disorder, inadequacy-immaturity, and subcultural (socialized) delinquency. Approximate administration time—two minutes.
	Rhode Island Pupil Identification Scale	Rhode Island College	Grades K–2. Multipurpose instrument for screening learning problems. Two areas: (1) measures observable behavior in regular classroom activities and (2) measures behavior through review of written work. Also employed as a basic screening instrument.
	Hahnemann High School Behavior Rating Scale	Hahnemann Medical College and Hospital	Grades 7–12. Reflects classroom adjustment in the following behavioral factors: reasoning ability, verbal interaction, rapport with teacher, originality, anxious producer, general anxiety, quiet-withdrawn, poor work habits, lack of intellectual independence, diagnostic-inflexible, verbal negativism, disturbance-restless, and expressed inability.
Reading	Spache Diagnostic Reading Scales	CTB-McGraw Hill Company	Grades 1–8. Comprehensive series of tests to evaluate oral and silent reading skills and auditory comprehension. It tests word recognition, phonics, and comprehension.
	Woodcock Reading Mastery Tests	American Guidance Service	Grades K–12. Battery of criterion referenced reading tests. Includes five individualized administered tests: letter identification, comprehension, passage comprehension, word identification, and word attack.
	Durrell Analysis of Reading Difficulty	Harcourt Brace Jovanovich, Inc.	Grades 1–6. Includes oral and silent reading, listening, flash words, word analysis, spelling, and handwriting.

	Test	Publisher	Description
	Mills Learning Test	The Mills School	Grades K–3. To determine ability to learn new words involving visual, phonics, auditory, kinesthetic, or any combination.
	Gates-Mac-Ginitie Reading Tests: Readiness Skills	Harcourt Brace Jovanovich, Inc.	Grades K–1. Readiness battery including listening comprehension, auditory discrimination, visual discrimination, following directions, letter recognition, visual-motor coordination, auditory blending, and total word recognition.
	Botel Reading Inventory	Follett Publishing Company	Grades 1–4, 1–6, 1–12. Includes frustrational, instructional and independent levels. Four tests: word recognition, word opposites, phonics mastery, and spelling placement.
Mathematics	Key-Math Diagnostic Test	American Guidance Service	Grades K–7. Comprehensive assessment in three areas: content, operations, and applications. Includes numeration, fractions, geometry, symbols; addition, subtraction, multiplication, division, mental computation, mental reasoning; word problems, missing elements, money, measurement, and time.
	Stanford Diagnostic Arithmetic Test	Harcourt Brace Jovanovich, Inc.	Grades 2.5–8.5 in two levels. Grades 2.5–4.5 include concepts (number system and counting, operations, decimal place value), computation (addition, subtraction, multiplication, division), and number facts. Grades 4.5–8.5 include concepts, computation, common fractions, decimal fractions, percent, and number facts.

Special Education Resource Programs in Maine; Rationale and Implementation, William E. Davis, Special Education Department, University of Maine, Orono, Maine, 1977.

REFERENCES

Davis, William B., *Special Education Resource Programs in Maine; Rationale and Implementation.* Orono, Maine: Special Education Department, College of Education, University of Maine, 1977.

———, *Screening Handicapped Children in Maine Public Schools.* Orono, Maine: Special Education Department, College of Education, University of Maine, 1974.

Functions of the Placement Committee in Special Education: A Resource Manual. Washington, D.C.: National Association of State Directors of Special Education, 1976.

Hammill, Donald, "Evaluating Children for Instructional Purposes." *Academic Therapy,* 6 (1971), 341–353.

Hammill, Donald, and N. Bartel, *Teaching Children with Learning and Behavior Problems.* Boston: Allyn & Bacon, 1975.

planning an IEP,
due process,
and parents' rights

3

WHAT IS AN IEP?

An individualized education program (IEP) is a written statement of the student's program and the manner in which the special education and related services will be provided. According to PL 94-142, all handicapped children must have an IEP. These are the most talked about three letters in the special education field today. Chances are, many school districts have already been doing IEPs without formalizing them according to the law. The law is specific as to who should be involved, what should be included, and when it should be done. There is, however, flexibility in the format of the written IEP. Examples of possible forms will be illustrated. (See Forms 3-1, 3-2, and 3-3.)

WHAT THE LAW REQUIRES

The term *individualized education program* as defined by PL 94-142 is "a written statement for each handicapped child developed in any meeting by a representative of the local educational agency or an intermediate educational unit who shall be qualified to provide, or supervise the provision of, specially designed instruction to meet the unique needs of handicapped children, the teacher, the parents or guardian of such child, and, whenever appropriate, such child."

The IEP must be written with the input of

1. A representative of the local educational agency or an intermediate education unit who might be the head of special services or the school principal
2. The teacher of the child, that is, the child's current regular classroom teacher and/or the special education teacher
3. The parent(s) or guardian of the child
4. The child, when it would be beneficial for the child to attend.

At the discretion of the parents and/or the public agency, others may participate in the IEP meeting. For example, the speech therapist or the reading specialist who is involved with the child may have important input into developing an appropriate program.

The IEP should include

1. "A statement of the present levels of educational performance of such child . . ." This could include test scores, current reading and math levels, and teacher observations as to the child's ability to perform in the classroom.
2. "A statement of annual goals, including short term instructional objectives . . ." Annual goals tell what the child should be able to do by the end of the year. For example, he/she will be reading on third grade level by June. The short-term instructional objectives are the steps that must be taken in order to meet the goal.

APPENDIX 2

SAMPLE INDIVIDUALIZED EDUCATION PROGRAM FORM

School District
Responsible _____

Date(s) of meeting: _____

_____

Student _____
(name or number)

_____

Current
placement _____

Eligibility
certified _____
(date)

Period of individualized education program

_____ to _____

Persons present	Relationship to child

Curriculum areas* requiring special education and related services	Present level(s) of performance	Annual goals	Short term objectives	Time required	Objectives attained (dates)		
Area 1							
Area 2							

*If more space is required, use an additional sheet.

FORM 3–1 (Torres, Scottie, ed., *A Primer on Individualized Education Programs for Handicapped Children* [Reston, Va.: The Foundation for Exceptional Children, 1977], Appendix 2, pp. 54–56.)

A. List any special instructional material or media necessary to implement this individualized education program.

Special education and related services recommended	Personnel responsible (name and title)	Date services begin	Duration
Curriculum area 1			
Curriculum area 2			

Student name or number _____

B. Describe the extent to which the child will participate in regular education programs.

_____

_____

_____

_____

C. Recommended type of placement: _____
   (include physical education)
   _____

D. Provide justification for the type of educational placement.

_____

_____

_____

_____

E. Actual placement: _____
   _____

F. List the criteria, evaluating procedures, and schedule for determining whether the short term objectives are met.

FORM 3-1 (cont.)

Short term objectives	Objective criteria	Education procedures	Schedule

Date of parental acceptance/rejection _____

Signature _____

Signature _____

FORM 3–1   (cont.)

```
INDIVIDUAL EDUCATIONAL PLAN

Name _____          Date _____

Grade _____ Age _____

    I   ANNUAL GOALS -- For the current school year.




   II   OBJECTIVES -- Specific intermediate steps to be followed to bridge
                      the gap between present performance levels and projected
                      goals.




  III   RECOMMENDED PROGRAM:

        A.  Rationale for type of program and placement including explanation
            of program's recommendation as "least restrictive environment."




        B.  Extent of participation in regular educational program.
```

FORM 3–2   (Special Education Resource Programs in Maine; Rationale and Implementation,
William E. Davis, Special Education Department, University of Maine, Orono, Maine, 1977.)

IV RELATED SERVICES:

    A. <u>Service</u>

        Speech

        Remedial Reading

        Title I/SCE

        Supplemental Gym

        Other

 V EVALUATION PROCEDURES AND SCHEDULE:

VI RESPONSIBILITIES FOR PROGRAM IMPLEMENTATION:

    Parent

    Teacher

    CST

    Other

IEP Development Meeting -- Date _____   Signature

Attendees: _____   _____

           _____   _____

           _____   _____

           _____   _____

           _____   _____

           _____   _____

           _____   _____

FORM 3–2 (cont.)

INDIVIDUALIZED EDUCATIONAL PLAN

NAME ___Doe, William___ BIRTHDATE ___8-10-69___ AGE ___17___ DATE ___9-1-76___

PARENTS ___Charles & Martha Doe___ ADDRESS ___1977 Main Street___

DISTRICT OF RESIDENCE ___Washington School Dist.___ COUNTY ___Hamilton___ PHONE ___588-8888___

RECOMMENDED DISTRICT OR EDUCATIONAL AGENCY OF ATTENDANCE ___Washington School District___ COUNTY ___Hamilton___

STATEMENT OF SPECIFIC EDUCATIONAL PROGRAM
Extent of participation in   Pupil will be enrolled in
regular educational program: Industrial Arts/and P.E./Health

Primary Program	Check Needs	Date To Be Initiated	Anticipated Duration	RELATED AND SUPPORTIVE SERVICES	Check Needs	Anticipated Needs
				Tutoring Program Participation		
Regular Education				Speech & Language Therapy	X	Traditional Artic.Correct.
Special Education	X	9-1-76	Indefinite Full Time	Occupational Therapy		
Home Based				Physical Therapy		
Residential				Attendant Service		
				Transportation		
LONG TERM PROGRAM GOALS				Orientation & Mobility		
1. Learn to communicate orally and in writing				Counseling	X	Supportive
2. Learn to communicate through reading						
3. Learn to communicate through arithmetic				Vocational Assessment	X	Pre-vocational
4. Learn to develop one's self potential						Work-Study
5. Learn to live and work in the world				Work Experience	X	Job

CRITERIA AND SCHEDULES FOR PERIODIC REVIEW

No later than 12 months from the above placement date, pupil's IEP and achievement of short term instructional objectives will be reviewed. Approximate review schedule will be April 1977. Parents will be asked to participate in review.

The above recommendations have been made by the Placement Committee and we feel this is the appropriate program placement.

_____
Placement Committee Chrmn.

Indicate who, by title(s) or position, will develop or implement the Individualized Educational Program:

Special Education Teacher
Occupational Counselor (Work-Study)
Speech Therapist

I have reviewed the above educational placement and
ACCEPT   DO NOT ACCEPT
recommendation of the Placement Committee.

_____ the
                                        Parent

FORM 3-3

46

EVALUATIONS COMPLETED AND INFORMATION GATHERED

6-10-75 WAIS Administered - results indicate moderate retardation.

5-15-76 Woodcock Reading Mastery Test - results indicate weakness in word attack & word comprehension skills, overall reading achievement is low compared to other 10th grade students in the district.

5-20-76 KEY MATH - results indicate deficiencies in mental computation & reasoning, multiplication concepts & inability to comprehend measurement concepts.

5-5-76 CALIFORNIA OCCUPATIONAL INTEREST INVENTORY - profile indicates specific interest in manipulative or mechanical skills. Likes taking things apart & putting them back together. Again indicates very low occupational skills in related occupational areas.

5-10-76 SPEECH & LANGUAGE EVALUATION - GOLDMAN-FRISTOE - articulation error on the "r" sound in conversation.

5-10-76 CARROW AUDITORY DISCRIMINATION - indicates difficulty in distinguishing consonant blends.

STATEMENT OF PRESENT LEVELS OF EDUCATIONAL PERFORMANCE

SOCIAL DEVELOPMENT - Limited positive behavior toward own peers and independence from authority figures.

MATH SKILLS - can add two column numbers, subtract three column numbers.

SELF-CONCEPT - perceives self as very inadequate and insignificant.

READING - Reading skills inadequate, unable to attack simple vocabulary words. Comprehends 50% of sentence and identifies less than 25% of main paragraph ideas.

VOCATIONAL READINESS & INTERESTS - Inability in completing class work tasks and assigned in-school jobs. However, does display some mechanical abilities.

ADDITIONAL SERVICES NEEDED FOR IMPLEMENTATION OF PROGRAM THAT WILL BE PROVIDED BY PARENTS AND/OR OUTSIDE PROFESSIONAL AGENCIES

FORM 3-3 (cont.)

ANNUAL EDUCATIONAL GOALS AND SHORT-TERM INSTRUCTIONAL OBJECTIVES

Directions: This sheet is to be completed by school personnel providing services to the pupil and the parent(s) together, in a conference at least 30 calendar days after initial placement into the program or within 30 calendar days after the beginning of school each year thereafter. The Annual Goals and Objectives are to be evaluated at the Annual Review Conference held in the spring. If any portion of the IEP is revised parents should be involved. Attach additional sheets if needed.

ANNUAL GOALS

Annual Goals(s) - are those expected educational performance levels to be achieved by the end of the school year under the child's individualized educational program.

1. Develop simple word attack, vocabulary, and comprehension skills.
2. Plan a developmental reading program in which sentence and paragraph comprehension will be improved.
3. Develop basic math skills in computation (adding, subtracting, multiplying, dividing) using practical application to improve deficits.
4. Provide preoccupational experiences in manipulative activities (assembly-sorting, etc.) and developing work attitudes in completing job tasks leading to part or full time employment.
5. Assist student in attaining self-confidence and personal independence.
6. To produce the "r" sound in all word positions and use in reading & conversation with 90% accuracy.
7. To distinguish & use consonant blends in conversation accurately.

SHORT-TERM INSTRUCTIONAL OBJECTIVES

Short-Term Instructional Objective(s) - are statements describing, in specific, objective and measurable terms, the intermediate steps in the accomplishment of the above stated annual goal(s).

I. The student will speak in a manner that reflects an understanding of proper word usage, employing correct grammar and sentence structure.
   A. ACTIVITIES - students will be grouped according to activity selected and peer group instruction will be under guidance of teacher.
   B. RESOURCES - the following language arts material will be used:
      1. Mott Basic Language Skills (Program 300)
      2. Ginn & Company "Help Yourself to Read, Write and Spell"

II. After listening to any paragraph or story read orally by the teacher, the student will correctly state the main idea of the selections.
   A. ACTIVITIES - teacher will develop a reading center or corner in room and use the tape recorder earphone listening lessons.

FORM 3-3 (cont.)

B. RESOURCES - teacher-made story lessons and short stories by Educational Foundation Corporation; Language Master & Listening Posts; Turner Livingston Communication Series; Reader's Digest Adult Readers.

III. When given orally or in writing, a story problem requiring subtraction, addition, division, the pupil will be able to on paper write the arithmetic process for the story problems and compute its correct meaning.
A. ACTIVITIES - practical exercises using computation problems from newspaper ads. Work sheets - computer device, etc.
B. RESOURCES - Newspapers, computer device, in-school work pay check stubs (checks, deposit slips). "Everyday Business Math for Living"; "Getting Ready for Pay Day."

IV. The student will be able to measure, using a 12 inch ruler or a 72 inch extension tape device, any specified object in the classroom within a specified length of time.
A. ACTIVITIES - Measure desk, paper, chair, window. Design a bulletin board using various measuring tools. Sheet completion - class project in industrial arts constructing a book shelf.
B. RESOURCES - Manipulative devices (tape measure, ruler); LaFollet "Measuring for Daily Living Workbook."

WORK STUDY GOALS

During the school hours, the student will demonstrate a knowledge of the concept of courteous behavior by consistently and without reminder, relating to all people he or she deals with in a courteous manner.
A. SUGGESTED ACTIVITIES - (1)observation on in-school part-time job; (2) placing student in work groups.

EVALUATION OF GOALS AND OBJECTIVES (Annual Review)

Evaluation - formal and/or informal to determine if the above stated goals and objectives were achieved. This section should be completed before the annual review conference.

1. Student has made some progress in object #1 & #2. However, future planning will need to look at reinforcing skills developed.
2. Student has not mastered to an 85% level in object #3. Teacher will need to continue with instructional objectives.
3. Student achieved measurement success using ruler in inches, quarter inches, and eighths.
4. Objectives #1 & 2 have been achieved; however, the Occupational Counselor needs to develop additional strategies for reinforcing objective #2 since the student occasionally completes work tasks.
5. Objective #3 - student seems to have overcome lack of self-confidence; however, Occupational Counselor needs to further assess next year.
6. Objective #4 student achieved success on one job only - will place again next year.

DEVELOPED & EVALUATED BY:	I have participated in the development of the above goals and objectives and/or I have carefully considered the goals and objectives and find them to be appropriate for my child's educational program. I also understand that I will participate in the annual review conference to evaluate achievement of these annual goals.

NAME_____ TITLE

NAME_____ TITLE

NAME_____ TITLE

NAME_____ TITLE

PARENT'S SIGNATURE   DATE

FORM 3-3 (cont.)

3. "A statement of the specific educational services to be provided to such child and the extent to which such child will be able to participate in regular educational programs . . ." Who will be working with the child and what percentage of the time will the child spend in the classroom and in the resource room?
4. "The projected date for initiation and anticipated duration of such services . . ." When will the child begin the program and about how long will the program last?
5. "Appropriate objective criteria and evaluation procedures and schedules for determining, on at least an annual basis, whether instructional objectives are being achieved . . ." How will it be decided if the child has reached the goals? Exactly what evaluation techniques will be used? (See Form 3–4.)

When Should the IEP Be Written?

Some districts have placed students in a special education program before the IEP is completed. The IEP should be developed *before* the child is placed in a special education program. One part of the IEP is the consideration of the type of placement that would provide an "appropriate" special education program.

The resource room teacher may find it difficult to help develop goals and objectives for students he/she has not yet taught. A suggestion might be for all "planners" at the IEP meeting to decide on long-term goals. The short-term objectives can be developed by the resource room teacher for each reporting period as he/she becomes better acquainted with the learning patterns of the child.

WHAT IS NEW ABOUT IEPs?

Historically, many special education programs have planned for children's progress by having professional educators set goals and short-term instructional objectives. Now planning must include parental input and, when possible, the child's input. This can be a startling change for parents, teachers, and administrators. However, parents have good reason to be involved in planning their child's program. They know their child better than anyone and will provide valuable information concerning the child's life outside the school. Often, when parents are "in" on the planning for their child's special education program, they will feel more involved in his/her learning. Children sometimes make better progress when the parents are working with the school in a cooperative effort.

Upper elementary and secondary students can successfully participate in developing their own IEP in most cases. There are many benefits from including the children.

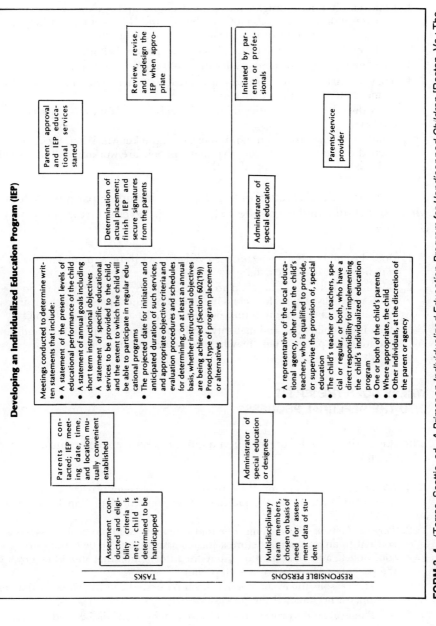

Developing an Individualized Education Program (IEP)

TASKS

Assessment conducted and eligibility criteria is met; child is determined to be handicapped

Parents contacted; IEP meeting date, time, and location mutually convenient established

Meetings conducted to determine written statements that include:
- A statement of the present levels of educational performance of the child
- A statement of annual goals including short term instructional objectives
- A statement of specific educational services to be provided to the child, and the extent to which the child will be able to participate in regular educational programs
- The projected date for initiation and anticipated duration of such services, and appropriate objective criteria and evaluation procedures and schedules for determining, on at least an annual basis, whether instructional objectives are being achieved (Section 602(19))
- Proposed type of program placement or alternatives

Determination of actual placement; finish IEP and secure signatures from the parents

Parent approval and IEP educational services started

Review, revise, and redesign the IEP when appropriate

RESPONSIBLE PERSONS

Multidisciplinary team members, chosen on basis of need for assessment data of student

Administrator of special education or designee

- A representative of the local educational agency, other than the child's teachers, who is qualified to provide, or supervise the provision of, special education
- The child's teacher or teachers, special or regular, or both, who have a direct responsibility for implementing the child's individualized education program
- One or both of the child's parents
- Where appropriate, the child
- Other individuals, at the discretion of the parent or agency

Administrator of special education

Parents/service provider

Initiated by parents or professionals

FORM 3-4 (Torres, Scottie, ed., *A Primer on Individualized Education Program for Handicapped Children* [Reston, Va.: The Foundation for Exceptional Children, 1977], inside front cover.)

1. Children often have insights into their strengths and weaknesses. When they have misunderstandings about their abilities, the IEP meeting may help them get a more realistic picture of what they can accomplish.
2. Children feel part of the team: "Lots of people are helping me."
3. They may be able to suggest ways that help them learn better.
4. They see that there are definite steps to reaching their goals. These goals may be more attainable than they had perceived.
5. They discover that what they think and feel is important to their parents and teachers.
6. Children often fear the unknown more than the known. When the doors are opened to them, they find out that many people are working on their behalf and it is not so frightening after all.

It is left to the discretion of the IEP team, including parents, to decide when to include children in the IEP meeting. Several factors need to be considered.

1. Does the child wish to be included? Even after a careful explanation, the child may not want to participate.
2. Do the parents want the child to be present? Some parents may not feel comfortable discussing their child in front of him/her. This is especially true if the parents have recently found out their child has a learning disability.
3. What is the child's age and maturity, and what is the severity of the handicap? The input of past teachers may help to make this decision.

WHERE DOES THE IEP FIT INTO THE REFERRAL PROCESS?

The stages that usually occur when a child enters a special education program include

1. *Identification*—A child may be referred by a classroom teacher, parent, guidance counselor, physician, judicial officer, or school principal. (See Form 3-5.)
2. *Parental Consent*—Parents must be told why their child has been referred and consent to an evaluation before a formal assessment can be conducted. Abeson, Bolick, and Hass (p. 45) outline the information that should be given to the parents. (Also see Form 3-6, p. 55.)
   a. The reasons the evaluation has been requested and the name of the person(s) who initiated the process
   b. The evaluation procedures and instruments that will be used
   c. A description of the scope of the procedures and the instruments that will be used
   d. A statement of the right to review the procedures and instruments that will be used

M.S.A.D. #29
HOULTON, MAINE

CONFIDENTIAL PUPIL REFERRAL FORM

Name _____ Date of Referral _____

Parent or Guardian _____ Telephone No. _____

Address _____ Age _____

School _____ Date of Birth _____

Teacher's Name _____ Grade _____

I. Background Information

    A. Child lives with: Mother _____ Father _____ Both Parents _____

       Mother/Stepfather _____ Father/Stepmother _____ Guardian _____

       Other _____

    B. Parents are: Living Together _____ Divorced _____

       Separated _____ Deceased _____ F _____ M _____

II. Teacher's Observation of Child As It Relates to the Following Areas:
(Please check only if condition appears excessive or abnormal to you
in comparison to other children.)

    A. Colds _____ Overweight _____ Motor Coordination _____

       Headaches _____ Underweight _____ Speech _____

       Earaches _____ Complexion _____ Hearing _____

       Sore Throats _____ Lack of Energy _____ Vision _____

    B. Comments: (Please expand on any of the above when it seems
desirable).

FORM 3-5

III. Reason for Referral

    A. Succinctly state your rationale for referring this child. (Describe behavior clearly)

    B. How long has this problem persisted? (Include comments from previous teachers if known by you).

    C. What kind of behavior change is desired in this student?

IV. Attempted Remediation

    A. What attempts (i.e., any particular steps or special services provided by parents or teachers) have been made to correct the problem?

    B. Are there any special services which the child now receives from professional personnel? (i.e., speech therapist)

FORM 3-5 (cont.)

Parental Approval for Individual Evaluation

Dear Parents:

    You have been informed of the school's concern for your child's educational progress and the need to gather further information so that the best possible program can be planned. State regulations require that you approve of any testing or other evaluation of your child. Please sign as indicated below. Your cooperation is appreciated.

****

A. Parent comments, concerns, etc.

B. This is to indicate that I have been informed and counseled regarding

    the referral of my child _____
                                (name of child)
    for individual testing or other evaluating using appropriate instruments

    and I do give my consent for such assessment by personnel of M.S.A.D.#29.

                        Parent _____
                                  (signed)

                        Date _____

FORM 3-6

    e. A statement of the right to review and obtain copies of all records related to the request for the evaluation and to give this authority to a designee of the parent as indicated in writing

    f. A description of how the findings of the evaluation are to be used, by whom, and under what circumstances

    g. A statement of the right to refuse permission for the evaluation with the understanding that the local education agency can then request a hearing to present its reasons and try to obtain approval to conduct the evaluation

    h. A statement of the right of the parent to obtain an independent educational evaluation, either from another public agency with the fee determined on a sliding scale, or privately at full cost to the parents

    i. A declaration that the child's educational status will not be changed without the parent's knowledge and written approval or completion of the due process procedures described in the right to hearing section of these procedures

    j. Identification of the education agency employee (chairman of the evaluation team) to whom the parent response should be sent and the deadline for response given in terms of the day, date, and time. In no case should the deadline be less than 10 school days nor more than 15 school days after receipt of the notice.

3. *Assessment*—According to PL 94-142, Sec. 5c, the child will be evaluated by one or more assessment procedures. For example, included in the assessment procedures in New Jersey will be a psychological profile, a learning evaluation, a social history, and possibly a medical examination. The resource room teacher in some states may be responsible for the educational assessment. (See Chapter 2, "Identifying Children for the Resource Room.")

4. *Team Conference*—The evaluation team, including the child's teacher, meets to review the testing results and to make tentative recommendations as to the necessity, amount, type, and duration of special education appropriate for the child. Parents should be included at this phase in order to understand the results of the assessment prior to the IEP meeting.

5. *Preparation for the IEP meeting*—Before the IEP meeting, some preparations are necessary. It is not reasonable to expect the participants to meet and make important decisions without prior contact. Since the entire IEP team ("a representative of the local educational agency . . . who shall be qualified to provide, or supervise the provisions of, specially designed instruction," teacher(s), parents, and possibly child) will have input into writing the IEP, each member needs to be prepared in order to run an efficient and productive meeting. The section of the IEP meeting which will require the most contribution from all members will be writing the long-term goals and objectives for the student. The following is a list of areas that could be considered for goal and objectives construction:

Reading

Language arts.

Math

Content areas (social studies, science, health)

Process areas (auditory, visual, perceptive, expression, languages)

Perceptual-motor areas

Social-emotional areas

Parents should be given time to consider the goals. This can be accomplished by sending a letter to parents in advance of the IEP meeting. This letter should include a brief explanation of the purpose and format of the IEP meeting as well as some examples of goals. This will give the parents an opportunity to decide what they want to see their child accomplish. (See sample letter, Form 3-7.)

The student who will participate in the meeting needs a chance to prepare. This could be accomplished by providing him/her with a goal checklist, a fill-in answer sheet or a teacher-student conference to discuss the goals. (See example of goal checklist, Form 3-8.)

Educators also need to prepare for writing long-term goals. For general preparation in writing all the IEPs, it is a good idea for the school district to sponsor in-service workshops on goal writing. In preparing for a specific IEP meeting, the staff members must be ready to suggest appropriate long-term goals for the student.

HOW DO YOU WRITE LONG-TERM GOALS?

Long-term goals reflect the educational expectations for the student for the current school year. These expectations will by necessity be educated guesses, based on the child's current level of performance. Also, the goals need to take into account the age, amount of time remaining in school, and how much time will be spent in the special education program (Torres, p. 16).

It is important for all involved in the goal-writing process to understand that goals are not "chiseled in stone." They can be reconsidered or altered as the year progresses. The teacher should not feel threatened by the long-term goals. They are the best expectations of what a child can achieve. Teachers are not required to "be held accountable if a child does not achieve the growth projected in the annual goals . . ." (Part 121a.349, "Individualized Education Program—Accountability, Education of Handicapped Children, Rules and Regulations," *Federal Register,* 42, no. 163 [August 23, 1977]). Many times children will achieve more or less than is expected.

There are many sources to help in writing long-term goals. Table 3-1 (p. 60) illustrates some of these sources and gives an example of a long-term goal.

Some long-term goals will be objectively measured, such as achieving a score on a standardized test. Other goals may have to be more subjective, such as goals concerning observable behavior. Examples of each type of goal are included in Table 3-1. As you think of possible long-term goals for a student, remember to keep the goal simple, concise, and appropriate. The long-term goal should enable the teacher, parents, and student to know where the student is going educationally.

```
                         SPECIAL SERVICES

                                              September, 19__

   Dear Parent,

   The child study team, your child's teacher, and your child will be meet-
   ing at _____ on _____ to review your child's individual
   educational plan (IEP) for the coming school year.

   We will be deciding on realistic goals and objectives that we will
   jointly try to help your child to achieve.

   It is my sincere hope that you will attend this meeting and help us
   plan your child's program.

   Enclosed is a list of sample goals and objectives which may be helpful
   to you.

   If you have any questions concerning this meeting please call me at
   (phone number).

                                      Sincerely,
                                      (name)
                                      Director of (agency)
```

FORM 3-7   (IEP Parent Letter)

GOALS CHECKLIST

NAME _____

This year I would like to:

    Improve my reading skills
    This is how: _____

_____

    Improve my spelling skills
    This is how: _____

_____

    Improve my handwriting skills
    This is how: _____

_____

    Improve my math skills
    This is how: _____

_____

    Improve my motor skills (sports, etc.)
    This is how: _____

_____

    Improve my ability to get along with friends
    This is how: _____

_____

    Improve my ability to get along with my teachers
    This is how: _____

_____

    Improve _____

_____

    This is how: _____

_____

    Signed _____

FORM 3-8

Table 3-1   Long-Term Goals

Goal Area	Source	Long-Term Goal
Reading	Specific reading program level	Joe will be able to read Scott Foresman, level 15 and score 70% oral on level 14 test.
	Independent reading skills	Joe will be able to read 5th grade social studies material and complete 75% of assignments with 70% accuracy.
	Standardized test scores	Joe will be able to score in the 70th percentile on Spring Iowa test.
	Classroom performance (reading group)	Joe will be able to read Scott Foresman level 15 orally with 70% accuracy.
Math	Specific math program	Joe will be able to complete all levels of Moving Up in Numbers (DLM) with 75% accuracy.
	Independent math skills	Joe will be able to complete morning work or homework with 80% accuracy.
	Standardized test scores	Joe will be able to score 4.5 grade equivalent on the Stanford Achievement Test.
	Classroom performance	Joe will be able to do math at the fourth grade level. Determined by Stanford Achievement Math Test.
Social studies/ science/other content areas	Assignment completion	Joe will be able to complete 85% of the social studies assignments with 70% accuracy.
	Test scores	Joe will score on an average of 70% on the science tests.
Perceptual skills	Specific material	Joe will be able to complete Level I of the DLM Auditory Discrimination Program with 90% accuracy.
	Classroom performance	Joe will be able to follow oral direction 80% of the time as determined by classroom teacher.
Social behavioral	Classroom functioning	Joe will be able to follow the class rules most of the time.
	Outside-of-classroom functioning	Joe will be able to eat lunch with the regular classroom without disruption.

HOW DO YOU WRITE
SHORT-TERM OBJECTIVES?

The short-term instructional objectives are the major steps that will begin with the current level of performance and end at the long-term goal. Many professionals feel the short-term objectives have to be a detailed day-by-day description of the child's special education program. This is not required and is not desirable. The local educational agency should decide upon a reasonable number of steps leading to the long-term goal (three or four). These objectives can be listed simply. For example,

> *Present Level:* Adds and subtracts numbers 1 through 10
> *Short-Term Objectives:* To be able to
>   –Read 2 and 3 place numbers
>   –Write 2 and 3 place numbers from dictation
>   –Add 2 and 3 place numbers
>   –Subtract 2 and 3 place numbers
> *Annual Goal:* Add and subtract 3 digit numbers without regrouping.

An effective way for the resource room teacher to develop, maintain, and use short-term instructional objectives is to organize them into a notebook or file for each student. The annual goal can be listed at the top of the page. Use a separate page for each area (Reading, Language Arts, and so on), where the short-term objectives are listed. (See sample Form 3–9.)

This file can serve as a daily or weekly place for comments on the child's progress and needs, a place to record test results throughout the year, and a very useful tool at parent reporting conferences and the annual review of the IEP.

Use curriculum guides, textbooks, and published lists of objectives to help you pinpoint the short-term objectives that are appropriate to the student.

USING THE IEP

A concise IEP can be most helpful to the teacher(s) who will be providing the day-to-day special education services. The IEP provides the resource room teacher with

1. A starting place for instruction. The IEP states that Johnny needs to learn all the consonants and short vowels in order to read vowel/consonant/vowel words during the year; thus, the starting place might be the introduction of a few consonants and one /a/ vowel to begin blending words.

```
┌─────────────────────────────────────────────────┐
│                                                 │
│  NAME _____    │
│                                                 │
│  SUBJECT _____    │
│                                                 │
│  GOAL _____    │
│                                                 │
│  OBJECTIVES _____    │
│                                                 │
│  _____        │
│                                                 │
│  _____        │
│                                                 │
│  _____        │
│                                                 │
│  _____        │
│                                                 │
│  _____        │
│                                                 │
│  _____        │
│                                                 │
│  _____        │
│                                                 │
│  _____        │
│                                                 │
│  _____        │
│                                                 │
│  TEST SCORES _____    │
│                                                 │
└─────────────────────────────────────────────────┘
```

FORM 3-9 (Educational Plan)

2. The IEP can assist the resource room teacher with grouping children. Several children may share similar goals and objectives. By comparing IEPs the teacher will be able to place several students in the same group for instruction.

3. The IEP will allow the teacher to predict what materials and methods will be necessary. It is a good idea to discuss at the IEP meeting any recommended specialized equipment that is not available. This helps the special education supervisor know what equipment or materials will be necessary to obtain before the school year is underway.

4. The IEP offers to teachers the support of the parents, other professionals, and, at times, the student. No longer can the responsibility for the child's goal achievement be confused. Many people share in the program planning, implementation, and evaluation.

5. The IEP can serve as the basis for reporting to parents. Referring to the IEP notebook regularly throughout the year is most helpful. It becomes a simple matter to review where the child was (compared with current performance level), where the child is presently functioning (short term objectives currently working on), and where the child is going (annual goal).

6. The IEP can be helpful when meeting with the regular classroom teacher and other professionals working with the child. Using the IEP at your conferences with the regular classroom teacher will help to focus on priority skills. This

will be easier for the regular classroom teacher to accept since the IEP was developed by an administrator, teachers, parents, and possibly the child. The IEP is not the suggestions of the resource room teacher alone.

When understood, the IEP can be a useful tool! When teachers, parents, administrators, and students experience the positive benefits from this truly individualized plan for special education, the fearsome three letters might also mean *Improved Educational Performance!*

DUE PROCESS AND PARENTS' RIGHTS

Public Law 94-142 sets down very specific guidelines to ensure parents the right to be informed and to disagree. The new law established certain rights for parents of handicapped children. These fall generally into three areas: the individualized education plan (IEP), confidentiality of information, and due process procedures. Individual states may add specific rights, but they cannot take away from the basic rights established by the federal law.

These rights, drawn here from issues of the *Federal Register* and compiled by Academic Therapy Publications, *Parents Rights Under the New Law: Public Law 94-142: Education for All Handicapped Children* (San Rafael, Calif.: Academic Therapy Publications, n.d.) are as follows:

The right to know what the policies are regarding storage, retention, or destruction of records on your child

The right to review and inspect records on your child

The right of interpretation of these records

The right to have a representative of your choosing inspect these records

The right to know who else, besides yourself, can inspect these records

The right to know all places where information on your child is stored

The right to have your permission granted before inspection is granted to any one other than officials and agents of the public agency (school district, for example) who would standardly use the information

The right to request, when information is no longer needed for storage or use by the public agency, that it be destroyed except for very basic information that may be required later, for example, for social security benefits, etc.

The right to be notified in advance of meetings pertaining to your child

The right to expect understandable language presentations in your native tongue at such meetings

The right to have all communications to you in your native language

The right to have your child tested in his/her native language

The right to an interpreter at meetings when language may be a barrier to understanding

The right to have an interdisciplinary team evaluate your child

The right to have an annual review of your child's educational program

The right to have educational placement for your child made by a team of people

The right to bring someone of your choice to all meetings to assist you

The right to have your child educated, when and where possible in a program as close as possible to your home

The right to a series of "related services" which may include such things as transportation, counseling, medical services, etc., which are written into the Individualized Educational Plan (IEP) and are free to the child and family

The right to a program, tailored to your child's needs, which includes services such as physical education, recreation, career and vocational education, etc.

The right to have your child placed in the "least restrictive environment" that is, placed in the best possible setting for him or her

The right to have your child evaluated on a series of tests that not only confirm that there is a handicapping condition, but help explain why and what can be done about it

The right to refer your child for education under the provisions of Public Law 94-142

The right to challenge any decision made regarding the identification, placement, and education of your child

The right to have, within 30 calendar days after your child has been diagnosed as handicapped by the evaluation team, an Individualized Education Plan (IEP) written on your child

The right to have tests used with your child that are not racially or culturally discriminating

The right to have your child tested in all areas related to the suspected disability, including, where appropriate, health, vision, hearing, social and emotional status, general intelligence, academic performance, communicative staus, and motor abilities

The right to a re-evaluation every three years

The right to participate in all meetings regarding the development, revisions, and review of the IEP on your child

The right to have an IEP include various alternative placements

The right to agree or disagree with ideas concerning educational plans for your child

The right not to be bound by what the public agency can offer in services that are needed, but the right to focus on what your child needs

The right to a fully paid private school placement if referred to such a setting because it is deemed in your child's best interests

The right to "due process hearings" should you disagree with any findings or recommendations regarding the identification, evaluation, or educational placement of your child

–This hearing must be conducted by the public agency

–The public agency must inform you of any free or low cost legal or other relevant services available in the area if you request it

–The right to have the hearing conducted by a person who is not an employee of the public agency

-The right to bring counsel with you to such meetings
-The right to see all information to be discussed at least five days prior to the meeting
-The right to bring your child and to have the meeting open to the public
-The right to record or tape the meeting
-The right to have a written copy of the results

The right to first request a fair hearing through the local public agency, and, if dissatisfied with the outcome, to request a fair hearing through the state office of special education. At the local level, you have the right that within 45 days after the receipt of a request for a hearing that a final decision is reached and a copy of the decision is mailed to you. Should the state be involved, the right that within 30 days after the receipt of a request for a review that a final decision be reached and that a copy of the final decision be mailed to you. (Note: The hearing officer may request a delay if all information is not available in the specified time.) Should you be dissatisfied with the state results, you may bring a civil suit.

This law has a strong provision mandating due process in all matters relating to decisions about special education. This assures that each state must follow specific procedures if and when significant changes are made in a child's school program. Implementation of this is assured by the fact that states are refused federal funding if these procedures are not written into the state education law.

It is certainly in the best interest of every teacher and parent to know what these parent rights and due process rights are. They are written as protection of the parents' right to be fully informed and to participate in all planning for decisions about their child's schooling.

Parents should be given the home state's guidelines governing due process in writing. All states do not follow this procedure however. Getting in contact with local or state parent groups such as the Association for Children with Learning Disabilities (ACLD) or Closer Look will usually provide parents with this information. The addresses of these organizations are listed under Special Education Organizations in Appendix E. Passing on this information to parents is important. Holding a parent's meeting where these guidelines are discussed and distributed in writing is yet another way to elicit parent cooperation and promote feelings of being included for parents.

REFERENCES

Abeson, A., N. Bolick, and J. Hass, *A Primer on Due Process: Educational Decisions for Handicapped Children*. Reston, Va.: The Council for Exceptional Children, 1975.

Parent Rights Under the New Law; Public Law 94-142: Education for All Handicapped Children. San Rafael, Calif.: Academic Therapy Publications, nd.

Torres, Scottie, ed., *A Primer on Individualized Education Programs for Handicapped Children,* inside cover, Appendix 2, pp. 54–56. Reston, Va.: The Foundation for Exceptional Children, 1977.

setting up
a resource room

4

KNOW THE LAW

Becoming familiar with both state and federal legislation is necessary before launching any new program. What you don't know *can* hurt you. You can save yourself much wasted time by doing some research ahead of time. (Refer to Appendix B, PL 94-142.)

Many states have specific regulations regarding the total number of students in the program, maximum amount of time allowed per day in the resource room, and the maximum number of students to be in attendance at one time.

Be sure you know your guidelines! If the law is vague, my recommendation is to have a maximum of twenty-five children in the total program. There should be no more than five to eight children in the room at one time. This affords the proper ratio of teacher to pupils and will allow for the most efficient rotation of groups.

LEARNING CENTERS

There are many ways to design and run a resource room. I have found the use of learning centers lends itself most effectively to this kind of program. The term *learning center* used in this book refers to a specific activity focusing on one skill, the result of which can be evaluated. It is a pupil-directed task. For ease of pupil flow, flexibility in programming, and maintenance of room attractiveness, learning centers are an excellent approach.

Each center can have activities geared to reinforce a specific skill on two or more levels. This can be done with phonic skills, spelling, following directions (verbal or written), math skills, and so on.

Learning centers can be made in just about any corner or available space in the room. Since a resource room is generally not a homeroom, closets designed for coats and boots can be used to house learning centers. Bulletin boards make an excellent backdrop for a learning activity, and the activity directions and possibly the task itself can be placed on the bulletin board. The blackboard can be used as part of an overhead projector station where the children respond by writing with chalk on the board. Cardboard dividers, bookshelves, chart holders, tri-wall, commercial dividers, and portable blackboards can all be used to section off a center area. Not only can these items be used as space dividers, but they make excellent "walls" for such items as pictures and direction cards (see Figure 4-1).

Let your creative imagination come up with as many novel combinations as possible. The more interesting and different the resource room is, the more exciting it will appear to the children. Learning centers are an excellent vehicle for this.

FIGURE 4–1 A Resource Room

Since students attending the resource room span many grade levels, the multilevel center is both efficient and self-rewarding. As students successfully complete one level of the learning center, they can be programmed into a more advanced level of the same center for further reinforcement. They can also be sent on to a new center for yet another skill on which to work.

By having a small number of children (one to three) meeting with the teacher at one time, each child gets individual attention. The remainder of the children will be working at stations designed to meet their individual needs. This almost eliminates classroom discipline problems since children are either with the teacher or working alone. The motivation level remains high as each new center is a new activity which is attractively presented. Properly prepared centers can even make that "old ditto" a rewarding evaluation of the center activity.

Do not overlook the fact that there are many excellent commercially prepared, inexpensive learning centers available. (See "Material List," p. 121. Specific center ideas and how to prepare and maintain learning centers are explained in Chapter 6, "Planning What to Teach." Check the *Reference* section for additional learning center books.)

DESIGNING THE ROOM

Choosing and implementing the design of a new resource room can be a rewarding experience. There is a great deal of satisfaction derived from changing four bare walls into an exciting and alive classroom.

Ideally, a resource room should be centrally located within a corridor of regular rather than special education classes. The thrust of recent legislation is to provide the least restrictive environment. Placement of the resource room should reinforce this. The room should be brightly lit, spacious, and colorful. If you have input into the decision about the room, a good argument is: ". . . the larger and more attractive the room is, the more respect the program will inspire."

Realistically we know that not all schools can provide an ideal room. We will try to help you get the optimum effect from any room to which you are assigned. Once you know where the room is, here is a checklist of what to consider.

1. *Where are the blackboards?* You will want to consider placing your small group activities here.
2. *Where are the outlets?* These are a must for your media centers.
3. *Where are the closets, shelves, and other permanent fixtures?* Learning centers as well as storage could be placed here.
4. *Where are the bulletin boards?* These make an effective backdrop for learning center activities.

5. *Where are the doors and windows located?* Consider how students will enter and leave the room, what possible distractions there are from the hallway and playground, and what additional light is available for working areas.

6. *Make a list of all built-in and large furniture in the room.* For example,
   6 small desks
   1 large built-in locker unit

✗ 7. *Make a list of furniture not in your room that you can request to be purchased, borrowed, or traded from another classroom.* (Refer to "Equipment List.")

✗ 8. *Draw a rough diagram of your room.* (See Figure 4–2.) Use your checklist as your guide.

✗ 9. *Draw in the room layout.* (See photo at beginning of chapter.) Using the blackboard for planning saves paper and time. Be sure to copy your final product on paper.

10. *Move the pieces of furniture to where they belong according to your diagram.* You will probably have to modify some of your ideas. Once the furniture is in place, new ideas may develop. Be flexible.

11. *Walk through a sample session as if you were the student.* Any flaws in your room plan will become apparent.

 EQUIPMENT LIST

   1 round or kidney shaped table
   several rectangular tables (depending on plan)
   several student desks (depending on plan)
   1 2-drawer file cabinet, with lock
   1 teacher's desk and chair
   book shelves (if not built in)
   portable blackboard
 * room dividers (tri-wall is good for this)
   pegboard (to hang clipboards) with daily plans (refer to Chapter 5)
   student chairs (number depending on plan)
 * study carrels
   clipboards
   cassette tape recorders (number will vary)
   head phones (or jack boxes and head phones) for each recorder
   overhead projector
   film strip previewer
   language master (optional)
   tutorgram
   large screen automatic cassette/filmstrip viewer (for group use)
   record player

   *There are companies who make durable cardboard carrels and dividers very inexpensively. Refer to "Materials List" in Chapter 7.

Utilize the days before school begins to plan your room and do the setting up. After school is in session, your time will be needed for scheduling, evaluating, and teaching.

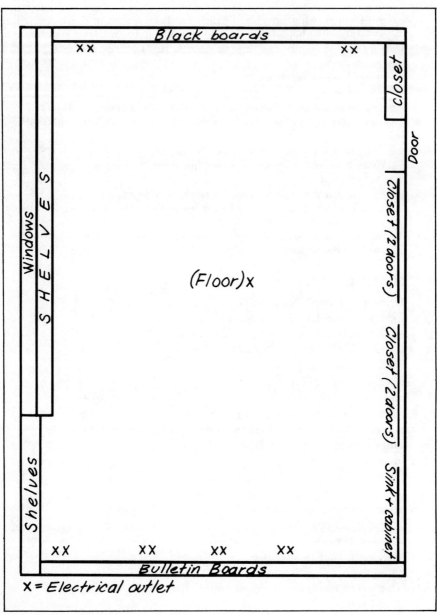

FIGURE 4–2 Room Diagram

SCHEDULING

Creating a schedule which will meet the needs of the students, keep the regular staff happy, and not run you ragged is quite a challenge. However, if the classroom is set up before school begins, it is possible to complete an operating schedule the first week of school. This will enable you to start your program along with the regular classroom schedule. In addition, if you finish your schedule early, you may not have to schedule around other support services such as speech or physical therapy which your students may be receiving.

Normally children assigned to a resource room will be scheduled for one to two hours per day. This is decided at the IEP meeting when the child's needs are reviewed and recommendations are made for programming.

You will have to consider the conflicting schedules and decide which ones take precedence over the resource room programming. Talk with other teachers and administrators to determine what should and should not be replaced by the resource room period. The resource room may be taking the place of reading and/or math sections of the regular class schedule. Thus, scheduling students for the resource room when their regular class is having these activities makes sense. You may want to schedule around gym, art, music, or other special activity times. Some states require children to attend certain special activities, such as gym.

Once you know what the priorities for most children are, here is what you do.

1. Arrange with the regular classroom teachers to meet with each child for a one-to-one evaluation. (See Chapter 2.)
2. Score tests and group children accordingly. (See Chapter 6, "Preliminary Grouping Worksheet.") Try to keep groups homogeneous according to age and ability. Sometimes a one-year span will work, but to put first and fifth graders together even if their abilities are similar could spell disaster.
3. Choose a teaching schedule format that best meets your needs. (See sample schedule, Table 4–1, p. 74.)
4. Obtain a master copy of the school's schedule for gym, art, library, and music classes.
5. Prepare a chart of each teacher's schedule of special activities. (See Form 4–1, p. 75.)
6. Write the names of the children in each group on a separate card. Place the teacher's name after each child. (See Form 4–2, p. 76.)
7. Make a blank schedule with only session times filled in. (Large graph paper is excellent for this.)
8. Arrange the teacher's schedule cards on one side of your schedule and the group cards on the other.
9. Begin placing your groups on your master schedule, moving each group around until it does not conflict with other scheduled activity times.

10. Don't despair. You can work the groups in. If necessary, alter your schedule plans for the children.
11. Send each teacher a note telling him/her exactly the times and days their students will be scheduled in the resource room. (See Form 4-3.)
12. Give each child his/her own copy of when he/she is scheduled to attend. (This can be copied by the child at a learning center.)
13. Send copies of your proposed schedule to your principal and director of special education. (Do not forget the school nurse, speech therapist, supplemental program teacher, and school secretary.)
14. Leave time each day for planning, preparation, enrichment activities, and student observation. An hour a day is usually adequate. Try to schedule this observation and planning period when you will be able to see your students involved in academics rather than when they are eating lunch or are at recess!

Flexibility is the key word to a successful program. You may have to make schedule changes for a variety of reasons. Be flexible.

Table 4-1   Sample—Schedule I

	Group Table	Individual Stations	Evaluation
8:30– 9:00	preparation		
9:00– 9:30	Group A		
9:30– 9:55	Group B	Group A	
9:55–10:00			Group A dismissed
10:00–10:25	Group C	Group B	
10:25–10:30			Group B dismissed
10:30–10:55	Testing or individual remediation	Group C	Group C dismissed
11:00–11:30	Classroom observation		
11:30–12:00	Enrichment Group		
12:00– 1:00	Lunch		
1:00– 1:25	Group I	Group II	
1:30– 1:55	Group II Read and dismiss	Group I	
1:55– 2:00			Group I dismissed
2:00– 2:25	Group IV	Group III	Group IV dismissed
2:25– 2:55	Group III Read and dismiss	Group IV	Group III dismissed
3:00– 4:00	Consultation with teachers		

TEACHER: *Miss Like*

STUDENTS: *John Doe, Ann Brown*

Monday: *art   2 - 2:50*

Tuesday: *gym   9 - 9:50*

Wednesday: *music 9 - 9:30*

Thursday: *library 10 - 10:30*

Friday: *nothing scheduled*

NOTES

*Lateral Reading
11 - 12
each day
Lunch
12 - 1*

FORM 4-1 (Classroom Teacher's Special Schedule)

CHILD: John Doe

TEACHER: Miss Like

Monday: Speech therapy 9 - 9:30
art 2 - 2:50

Tuesday: gym 9 - 9:50

Wednesday: Music 9 - 9:30
flute 2 - 2:20

Thursday: library 10 - 10:30

Friday: Title I Math 9 - 9:30

NOTES:

Lat. Rdng 11 - 12
Lunch 12 - 1

Fri. P.M.
doctor appt.
1st + 3rd wk.
of each month

FORM 4-2 (Individual Student's Special Schedule)

```
                       RESOURCE ROOM
    Dear
    _____

    _____

    is/are scheduled to attend the resource room at the following times:

    Monday _____

    Tuesday _____

    Wednesday _____

    Thursday _____

    Friday _____

    Every effort has been made not to conflict with previously scheduled
    activities.  If a conflict in scheduling does occur, please contact me
    as soon as possible.  Thanks for your cooperation.

                                  Sincerely,
```

FORM 4-3 (Resource Room Schedule Notification)

getting off to a good start

5

As a member of the teaching staff, it is a good idea for you to begin teaching when all the other teachers begin. Starting the resource room that first day of school will inspire respect for the program and immediately establish the resource room as an essential part of the child's daily routine.

Of course the first week will be spent informally evaluating children, talking with teachers, and drawing up the schedules, but that week should also include formal student contact time. Reading pupil files, setting up the room, and lengthy conferences should be done before school opens.

A resource room program will only be as important and successful as the resource room teacher believes it to be. A successful program does not have room for an inferiority complex. Your attitude about the program will be quickly transmitted to the staff. Think positively.

WHAT TO DO BEFORE SCHOOL BEGINS

1. Read each child's school record and take notes about learning strengths and weaknesses, reading and math levels, programs used in the past, and any pertinent family information. (Some teachers prefer doing this after they meet the child.)
2. Set up the room. (See Chapter 4.)
3. Set up the schedule. (See Chapter 4.)
4. Plan and set up learning centers for the first two weeks. (See Chapter 6 for suggestions.)
5. Plan group activities for the first week. (See Chapter 6.)

WHAT TO DO WHEN SCHOOL BEGINS

Put aside the first day or two for teaching each child how to use the resource room. Taking time at that point to explain and walk through the daily routine will insure a smooth-running program. Most children with learning problems need extra time to adjust to new situations and that is what you can provide. Here is what you should cover with each child on the opening days.

1. *How to get to the resource room on time.* Place the responsibility of being on time on the child. You can give a picture of a clock with the time drawn to a younger student. The older students can be given a copy of their schedule to take to their desk. Make sure they understand that the excuse, "my teacher forgot to send me," is unacceptable.
2. *How to enter and leave the room.* Point out that others will be working, and it will be necessary for students to enter quietly. Some may need the actual practice of doing this.
3. *Where to go for assignments and materials.* With each child go through the routine of
   a. Picking up the assignment sheet (see Figures 5–1, p. 81, and 5–1A, p. 82)

    b.   Checking center assignments

    c.   Doing work independently when not at a group activity

    d.   Finding and reading direction cards at each center (see Figure 5–2, p. 82)

    e.   Locating dictionaries, encyclopedias, and other references

4.   *How to ask for help when the teacher is busy.* The children should understand that the teacher is not to be disturbed while a group is in progress. This inspires respect for what is going on at the group activities and is less distracting to the group. Students should be asked to go on to the next problem if they are "stuck." They should wait to ask the teacher for help when he/she is free. It is essential that proper directions for each center be given *before* the child begins. It is a good lesson in reality testing when a child neglects to ask questions at the proper time and must wait out a work period for the teacher to reexplain. Every lesson a child learns independently is truly learned.

5.   *How to move from center to center.* The first day can be a treasure hunt to find the properly numbered center. When students find the center, encourage good housekeeping. Be sure to have labeled storage places at each center for materials such as markers, scissors, and papers. Practice sliding chairs in and moving on to the next activity. Young children will enjoy this role playing.

6.   *What will occur during group time.* Tell students why they are attending the resource room and why they will be working together as a group. Sit at the table where the work will take place and share a few of the materials you may be using. Do not be afraid to discuss their deficit areas with them. They are living with these disabilities and will welcome the opportunity to share their feelings about them.

7.   *How will each day's work be evaluated.* Remind the students that you are partners in learning. They will help you to check their work, decide what was accomplished, and plan the next day's activities. Practice bringing work to the designated place and do a make-believe evaluation. Such questions as, "What did you like about this work?," "What did you do best?," and "What could you improve on?" will help focus the child's attention on his/her work. Rewording a problem and asking students to answer it will double-check their comprehension. Show the stamps, stickers, or buttons you plan to use to reward daily work. Children like tangible recognition for their effort.

8.   *How to return to class.* Younger children may need to practice the route back to class. Older students should be encouraged to walk rather than run in the halls (for safety reasons). They have a full schedule and will not want to delay their return for the next part of their program.

HOW TO GIVE DIRECTIONS AND DEFINE EXPECTATIONS

Each task given to the child should be clearly defined both in writing and verbally. Knowing each child's deficit areas will tell you the proper learning channel to use when explaining the task. The child who is auditorally impaired will need mostly visual clues. The child who is visually impaired should receive a strong auditory approach. Using both the visual and auditory channels simultaneously is usually the safest bet. This way you are reaching the child's area of strength, and you are exercising his/her deficit areas. A good technique to make sure the child understands your directions is to ask the child to reexplain those directions. Learning disabled children often say they understand when they do not. This is important to check.

Be sure the child knows what is expected. For example,

1. How many pages should be finished?
2. Should the writing be in script or print?
3. How much time should be spent on each task?
4. How many problems should be correct in order to progress to the next level?
5. Where are the reference books that will be needed?
6. How much progress can be expected in a set period of time?

Establishing the above routines will help learning disabled children to become independent. This is an important part of their overall development. Expect to go over many of the above points more than once. Helping the children to establish good work habits will need consistent reinforcement from you.

STAT.	MONDAY	TUESDAY	WEDNESDAY	THURSDAY	FRIDAY
1A 1B 1C					
2A 2B 2C					
3A 3B 3C					
4A 4B 4C					
5A 5B 5C					
6A 6B 6C					

NAME _____ ASSIGNMENT SHEET
WEEK OF: _____

FIGURE 5–1 Assignment Sheet

FIGURE 5–1A Assignment Sheet

The assignment sheet reads:

NAME Bonnie

WEEK OF: Oct. 7

STAT.	MONDAY	TUESDAY	WEDNESDAY	THURSDAY	FRIDAY
1A 1B 1C 2A 2B 2C 3A 3B 3C	Spelling Don't forget to say each sound as you write the words.	Creative Writing Good I really liked your story!	Classroom work (study your spelling list.)	Punctuation O.K.	Adjectives Do Over! See me
4A 4B 4C 5A 5B 5C 6A 6B 6C					

VOWEL ACTIVITY a e i o u

DIRECTIONS:

1. Listen to the taped recording. (Be sure to rewind the tape before you begin.)

2. Answer the questions on the worksheet as the recording is playing.

3. Put your finished worksheet in the finished work box.

HAVE FUN!!!!!

FIGURE 5–2 Sample Direction Card

planning
what to teach

6

HOW TO BEGIN

Teaching a resource room may appear to be an overwhelming task. The range and spectrum of teaching requirements are indeed great, but as with every endeavor, there is a beginning. Once you have your class list and have possibly participated in IEP meetings, you must begin planning for each day. You may feel like calling "help," but there are some basic steps you can take to get your program running smoothly and effectively.

Try to have each student visit the resource room before school begins. This will give you a headstart on the assessment procedure. The visit can be very informal. Here's how to do it.

1. Invite each set of parents and their child to visit the resource room the week before school begins. (Parents will enjoy the chance to get a preview of the room and to meet the teacher.)
2. During the visit, encourage the parents to look at the materials in the room while you do a five-minute evaluation with the student. Give the student a 6 × 8 inch index card and ask him/her to fill out the card according to age or ability level. (See examples.)

Lower Elementary Draw a picture of your family.	*Upper Elementary* Name _____ Age _____ Address _____ Brothers or Sisters _____ Pets _____	*Jr. High/H.S.* Same Favorite Subject _____ Best Sport _____ Favorite T.V. Show _____

STEP I—WHAT? MORE TESTING!

Yes, probably the first week of operation, it is a good idea to give a battery of diagnostic assessment tests. These can be commercial tests or teacher-made tests. The IEP that has been written on each student may state that a particular test be used to evaluate the annual goals. That test should be administered in the fall and an alternate form of the same test given in the spring to compare growth.

The testing situation is an excellent way to find out how students operate in a structured situation. The main purpose is to get enough detailed information to help individualize the instruction for each child.

We will not attempt to delve into the complex area of testing. There are many excellent references to help you decide what test to use. (See Appendix C and the list of tests in Chapter 2.)

Besides the official results of the test, the teacher can learn much about the child by his/her behavior during the test. The following list shows some things the resource room teacher should observe during test taking:

1. Is the student holding the paper or book in an unusual way? (Sideways or upside down?)
2. How is the student's posture? (Is he/she leaning to one side or tilting the head?)
3. What are the body movements like? (Are motions too rapid or slow?)
4. What is the student's attitude like? (Does he/she appear cooperative or unhappy?)
5. Is the student squinting?
6. How is the student's pencil grip?
7. What is the student's handwriting like?
8. Does the student read smoothly? (Does he/she read with expression, self-correct, skip words, apply phonic skills?)
9. Is the student able to follow oral directions?
10. Is the student able to follow written directions?
11. Does the student work independently?
12. Is the student easily distracted?
13. Does the student wear glasses, hearing aid, and so on?
14. Is the student right- or left-handed?
15. What is the student's general appearance?
16. Does the student make eye contact?
17. Does the student have nervous habits?

Considering these behavior characteristics will help you gain a better perspective on the child's handicap. It will help in planning for each child's unique learning style. For instance, if the teacher notices that a child is laboring with handwriting on the test and is using a maladaptive pencil grip, the remediation for this problem begins by establishing a proper grip. This could be done by using a mechanical device on the pencil, child awareness, behavior modification, and/or strong reinforcement in the resource room, classroom, and at home. Many of the above behaviors can signal similar remediation beginning with teacher awareness.

HOW TO ARRANGE FOR TESTING

Once school has started there are several ways you can arrange to do testing.

1. Schedule children by grade level. Taking all the third graders at the same time may be the easiest way. If all the third graders will not be taking the same test, arrange for some independent activity at a learning center while you test individuals or a small group. This gives the children a chance to get used to the resource room and the idea of rotating activities.

2. Arrange with the classroom teacher to see students one at a time. (This may be easy to arrange but is the most time consuming.)
3. Schedule groups of children according to the test they will be taking. For instance, Mon. 10:00–11:00, three fourth graders, two fifth graders—Stanford Diagnostic Test of Reading Skills.

When the testing is concluded, and the results have been tallied, a meeting should be scheduled with each student to share the test results. This should be done according to each student's ability to deal with the information. It is not always necessary to tell a student exactly what his/her grade equivalent is; however, the student should know in which skill areas he/she is strong and in which areas more work is needed.

Keeping the completed tests in the child's folder allows him/her the opportunity to look over the tests throughout the year. (Remember, the diagnostic tests are not the same as the tests given to identify children for the resource room.)

STEP II—WHAT ARE THE TEACHING PRIORITIES?

For those children with many learning deficits, decisions must be made about where to begin. Many areas can be remediated simultaneously while using one or more subject areas as vehicles. To help you decide which subjects to concentrate on you may want to fill out a Teaching Priority Form (see Form 6–1).

TEACHING PRIORITY FORM

Name _____   Grade _____ Age _____

Reading Level _____   Behavior Characteristics _____

Math Level _____   _____

Spelling Level _____   Physical Disabilities _____

Process Area Deficits   _____

    Auditory _____

    Visual _____

    Motor _____

FORM 6-1

Then make your priority decisions based on the following planning information:

1. What are the goals set down in the child's IEP?
2. How essential is each deficit area to learning in the classroom?
3. How much below grade level is the child?

4. How strongly does the child feel about learning this subject area?
5. What will be the most effective way to teach the child (based on test results of process skills)?
6. How frequently will you need to see the child to help build the needed skills?
7. What is a reasonable goal to expect the child to achieve? (See McGraw-Hill Management Checklist, Form 6-2.)

STEP III—INDIVIDUALIZING

Individualizing instruction is providing the educational program that is appropriate for each student. This can be done in several ways.

1. *Small Group Activities.* Grouping children with similar learning problems is an efficient way to meet individual needs. The interaction between the children can be a positive learning experience for the child. Frequently, learning takes place not only with a one-to-one confrontation but by being a listener and observing responses of others.

2. *One-to-One Instruction.* There are some children who derive the maximum benefit from a one-to-one situation. Sometimes they are distracted by others in a group situation or they disrupt the progress of others. These children must have the teacher's undivided attention in order to learn.

3. *Independent Activities.* Having independent activities available to reinforce each child's skill area is a good individualization technique. Generally the use of learning centers or activities that can be set up ahead of time is most effective. This eliminates time loss as the child is preassigned to a center and knows where to go. This is an added benefit in planning since the stations can be geared specifically to meet each individual's current needs. (See Weekly Assignment Plan in Chapter 5, p. 81.)

4. *Home Assignments.* Some children work most effectively with their parents at home. Sending home reinforcement activities to be done after school hours can be most beneficial if the attitudes of the child and the parents are conducive to this arrangement. Those children who are resentful of added homework or whose parents do not seem to work in a positive fashion with them should not have home assignments.

5. *Modifying Regular Class Assignments.* Changes in the regular classroom program will be very important for many students who attend the resource room. This will be done on an ongoing basis throughout the year in consultation with the classroom teacher. (See Chapter 9, "Supporting the Regular Class Program," for several ideas on modifying regular class assignments.)

6. *Modifying the Resource Room Program.* Frequently changes must be made in the resource room program to accommodate individual differences among children. For example,
   a. Working in a study carrel
   b. Working in close proximity to the teacher
   c. Working with another child
   d. Working with a timing device (egg timer)
   e. Using a time-out area
   f. Working with earphones on to block out distractions

IEP MANAGEMENT CHECK LIST

To the Teacher: The items on this check list can help you structure the learning environment in the classroom for the student to insure his or her success in mastering the IEP's annual goals and short term objectives.

1. Place a (+) for the instructional setting which is the most appropriate for the student; place a (−) for the setting least appropriate.
   ___ Group Instruction
   ___ Individualized Instruction
   ___ Individual Tutoring
   ___ Learning Center
   ___ Peer Tutoring
   ___ Other (specify)_____

2. List the cognitive skills in which the student has strengths.
   _____
   _____

3. List the cognitive skills in which the student has deficits.
   _____
   _____

4. List the learning approaches which the student responds to most readily.

Presentation to task	Student performance
___ Visual	___ Visual
___ Auditory	___ Auditory
___ Auditory/Visual	___ Auditory/Visual
___ Kinesthetic	___ Kinesthetic
___ Tactile	___ Tactile
___ Motor	___ Motor

5. List the student's hobbies or special interests that can be used as a motivation technique.
   _____

Student's Name _____

Date _____

6. Types of instructional materials best suited to match the student's learning mode.
   ___ kits   ___ task cards
   ___ special toys/games   ___ workbooks
   ___ spiritmasters   ___ experience charts
   ___ transparencies
   ___ supplementary textbooks
   ___ AV materials (filmstrips, cassettes, etc.)
   ___ other (specify)_____

7. List the primary reinforcers that can be used to reward the student for good behavior and completing assignments.
   _____

8. List the part of the school day in which the student is more attentive for doing academic work.
   _____

9. List the non-academic classes in which the student performs well.
   _____

10. List the names of classes for which the student should be considered for mainstreamed placement. Identify the name of the teacher for each class.
   _____

Teacher's Signature _____

The Webster Division has designed this checklist for your use, and it may be reproduced for each student in your class.

FORM 6–2

g. Using a tape recorder to give answers rather than writing
h. Using manipulative materials such as clay, shaving cream, or textured letters
i. Having reading assignments on tape
j. Using a combined audiovisual approach
k. Using graph paper or wide-spaced paper for writing and math
l. Using a typewriter to reinforce handwriting and spelling
m. Using all modalities (visual, auditory, and so on) when teaching
n. Getting frequent student feedback to assure comprehension
o. Using reward system for modifying learning and social behavior
p. Using contracts
q. Using frequent home reports to modify behavior
r. Using peer tutoring for reinforcement and ego boosting.

7. *Choosing a Reading or Math Program.* Several factors must be considered when choosing an individualized program for each child.

a. *Learning strengths and weaknesses.* For instance, if the child has an auditory discrimination deficit, you would not want to choose a program that uses a strong phonics approach. A sight-reading approach would probably be more effective. On the other hand, a child who has a visual memory problem and adequate auditory skills would be a good candidate for a strong phonics reading program. (See Materials List, Chapter 7, for available programs.) Using a manipulative math program where number values can be seen and felt is excellent for a child who is weak in abstract thinking. Some children respond well to learning via many modalities, that is, auditory, visual, tactile, and kinesthetic. Finding a program that capitalizes on the child's strongest learning modality is usually the best technique for teaching.

b. *The reading or math program being used in the regular classroom.* If a child is participating in some part of the reading or math program in a regular classroom, you may want to support that program by doing preclassroom lessons or follow-up lessons. Also find out which skill areas the regular classroom reading or math program may not emphasize enough so that you can supplement with additional help.

c. *The reading and math materials available to you.* Despite the resource room teacher's best efforts at providing a wide variety of materials by using the "beg, borrow, or steal" method, there will be some limitation on what programs are available. It is always possible to make modifications to a less than perfect program. Modifying available programs is an excellent individualizing device.

STEP IV—GROUPING

Once learning priorities have been established and appropriate teaching programs have been selected, you are ready to begin preliminary grouping.

There are many ways one can group children for instruction.

1. Test scores
2. Age

3. Grade
4. Disability
5. Compatibility
6. Random

In a school district where you must schedule around special subject areas, the most effective way to group seems to be by grade. Not only is this often necessary for efficient scheduling, but it is the most acceptable method to the children attending the resource room. If the ability level of the child is drastically below that of his/her grade-level peers, an exception may have to be made. Either this child will have to be taught alone while the others are working independently, or the child will have to be scheduled to attend with a lower grade. To have a child combined with children more than one year below his/her present grade is usually not a good idea. The child sometimes feels so embarrassed and resentful that he/she is not in a teachable frame of mind. It is less disruptive to the regular class if all the children of a particular grade leave at the same time. It also enhances peer relationships among the children. The following questions must be considered about each child as you make grouping decisions:

1. What are the most important subjects to teach this child?
2. How much time should be spent on each subject area?
3. Can the child work more effectively in a small group or one-to-one?
4. Can the child's program be supplemented with home instruction?
5. How can the child's classroom situation be coordinated or modified?
6. Which reading or math program will be best?

Grouping children from each grade can be effectively done by using all of the measuring criteria previously mentioned.

Children should be told before the groups are announced that there may have to be some changes. Once the children have been placed in preliminary groups by the resource room teacher, it must be decided if each child is appropriately placed. If a child has been placed in the wrong group because of academic, social, or emotional reasons, it will be quickly discovered.

The child who is afraid to read or answer questions in a group may need more time to adjust. The child who just cannot keep up with the reading or math level will be very obvious in a small group. This child may need some individual instruction to bring him/her up to the level of the group or may indeed need to be placed with a lower level group. (See Table 6–1.)

LESSON PLANNING

Efficient planning is essential to a well-run resource room program. Knowing ahead of time exactly what will be done and what will be used and when for each teaching day saves time and affords the child the best quality program. Materials such as books, paper, and pencils should all be prepared and ready for the lesson *before* it begins. Wasting precious teaching time looking for materials is a sign of poor planning and a disorganized program.

Deciding on what your lessons will contain and how to plan your learning centers will depend on the needs of the individual children and groups.

There are some guidelines to follow when choosing group and center activities. It makes sense to plan activities which build needed learning skills for handicapped students. Some of these basic thinking skills in order of difficulty are: identifying, naming, classifying, describing, contrasting, constructing, demonstrating, stating rules and drawing conclusions, and finally applying a rule or concept.[1]

Learning centers provide a wide variety of activities that can tap many modalities. When planning center tasks that reinforce small group instruction, put them into a useful format by using some of the above techniques. For instance,

Identifying
"Identify the capitals of the states on this map."
Naming
"Name the short vowel sounds in the following words . . ."
Classifying
"Put all the words that describe *why* in column one. Put all the words that describe *what* in column two. Put all the words that tell *where* in column three. Or, put all the *odd numbers* in one box. Put all the *even numbers* in another."
Describing
"Describe what the student next to you is wearing. Be sure to tell colors and textures."
Contrasting
"Find homonyms for the following words . . ."
Constructing
"Draw a picture of your family. Make a diorama of a scene in a book you just read."
Demonstrating
"Show or tell oral book report."
Stating a rule or drawing a conclusion
"What is a noun? Underline the nouns in the following sentences."
Applying a rule or concept
'Write a creative story. Do a math assignment."

Many of the lessons and learning stations presented in the sample lesson plans are examples of activities exercising the basic skills needed for learning.

[1]From notes taken at Association for Children with Learning Disabilities Convention, March 1979, San Francisco, California.

The lesson plans are set up to show small group lessons with the resource room teacher while simultaneous activities are being done at the learning centers by others. For each lesson shown, appropriate learning centers to reinforce that lesson are listed by letter names (to be found on weekly lesson plan list).

Sample worksheets are provided to accompany [*] activities in the "Learning Centers" list on pp. 96 and 112. The sample lesson plans are designed for the beginning of the school year.

Table 6–1 Preliminary Grouping Worksheet

9:00–10:00		*Language Stimulation Group*
5 First Graders	I Gail George	Referred by speech therapist. Test results on Peabody and Wepman showed below age expectancy—auditory discrimination low. UTAH Test of Language Development—vocabulary and concepts, scores low. Unable to take assessment tests.
	II Mary Kate Donald Brian*	Below grade level one year or more on Metropolitan. Sound symbol on Stanford kindergarten level. Bottel Reading Inventory Primer Level except Brian scored Pre Primer. Boehm Test of Basic Concepts showed all three to be deficit.

*Watch Brian, may need one-to-one rather than group. Lower than others.

10:00–11:00		Stanford Reading	Stanford Math	Bottel Word Rec.	Kottmeyer Spelling
3 Third Graders 4 Fourth Graders	III (3) Blake	2.0	2.5	2.0	1st
	(4) Magen	1.5	3.0	1st	1st
	(4) Craig	1.9	3.5	1st	1st
	(3) Stanley*	1.9	2.9	2.0	1st

*Stanley, Craig, and Liz above others in Math. Group for Math separately.

Reading M, W, F Math T & Th.	IV (3) Georgia	2.5	1.9	2.0	2nd
	(4) Liz	2.5	3.5	2.0	3rd
	(4) Sue	3.0	2.5	2.0	3rd

I Stanley, Craig, Liz
II Blake, Magen, Georgia, Sue

11:30–12:00		*Emotional Support Group*	
3 Fifth Graders 3 Sixth Graders	V	Jeff Kathy Laura Freda Mark Bill Bert	Historically, kids who are in trouble. Some poor home situations. Referred by Special Services for emotional awareness training. Experimental group. Use DUSO Kit—meet with school psychologist on regular basis to discuss problems.

1:00–2:00		*Language Development*				
3 Kindergarten 2 First Graders 1 Second Grader	VI	(K) Sara (K) Marilyn (K) David	Recommended by Speech Therapist. Boehm scores and UTAH scores low in process areas.			
		Slow Learners *(border line)*	Stanford reading	Stanford math	Bottel word rec.	Kottmeyer spelling
	VII	(2) Erwin (1) Jack (1) Morrie	K K K		Pre P Primer Pre P	— — —
		Metropolitan scores all 1+ years below grade level on reading and math.				

2:00–2:30		*Perceptually Impaired*				
3 Second Graders	VIII	Marcia Eddie Sam	1.0 1.5 1.5	1.0 1.8 1.9	1st 1st 1st	1sr 1st 1st
		Metropolitan scores 1+ years below grade level. Team recommendation—all three perceptually impaired. Stress visual, auditory kinesthetic program. (Intersensory Reading Program)				

Table 6-2 Orientation Day—Monday

Time	Group	Lesson or Activity	Recommended Learning Centers (Centers A–O are described on p. 96.)
9–9:30	I II Lesson	Group I-II— Language Impaired & PI 1st Graders. Pick up in regular classroom. Discuss walking quietly, location of bathroom, water fountain. Show around the resource room. Talk about rules.	All children at group activity.
9:30–10	Learning Center	Teacher will spend time at learning center helping children with activities.	I and II A, D, J, M
10–10:30	III IV Lesson	III & IV 3rd & 4th Grade Group (PI). Give a tour of the room stopping at each station to answer questions. Show where their clipboards holding their weekly plan will be kept. Put weekly plan on overhead projector on blackboard. With chalk write in sample assignments as you explain. Talk about bathroom sign-out, etc.	All children at group activity.
10:30–11	Learning Center		III and IV B, E, H, K, N
11–11:30		Planning Period (Work on learning centers.)	
12–1:00		Lunch	

			VIII
1–1:30	VI VII Group Lesson	VI–First Grade, VII Kindergarten Language Stimulation Group Pick up at their rooms. Read story about first day at school. Encourage the children to say something about their families. Use Peabody Language Kit, puppet to encourage verbal response from them. Let them draw a picture of something about school. Put pictures on the bulletin board with their help. Walk them back to their rooms.	Study carrels (2 physically handicapped youngsters who use room to study while class is at gym.)
1:30–2		Planning Period (Meeting with Learning Consultant to go over assessment test scores for grouping.)	
2–2:30	VIII Study Carrels IX Group Lesson	IX–2nd Grade Group (Perceptually Impaired) Give tour of resource room. Show film strip of *Benjy* on automatic viewer. Explain that soon they will be going to stations by themselves and learn how to work the equipment independently.	
2:30–3		*Teacher conference time.* Have materials and books ready to lend out to teachers. Give a quick tour of the room to those who come. Allow them time to peruse and choose materials they may need.	

Note: The first week of regular resource room scheduling is for orientation purposes. Therefore, one joint lesson is given at each time segment rather than in ability skill groups.

To have the children leave the room with a positive attitude to start the year is the main goal of this week's planning.

LEARNING CENTERS

Orientation Week

A. *Build the School.* Using toy blocks, people, buses, cards—build the school, put in students, cars, and buses. (toys and blocks)

*B. *Map of School.* Use tape recorded instructions to locate important places on a map of the school. (prerecorded cassette, tape recorder, earphones, map, worksheet, and crayons)

*C. *Map of School.* Following written directions, locate places on a map of the school, use directional key to tell the directions. (map, worksheet with instructions, and pencils)

*D. *Time Schedule.* Using ditto with time schedule drawn in, copy the schedule. (schedule for each child, schedule worksheet, pencils)

*E. *Time Schedule.* Locate the index card with your name and schedule, stamp the clock, and draw in hands on a worksheet showing the correct time. Replace index card in alphabetical order. (index cards of each child with time schedule, file box, stamp pad, clock stamp, worksheet, and pencils)

*F. *Time Schedule.* Locate index card with your name and schedule on it in card file, copy schedule, state beginning and ending times, calculate length of session in resource room. Replace card alphabetically. (prepared index cards of child's schedule, file box, and worksheet)

G. *Resource Room Rules.* Following tape recorded directions, draw pictures demonstrating correct resource room procedure. (prerecorded cassette tape, crayons, tape recorder, earphones, and drawing paper)

*H. *Resource Room Rules.* Follow directions written on index cards. Carry out the task such as, "using the check-out, leave the room and walk to the restroom." Check off each task on the worksheet. (index cards of tasks, worksheet, and pencils)

*I. *Resource Room Rules.* Complete worksheet on resource room procedures. (worksheet and pencils)

*J. *Learning Centers.* Use a map showing learning centers, find each center and pick up a worksheet from each center. (map worksheet, folders, and pencils)

K. *Learning Centers.* Following a map of the resource room, find listed centers, and write in on the map. (map worksheet, master map, and pencils)

*L. *Learning Centers.* Following a list of directions, draw a floor plan of the room and show correct placement of learning centers. (floor plan, worksheet, and pencils)

M. *Learn about Others in Resource Room.* Draw a picture of one person in your resource room group. Put the name at the bottom. (drawing paper and crayons)

*N. *Learn about Others in Resource Room.* Interview another child. Tape record the interview. Find out where the child lives, what his/her pets and hobbies are. (interview worksheet, blank cassette tapes, tape recorder, and microphone)

O. *Learn about Others in Resource Room.* Write out questions to ask another person. Have him/her fill out your questionnaire. (questionnaire worksheet, pencils)

*See accompanying example

1. Hi! Welcome to the Resource Room. Find the Resource Room on your map. Color the happy face yellow. Is your face a happy face? (pause)

2. Find the Boy's Room. Color it blue. (pause)

3. Find the Library. Color the globe on the bookcase orange. (pause)

4. Is your classroom on the map? If it is, write your name on your classroom. If your classroom isn't on the map, write your name on the Resource Room. (pause)

5. Find the Girl's Room. Color it green. (pause)

6. Find Miss Fritz's room. Put a happy face in her room. Color it yellow. (pause)

7. Be sure to put your name on your map and turn it in to your Resource Room teacher. What is her name?

FIGURE 6–1 Teacher Cassette Dialogue

FIGURE 6–1A Worksheet

Name _____

1. Find the resource room on your map. What is the answer to the problem found there? _____

2. Find the library on the map. Is it north, south, east, or west of the resource room?

3. Find the gymnasium. Which three classrooms are south of the gym? _____, _____, _____.

4. Find the library. Which letter is missing from the word found there? _____.

5. On what floor is the auditorium located? _____.

6. On what street is the school located? _____.

FIGURE 6–2 Map Directions

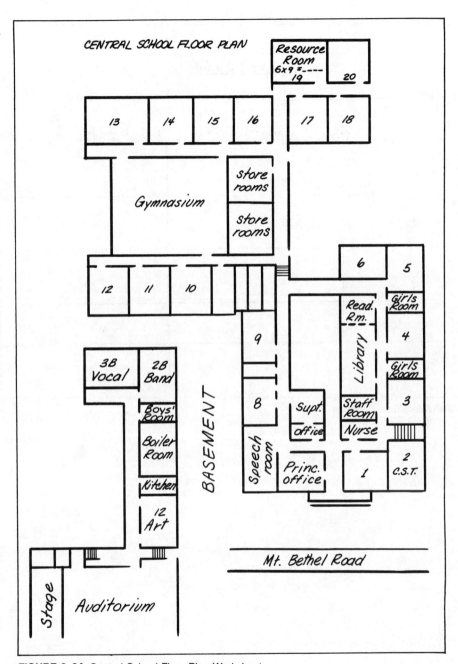

FIGURE 6–2A Central School Floor Plan Worksheet

Resource Room
Time Schedule   Station "D"

name _____

	I arrive:	I leave:
Monday		
Tuesday		
Wednesday		
Thursday		
Friday		

FIGURE 6–3 Time Schedule

name _____   Resource Room   Station "E"
                           Time Schedule

Directions:
1. Stamp each day with the clock stamp.
2. Find your name on an index card in the File box. (alphabetical order)
3. Make each clock tell when you arrive at the Resource Room and when you
4. Return the index card when you finish.   leave.

Monday	Tuesday	Wednesday	Thursday	Friday
I arrive at:	I arrive at:	I arrive at:	I arrive at:	I arrive at:
I leave at:	I leave at:	I leave at:	I leave at:	I leave at:

FIGURE 6–4 Time Schedule

Resource Room
Time Schedule

Station "F"

name _____

Directions:
 1. Find the index card with your name and schedule. (alphabetical order)
 2. Copy your schedule on the grid below.
 3. Calculate the number of minutes per day you will be in the Resource Room.
 4. Total the number of minutes per day to give a weekly total.

Example: From 10:00
           to   11:00
         total 60 minutes

* Do your figuring on the back.

Monday	Tuesday	Wednesday	Thursday	Friday
From:	From:	From:	From:	From:
To:	To:	To:	To:	To:
Total:	Total:	Total:	Total:	Total:

Weekly total:

I attend the Resource Room _____ hours per week

FIGURE 6–5 Time Schedule

```
                                                                    Station H

    Card 1.......
    Write your name on the "excused board."  Take the key and go to the rest-
    room.  Be back as soon as you can.

    Card 2.......
    Go to the Clipboard Center and find a clipboard with your name on it.
    Walk to each assigned station.  Mark your worksheet appropriately.

    Card 3.......
    Replace your clipboard.  Turn in your worksheet and wait for your teacher
    to evaluate your work.
```

FIGURE 6-6 Tasks for Index Cards

```
                                                                    Station H


    CARD 1 TASK                      I completed this task in _____
                                     minutes.


    CARD 2 TASK                      I went to stations:  _____, _____,
                                     _____, and _____.


    CARD 3 TASK                      _____

                                     completed this station

                                     _____

                                     _____.


                        Signed _____
```

FIGURE 6-6A Worksheet

Directions: Complete each question. You may look at the rule chart for help.

1. I must _____ when I want to talk.

2. My name must be written at the _____ when I leave the room.

3. I must get my _____ as soon as I walk into the resource room.

4. If I need help with a station assignment, I must _____
    _____.

5. I always _____ my _____ when
    I am ready to leave for the day.

FIGURE 6–7 Resource Room Rules

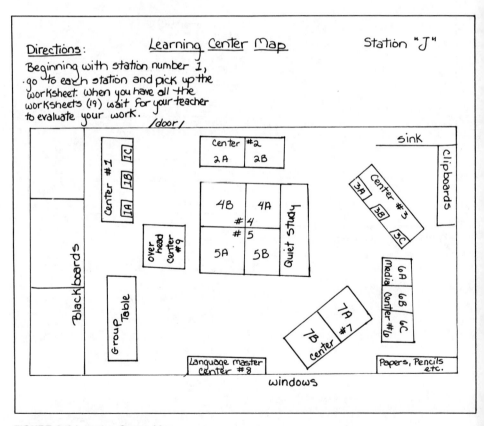

FIGURE 6–8 Learning Center Map

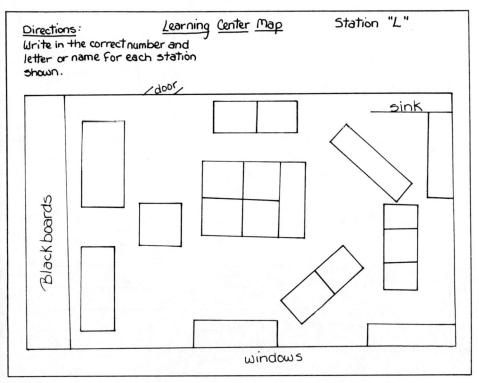

FIGURE 6–9 Learning Center Map

Name _____

1. What is your full name? _____

2. Where were you born? _____

   _____

3. How old are you? _____

4. How many brothers do you have? _____

5. How many sisters do you have? _____

6. What is your favorite subject? _____

7. Why do you attend the resource room? _____

   _____

8. What do you do for fun? _____

   _____

9. Where have you gone on vacations? _____

   _____

10. Who's your favorite person? _____

11. Do you have a pet? _____ What is it? _____

FIGURE 6–10 Interview Worksheet

Table 6–3 Lesson Plans for Day #1

Time	Group	Lesson or Activity	Recommended Learning Centers (Centers A–P are described on p. 112)
9–9:30	I Station		I
	II Group	II–Primary PI Sound symbol lesson. Presenting the vowel sound short /a/. (1) Show letter. (2) Pass out sandpaper letters. (3) Say sound. (4) Children repeat. (5) Draw letter on board. (6) Children draw letter on the board. (7) Draw short /a/ figure pictures.	D, E, A
9:30–10	I Group	I–Sound Discrimination Lesson (1) Using DLM buzzer board, ask children to tap out on the table the same sound pattern they hear on the buzzer board. (2) Allow children to take turns making buzzer patterns for the others to reproduce. (3) Say list of short vowel words and have them raise their hand when they hear short /a/ word. Write words on the board.	II
	II Station		A, B, C
10–10:30	III Group	III–Intermediate PI Group Palo Alto Reading Program Book 12 and workpad. Read story pp. 16–32. Discuss story. Ask comprehension question of each child. Ask them to consecutively take turns retelling the story. They may work on workpad pp. 17–20. They will be checked tomorrow. Work with individuals as needed.	IV
	IV Station		F, G, H

Table 6-3 (cont.)

Time	Group	Lesson or Activity	Recommended Learning Centers
10:30–11	III Station	IV–Intermediate PI Boning Skill Booster Booklet (comprehension) pp. 1-5. Children read selections out loud each taking a turn.	III
	IV Group	Let children answer questions independently in the book. Discuss questions and answers together.	F, G, H
11–11:30		Planning Period Observe in Mrs. Caviar's room—15 min. Observe in Mr. Young's room—15 min. (Don't forget to make out observation form for folder.)	
11:30–12	V Group	V–5th–6th Grade Emotional Growth Group DUSO Lesson on self-awareness. (1) Read Role Playing card to children. (2) Let each one take a role and act out problem situation. (3) Let groups rotate to each problem to role play. Have whole group discussion.	No Centers
12–1:00		Lunch Duty	
1–1:30	VI Station	VII–Primary-Language Peabody Language (K-level) lesson on naming fruit. (1) Show plastic fruit and have children name each (go over several times). (2) Let each child hold and touch fruit as they say the name (repeat until each child knows the names of the fruit). (3) Put fruit in canvas bag. Let each child take turns putting hand in bag and naming the fruit by feel. (4) Color ditto with fruit pictures on it.	VI
	VII Group		E, D, A, J

1:30–2	VI Group	VI–Primary PI	VII
		Lesson on following simple verbal directions. (1) Have each child sit with feet on the floor and hands folded and eyes closed. (2) Tell them you will give a direction—they are to listen and do what you say. (3) Give 1 task direction first: *Stand up* or *Lift your arms.* (4) Increase: *Stand up and hop.* (5) Give a task: *Walk to back of the room.* (6) Increase: *Walk to back of the room and return.* (7) Give much positive reinforcement. Stop at level of success and reinforce.	
	VII Station		B, D, I
2–2:30	VIII Group	VII–*Primary*	No centers
		Pollack reading lesson (using concrete objects) (1) Name apple. (2) Hold apple. (3) Say short /a/ sound—reinforce and repeat. (4) Name other /a/ words. (5) Put apple with /t/ toy. (6) Work out word AT. (7) Put apple with /m/ toy, work out AM. (8) Put apple with /s/ toy, work out AS.	
2:30–3		Teacher Consultation Time	
		(1) Check out materials. (2) Help teachers with ongoing problems.	
3–3:20		Conference with Mr. Jones in office.	

Table 6-4 Lesson Plans for Day #2

Time	Group	Lesson or Activity	Recommended Learning Centers
9-9:30	I Group	I-Primary-Language Stimulation Counting Lesson (1) Using Stern rods (large ones) count out loud while giving each child a set as you count (establish one-to-one correspondence). (2) While you are counting slowly again have one child at a time hand you one rod with each number. (3) Place the rods on the table as you receive them. (4) Have child take the rods one at a time while he/she counts. (5) Free time to build with the rods independently.	II L**, K, B
	II Station	II-Sterns math lesson on number value. (1) Take out one rod. Have child find rod from pile of multivalues which is the same. (2) Take out 2 rods, have children guess how many ones will fill it up. (3) Continue in this manner up to 10. (4) Take rods out of number sequence and see how many can tell you the correct number. (5) Do workbook page.	I K, L**, I, O**
9:30-10	I Station		
	II Group		
10-10:30	III Group	III-Intermediate PI—Math (Stanley, Craig, & Liz) Review multiplication tables. (1) Using flashcards give each one a turn to respond. Those they cannot answer they hold onto. (2) Let them test each other. (3) Play "Fish" using the flashcards with the problems on the outside and the numbers inside (Do you have 6x7?). (4) Let them work out tables on the board for reinforcement.	IV L**, O**
	IV Station		
10:30-11	III Station	IV-Intermediate—low math. Lesson on subtraction using borrowing. (1) Put problem on the board (write big numbers); have them work each step with you. (2) Stop at each step and have a child explain what comes next. (3) Put 3 problems on the board—assign each child a problem to work out in front of you. (4) Work	III L**, M & N, O**
	IV Group		

110

11–11:30		Observe Miss Craigmore—3rd Grade. (Work with low math group on borrowing.)	
11:30–12		*Enrichment Group*—12 Fifth Graders. Mr. Davis is giving talk on stars and Plutonian telescope next week. (1) Prepare questions on oak tag that group wants answered by Mr. Davis (use for reference when speaker is there). (2) Assign books on topic to have each one read before next session to gather resource information before lecture. (3) Group discussion on stars, etc.	
1–1:30	VI Group	VI–Following Directions and Beginning Counting. (1) Have children seated facing the teacher and ready to listen. (2) Start out with one task direction: *Hold up one finger* (give positive reinforcement). (3) *Hold up two fingers.* (4) *Stand up and hop one time.* (5) *Stand up and clap four times.* (6) If children cannot carry out directions, simplify them.	VII L**, K, P
	VII Station		
1:30–2	VI Station	VII–Counting Lesson—using artificial fruit from Peabody Language Kit. (1) Have children repeat the names one at a time saying the name of each fruit. (2) Have children repeat the names for review. (3) Count the fruit as you put each one on the table. (4) Count three fruits as you give them to each child. (5) Have child count as they give the fruit back to you. (6) Take the fruit from each child and count them aloud as you do—put them in a line on the table. (7) Have children practice counting. (8) Repeat several times.	VI P, K
	VII Group		
2–2:30	VIII Group	VIII–Reading—Continue Pollack reading program. (1) Review short /a/ sound. (2) Review consonant toys and sounds. (3) Work out short word combinations.	
2:30–3		*Teacher Consultant Time* (1) Check out materials (2) Consultations	
3:00		Staff Meeting	

**Specific lesson must be assigned (multilevel station).

LEARNING CENTERS
Regular School Schedule

A. *Short /A/ Station.* Milton Bradley short vowel tape and worksheet. Listen to tape while answering questions on the worksheet. (tape recorder, earphones, tape worksheet, pencil, erasers)

B. *Visual Discrimination Station.* Tutorgram and visual discrimination station cards. Find the symbol on the top of the card and match it.

C. *Writing Station.* Practice writing figures on Dubnoff (wipe-off acetate) worksheet. Include short /a/ letter. (worksheets, acetate, grease pencil)

D. *Listening Station.* Listen to prerecorded story *Mac and Tab* (Educator Publishers) on tape recorder. When story is finished, have child tell story in his/her own words on another tape. (Book of *Mac and Tab,* tape of story, blank tape, earphones)

E. *Listening Station.* DLM auditory discrimination tape and worksheet (Primary Level). (tape, worksheet, pencil, earphones)

F. *Comprehension Station.* See filmstrip on *Charlie and Chocolate Factory* by *Movie Strip*®. See film and do two activity cards on worksheet. (filmstrip, cassette tape, activity cards, worksheet, paper, automatic viewer)

G. *Paragraph Comprehension.* Instructo Learning Center on Comprehension. Read poster on the bulletin board—answer questions on prepared ditto worksheet. (Instructo poster, worksheet, pencil)

H. *S.R.A. Reading Kit Station.* Read two stories on your level.* (*prearranged by first week assessment) Answer questions on S.R.A. answer sheet. (S.R.A. reading box and worksheets, pencils)

*I. *Naming and Coloring.* Color fruit on the worksheets. Cut out the fruit and paste it in correct outline in prepared booklet. (fruit worksheets to color, booklet to paste in fruit, crayons, scissors, paste, wastebasket)

J. *Listening Station.* Media Materials Following Directions tape and worksheet (Primary Level). Listen to tape and answer questions on the worksheet. (tape, worksheet, pencils, crayons)

K. *Counting Station.* Place each rod on the drawn box on the worksheet. Outline in pencil the dotted numbers. Color each box. (10 Stern rods, prepared worksheet, pencil, crayons)

L. *Sterns Arithmetic Station.* Using rods, have children do the problems on the prepared assigned workbook page. (assigned worksheets, Sterns student rods, pencil)

M. *Multiplication Review.* Listen to record on multiplication tables. Answer multiplication problems on worksheet. (record, record player, earphones, worksheet, pencil)

N. *Instructo Learning Center on Multiplication.* Play game provided on multiplication problems. Do the maze worksheet. (Instructo Multiplication Learning Center, worksheet [with kit], pencil)

O. *Moving Up in Numbers (DLM).* Do assigned activity cards. Be sure to put your answers on the answer sheet provided—not on the card.

*P. *Listen and Do (counting).* One pre-prepared tape. State simple counting directions: (1) Hop 2 times. (Leave time in between.) (2) Jump 3 times. Listen to the tape and follow the directions carefully.

name_____   Station I

Directions: 1. color the fruit on page 2
            2. cut the fruit out.
            3. Paste them above their names.

                                        apple

        banana

                                    orange

        grapes

FIGURE 6-11 Naming and Coloring

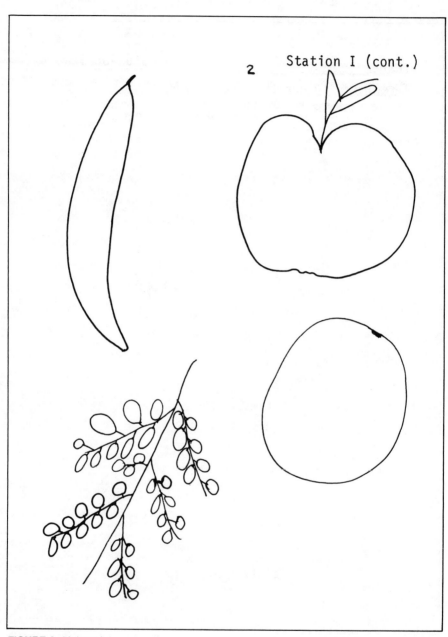

2   Station I (cont.)

FIGURE 6–11 (cont.)

1. "Hello! You are going to listen very carefully to the directions and do exactly as I say.

2. First... Turn off the tape recorder and take off your earphones as soon as you get your directions. Get ready... Hop 2 times.

3. Good!.... Now, you remember to turn off the recorder and take off your earphones as soon as you get your directions. Get ready... Jump 3 times.

4. Good!.... Get ready... Tap your finger on the table 4 times.

5. Good!.... Get ready... Tap your finger on your nose 5 times.

6. You are doing just fine. Now get ready for the last time... Turn off the tape recorder, return the earphones, and go to the group table. Bye.

FIGURE 6–12 Interview Dialogue Worksheet

REFERENCES

IEP Management Check List. Inside Back Cover—Materials Catalogue. New York: Webster Division, McGraw-Hill Book Company, 1978.

choosing materials and equipment for the resource room

7

Materials and equipment for the resource room can be gathered from many sources. These sources vary from school to school, district to district, and state to state. We will list the most common places to acquire equipment. Each resource room teacher must then peruse his/her own school district to find local sources to help supply the program and procedures for acquiring materials.

Knowing your resource room enrollment and becoming familiar with the prescriptions on each child are necessary before looking for materials. You will want the materials and equipment you obtain to reflect the individualized programming you have planned for each child.

SOURCES FOR MATERIALS AND EQUIPMENT

1. School Library. Frequently school libraries not only house useful books but also filmstrips, films, cassette programs, overhead projectors, record players, filmstrip projectors, cassette tape recorders, movie projectors, tachistoscopes, and so on. There are procedures for teachers to use this equipment on loan. Some schools will lend out machinery for the year (if there is ample quantity to go around). If not, the equipment can be taken out for short periods of time, and the learning centers must be planned accordingly.

A school library is an excellent place to find learning center activities. Do not overlook professional magazines that may be received by the library. These often have excellent ideas and are a good resource for teachers.

2. Local Library. Sometimes forgotten, the local city library is an excellent resource for materials. Many city libraries also lend out audiovisual machinery. They may have many of the same materials discussed under school libraries. Often, local libraries are affiliated with larger city libraries and have a retrieval system for materials they may not have on hand. Check into this.

3. School Storage Room. Most schools have a storage room. Try to gain permission from the principal or custodian to go browsing. Often there is usable equipment, such as desks, portable blackboards, room dividers, and tables. Even old text books or dated unused workbooks make excellent reinforcement materials for learning disabled children. Entire resource rooms have been known to be equipped just from the use of furniture and materials stored away.

4. Remedial Reading Teacher or Speech Therapist. If your school has a remedial reading program or speech therapy program in addition to the resource room, these are good sources for materials. Since these programs also service children with learning difficulties, the materials are often excellent for resource room use. Check into borrowing books, dittos, reading programs, skills series, tachistoscopes, tapes, and films. By making your resource room materials available to the reading teacher and speech therapist, a mutually beneficial arrangement can be established.

5. Special Services Department.   Many times special services departments have a library of materials available to loan to teachers, supplemental instructors, and parents. Check with your special services team to see if such a library exists.

6. Government Funded Resource Centers.   Special education materials centers or regional materials centers are located throughout the country. These are a marvelous source for resource room programs. They usually loan out materials and some hardware to area teachers. Not only are these materials useful in the classroom for individualizing, but they give the teacher an opportunity to see and use materials before ordering them from a catalogue. Also, some resource centers provide in-service materials and consulting services to schools. It really is worth looking into.

Since funding for these programs is often through grants, their names and availability have a tendency to change. The best way to find the closest materials center is to write to your own state's special education department and ask for information. The names and addresses of all the state agencies can be found in Appendix A.

7. Handmade Materials.   One of the best sources for individualized materials are those made by the teacher, an aide, or a volunteer. Many books are available to suggest ideas for handmade goods. The *Kids Stuff* series by Incentive Publications in particular is invaluable to this sort of endeavor. See Appendix C for more suggestions and addresses.

Do not forget to check local service organizations who are looking for projects for their volunteers. Senior citizens groups and college clubs, for example, can sometimes offer excellent service in making materials, and at the same time this practice encourages cooperation between the school and the community. Be sure to consider older children in your own school, especially the gifted and talented, to make materials for you.

8. Regular Classroom Materials.   With some resource room children the use of regular curriculum materials to reinforce classroom work will be necessary. Be sure you requisition for those textbooks, workbooks, and teacher guides that you need.

Things like paper, pencils, scissors, crayons, rulers, ditto masters, erasers, and chalk are usually available in the school stock room. Generally, a procedure is set up for obtaining these materials. Be sure to request enough materials to stock all the learning centers as well as the group activity centers.

9. Other Teachers.   Eliciting the support of other teachers can yield extra materials for the resource room. Those teachers who are retiring or changing grade level or have duplicate materials on hand are often willing to loan them. Be alert and not afraid to ask.

10. Catalogue Materials.   There are lists and lists of materials available for both regular and special education. Unfortunately, the usual procedure is that a resource room teacher is given a budget amount, a stack of materials catalogues, and some requisition blanks. Teachers who have never taught in a resource room before then begin taking educated guesses and place their orders.

To avoid making what can be a costly mistake, you may want to consider the following information. I have provided a list of priority materials according to budget amounts. These are materials that the author (through educated guessing and missing) has found to be effective in working with resource room children in grades K–6. Materials for secondary level resource rooms will be found in Chapter 8. Other recommended materials will be found in the Materials List (Table 7–1, p. 121).

Understand that it is impossible for any teacher to have tried all available material on the market. I can only suggest those with which I am familiar. If you have found materials that work for you, please substitute them. The priority materials list is presented as a guide in planning materials for a new resource room or adding to established programs ready for new materials.

There is an organization called the National Information Center for Special Education Materials (NICSEM). NICSEM has catalogues which list every available special education material and where to purchase it. See Appendix C for addresses and phone numbers.

There is a checklist for evaluating materials at the end of this chapter. (See From 7–1, p. 143.) This is helpful when making decisions about what to order.

BUDGET: Up to $300.00

1. Cassette tape recorder	$39.95
2. Blank tapes (30 min.)	10.00
3. 3 sets of headphones	32.00
4. Corrugated paper goods (shelves, dividers, carrels, etc.) Calloway House	20.00

5. Frank Shaefer Primary Special Ed Learning Center: 39.95
   5 activity books, 3 card sets, 5 game boards (good
   material for learning centers)
6. Palo Alto Sequential Steps in Reading Program   50.00
   Readiness–Third Grade
       Books 1-21
       Workbooks 1-21
       Teacher Guides 1-21
   (good basic reading program)
7. DLM Peg Boards and Pegs (good perceptual training)   7.25
       2 boards $1.75 ea.
       1 box pegs $3.75
8. DLM Moving Up in Grammar (sequential   25.00
   activity cards—good for ongoing station)
9. DLM Sound Foundations Program Level I   19.00
   (spelling activity cards with reproducible answer sheet) Grades 1-2
10. Math Resource File for Individualization, Wayne Township,
    Board of Education, Wayne, New Jersey
    150 card resource file for individualization
    Primary Level ages 6–8   12.00
    Intermediate ages 8–12   12.00
        110 cards
11. Magnetic numbers and symbols, Child Guidance   1.25
    Products, Bronx, NY 10472
12. Wooden Rods   25.00
    Sterns Structural Arithmetic (Houghton Mifflin)
    Teacher's guide   5.00

BUDGET: Up to $500.00

Items 1 through 12 plus:

13. Cambridge Press Math Workbooks $20.00
14. Filmstrip previewer   25.00
15. Sterns Structural Arithmetic (Houghton Mifflin)
    Level 1
          6 workbooks   12.00
    Level 2
          6 workbooks   12.00
    Level 3
          6 workbooks   12.00
        2 teacher guides   10.00
16. DLM Moving Up in Numbers (ongoing learning center)   25.00
17. DLM Sound Foundations Program, Level II, Grades 3-4   19.00
18. Instructo Learning Centers   30.00
    3 @ $10.00 each
19. Milton Bradley Duplicating Masters (wide variety available) 25.00
    5 books @ $5.00
20. *One Hundred Ways to Enhance Self-Concept in the Classroom* 5.56
    (a handbook for teachers and parents, Prentice-Hall)

BUDGET: Up to $800.00

Items 1 through 20 plus:

21. DUSO Kit (Developing Understanding in Self and Others) 2–4	$125.00
22. DLM Handwriting Slantboard	13.00
23. Media Materials skill kits with worksheets and cassette (five kits in a variety of areas)	50.00
24. Dubnoff Handwriting Program	35.00
25. Typewriter (used)	75.00

Table 7-1 Materials List

Title and Description	Publisher
Reading	
BARNELL LOFT'S SPECIFIC SKILL SERIES	Barnell Loft
Nonconsumable booklets highlighting eight important reading skills. Each booklet concentrates on one skill. Grades Pre-one–nine	
Price Range: Complete set $100.00	
BE A BETTER READER	Prentice-Hall
Basic Skills Edition. Develops special skills in content areas: social studies, science, math, and literature. Levels A, B, and C.	
Price Range: $4.00 each	
CHECKERED FLAG READING PROGRAM	Field Educational Publications
High interest—low reading level. Cassette and book. Four titles in each series. Kits A and B.	
Price Range: $100.00	
DISTAR READING	Science Research Associates (S.R.A.)
Levels I, II, and III. Provides basic reading and reading comprehension instruction. Readiness–3rd grade	
Price Range: $110.00–$140.00 per kit	
I CAN DO IT	Bowmar Publishers
Early Concepts introduced. Three dimensional, study, supplemental books. Grades K–3.	
Price Range: $10.00 each	
I CAN READ—FOR RELUCTANT READERS	Perma Bound
31 easy-to-read books. Excellent supplemental program—grades 2–4.	
Price Range: $85.00	

Table 7-1 (cont.)

IDEAL CASSETTE Worksheets and Tapes 12 cassettes per case Price Range: $30.00 and up	Ideal School Supply Co.
INTERSENSORY READING PROGRAM (Individual) Developed by Cecelia Pollack. Build simple words by manipulating toy objects that represent letter sounds. More than 250 words are built in this manner. 1 set large letter cards; 1 copy child workbook; 1 book; and teacher's manual. Grades K-1. Price Range: $11.00	Book-Lab, Inc.
INTERSENSORY READING PROGRAM EVALUATION SET (Cecelia Pollack) 1 Phonics Readiness Set; 1 set large letter cards; 1 copy *My Own Reading Book;* 1 copy *My Own Writing Book;* 1 copy *My Own Reading Workbook.* Volume 2 Teacher's Manual. Grades K-3. Price Range: $14.00	Book-Lab, Inc.
INSTRUCTIONAL AID PACKS Diagnostic and prescriptive decoding program designed for small groups and individuals. Grades K-9. Price Range: Total program $380.00 　　　　　　 Each Pack $6.00	Dexter & Westbrook
NEW OPEN HIGHWAY PROGRAM Basal reading program, phonics approach, slow pace. Grades K-8. Price Range: Workbooks $1.75 each 　　　　　　 Texts $8.50 each 　　　　　　 Teacher's Guide $6.50	Scott, Foresman & Co.
OPEN COURT FOUNDATION PROGRAM A sequential introduction to sounds and their spellings. Multisensory, multipath approach to learning with lots of structure and positive reinforcement. Primary level. Price Range: Varies	Open Court Publishing Co.
PALO ALTO SEQUENTIAL STEPS IN READING 3rd Edition Linguistic approach to reading stressing sound/symbol relationships. Develops decoding and comprehension. Short sequential success steps. Grades 1-3 (remedial levels up to grade 5). Price Range: $1.50 per workbook and soft cover texts. Levels 1-21.	Harcourt Brace Jovanovich, Inc.

PEABODY REBUS READING PROGRAM   American Guidance
Programmed introduction to reading. Pictures   Service
symbols and words used sequentially. Grades K–2.
Price Range: $12.00 for examination set

PICTO-VOCABULARY SERIES   Barnell Loft Ltd.
Individualized vocabulary program. Grades 1–2.
Price Range: $49.95

PROGRAMMED READING by M. W. Sullivan and   Behavioral Research
C. D. Buchanan   (Division of McGraw-
Programmed format allowing each student to move at   Hill Publishers)
his/her own pace. Readiness–3
Price Range: $3.00 per book. Wide variety of prices
and materials available.

READ BETTER, LEARN MORE   Ginn and Company
Content areas covered with reading skills
emphasized. Text/workbook format. Grades 4–7.
Price Range: $3.50 per book
             $4.50 Teacher's Guide

READING INCENTIVE PROGRAM   Bowmar Publishing
High interest—low reading level. Action oriented   Corp.
with documentary photos. Books, records. tapes and
filmstrips. Grades 3–High School.
Price Range: $400.00 entire series

SCHOLASTIC GO: READING IN   Scholastic Book
THE CONTENT AREAS   Services, Inc.
Each text workbook is organized into 4 content areas:
literature, social studies, mathematics and science.
Grades 4–8.
Price Range: Skills Text $3.00
              Ditto Masters $12.50
              Teacher's Guide $5.00

SCHOOL HOUSE: A WORD ATTACK   S.R.A.
SKILLS KIT
Sequential approach to word attack skills. Dittos,
plastic response cards, markers, progress sheet pads,
and teacher's guide. Grades 1–3.
Price Range: $130.00

SCHOOL HOUSE COMPREHENSION   S.R.A.
PATTERNS
195 activity cards. Grades 3–6.
Price Range: $135.00

Table 7-1 (cont.)

SPRINT MAGAZINE	Scholastic Book Services, Inc.
High interest—low reading level subscription newspaper. Skill activities included. Grades 3–5.	
Price Range: $2.10 per student copy per year	
S.R.A. LISTENING LAB	S.R.A.
A tape cassette series of directed listening experiences. Grades 1–6.	
Price Range: $305.00	
S.R.A. SKILLS SERIES: PHONICS	S.R.A.
48 lesson plan cards, 10 student magazines, 48 cassette lessons, 96 ditto masters, tests, student folders and teacher's guide. Grades 1–3.	
Price Range: $300.00	
S.R.A. READING LABORATORY	S.R.A.
150 power builders each with a key card; 150 rate builders; 30 rate builder key booklets; 150 skill development cards; 4 cassettes and teacher's guide. Grades 1–3.	
Price Range: $225.00	
MCP SKILL BOOSTER SERIES	Modern Curriculum Press
Consumable skill booklets. Includes word power, comprehension, facts and details, organizing information and using references. Grades 2–5.	
Price Range: $2.10 per booklet	
S.R.A. SKILLS SERIES: STRUCTURAL ANALYSIS	S.R.A.
48 lesson plan cards, 10 student magazines, 48 cassette lessons, 96 ditto masters, tests, student folders, and teacher's guide. Grades 3–7.	
Price Range: $300.00	
S.R.A. SKILL SERIES: COMPREHENSION	S.R.A.
48 lesson plan cards, 10 student magazines, 48 cassette lessons, 96 ditto masters, tests, student folders, and teacher's guide. Grades 4–8.	
Price Range: $300.00	
READING SKILLS PRACTICE KIT I	Curriculum Associates
200 usable activity cards in a sturdy classroom box. Teacher's guide included. Main idea, story analysis, comprehension, structural analysis, study skills, and vocabulary. Grades 2–4.	
Price Range: $30.00	

SUCCESSFUL LEARNING KIT

Love Publishing

Hundreds of items to individualize instruction. Good resource materials for variety of learning centers. Primary–Intermediate.

Price Range: $80.00

SUPPORTIVE READING SKILLS SERIES

Dexter Westbrook Ltd.

Diagnostic, prescriptive reading program. Focus on key sub skills. Pretest and posttest included. Grades 1–9.

Price Range: $10.00

SYLLABLE SCORE BOARD

DLM

Basketball game of syllabication. Four spirit masters and game board. Ungraded.

Price Range: $10.00

THE BIG BOOK SERIES

Prentice-Hall

Collection of ready-to-use hands-on activities in easy-to-assemble form. Grades 3–6.

Big Book of Writing: Games & Activities (Elementary)

Big Book of Collections: Math Games & Activities (Primary)

Big Book of Independent Study

Big Book of People and Words

Price Range: $18.00

THE NEW SPECIFICS SKILLS SERIES

Barnell Loft Ltd.

Nonconsumable reading program. Development of eight crucial reading skills. Placement tests, structural reading program. Grades 1–12.

Price Range: $20.00 for one of each series.

THE TEACHING BOX

Educators Publishing Service

A basic phonetic program for children with a specific language disability. Provides a consistent order of teaching and carefully correlated materials. Primary level.

Price Range: $85.00

TUTORGRAM

Enrichment Reading Corporation of America (ERCA)

Compact electrovisual teaching aid which is easily portable and lightweight. It operates on 2 "D" cell batteries and standard flashlight bulb. Many programs available (54 cards in each). Ungraded.

Price Range: $40.00

Table 7-1 (cont.)

TUTORGRAM SELF TEACHING PROGRAMS	ERCA

54 question cards on large variety of skills. When question card is placed on the tutorgram, the child places the pointer into a hole next to the answer. If the answer is correct, a light and buzzer are activated. Grades K–5.

Price Range: $11.00 per set

VOCABULARY DEVELOPMENT	Milton Bradley

Tapes, worksheets, and response sheets. Covers abbreviations, contractions, prefixes, suffixes, synonyms, antonyms, homonyms, word endings. Grades 3–6.

Price Range: $65.00 per set

WEBSTER'S NEW WORLD DICTIONARY	Prentice-Hall

Good dictionary geared for grades 3–8.

Price Range: $8.00

WHERE I AM	Developmental Learning Materials (DLM)

Independent map and orientation activities. 32-page workbook. Set of 15. Ungraded.

Price Range: $15.00 per set

WORLD MAP GAMES	DLM

Develops math skills and geographical concepts. Six maps, three posters—game format. Ungraded.

Price Range: $8.00

WORD SPY: LANGUAGE AND LEARNING ACTIVITIES	Continental Press

One teacher's guide, 24 spirit masters. Grade 4.

Price Range: $5.00

Language Arts and Learning Centers

CAPITALIZATION & PUNCTUATION	Barnell Loft

12 nonconsumable books with duplicator worksheets and tests. Grades 1–9.

Price Range: $30.00 per level

CHARLIE BROWN DICTIONARY by Charles M. Schulz	Prentice-Hall

Peanuts characters introduce young people to the dictionary. Grades K–3.

Price Range: $7.00

DUPLICATING MASTERS   Milton Bradley

Books of Reading, Math, Perception, Spelling, and
Language Arts. Readiness–12.

Price Range: $5.00

EXPLORING LANGUAGE WITH THE   Prentice-Hall
DICTIONARY

Consumable format. Presents basic dictionary skills in
a total language arts context. Levels A–D.

Price Range: Text $2.00
              Teacher's Guide $2.25

GOAL: LANGUAGE DEVELOPMENT   Milton Bradley

Games oriented activities for learning. 337
lesson-planned cards based on ITPA test. Grades
K–6.

Price Range: $125.00

IDEAL CASSETTES AND WORKSHEETS   Ideal

Modular program. Each unit has cassette tapes, a
duplicator workbook and teacher's manual.
Primary–Secondary levels.

Price Range: Depending on number of cassettes and
worksheets in set: $18.00–$66.00

INSTRUCTO LEARNING CENTERS   Instructo

Kits in strong plastic packaging for storage.
Three-dimensional visuals (easy to assemble), games,
and worksheets. Available on variety of subjects and
levels. Grades K–6.

Price Range: $10.00 and up

KNOW IT ALL   Educational
                                                        Insights, Inc.
Plastic case houses a disk which questions skill areas.
Self-checking, easy to operate. Grades K–3.

Price Range: $10.00 per set. Includes 5 discs.

LANGUAGE PATTERNS/A SELF   Milton Bradley
INSTRUCTIONAL MODALITY

Multisensory approach to linguistic structure. 10
prerecorded lessons. 5 student manipulatives and 10
packs of 2 worksheets. Intermediate level.

Price Range: $65.00

LEARNING CENTER SETS   Frank Shaefer

Special collection of activity cards, game boards, and
books. 8 different collections. Grade K–8.

Price Range: $40.00

Table 7-1 (cont.)

MAGICAL SILENT E	DLM

Game format for reading long vowel sounds with silent /e/ on the end. Ungraded.
Price Range: $10.00

MEDIA MATERIALS — Media Materials Inc.

Each kit contains worksheets, posttest for reproducing, and cassette. Many available on prereading recognizing words, basic vocabulary, reading comprehension, grammar and usage, written expression, and word-related skills.
Primary–Intermediate.
Price Range: $10.00 per set

MOVIE STRIP™ — Films Inc.

Conveniently boxed film strips and cassettes of children's favorite stories like *Charlie and the Chocolate Factory*. Includes activity cards suggested worksheets.
Grades K and up.
Price Range: $60.00–$100.00

MOVING UP IN GRAMMAR — DLM
(Capitalization and Punctuation)

Sequential activity cards for student use. Practice and reinforcement for capitalization and punctuation.
Primary–Intermediate.
Price Range: $25.00

PEABODY LANGUAGE DEVELOPMENT KIT — American Guidance Service

Designed for oral language and concept development. Metal kit, manual, stimulus cards, posters, tapes, puppets, etc. Grades K–3.
Price Range: $100.00

PICTURE A VOWEL SOUND — DLM

12 posters, 12 spirit masters. Language and short vowel review. Ungraded.
Price Range: $14.00

FRANK SHAEFER ACTIVITY BOOKS — Frank Shaefer

Available in a wide variety of math and language arts skill-reinforcement activities. Designed to be reproduced. 48 or more pages in each book. Grades K–6.
Price Range: $4.00 per book

FRANK SHAEFER ACTIVITY CARDS

Frank Shaefer

Each packet contains 48 reusable cards. Emphasis on skill reinforcement for language arts, math, and content areas. Grades K–8.

Price Range: $5.00 per packet

FRANK SHAEFER LEARNING CENTERS

Frank Shaefer

Complete learning center materials in each packet: game boards, reproducible worksheets, etc. Grades K–8.

Price Range: $39.95 each level

SKILL-PACS

Prentice-Hall

Games, puzzles, and activities ready to use. Reproducible format. Readiness–intermediate reading and math.

Price Range: $30.00–$40.00

STRATEGIES IN STUDY SKILLS

Milton Bradley

Tapes, worksheets, and response sheets included. Available on dictionary skills, reference, information, sentence composition, and paragraph composition. Grades 3–5.

Price Range: $65.00

FLASH X

Educational Development Laboratories

A mechanical flash card. It presents material for exactly 1/25th of a second. Discs available for reading, spelling, arithmetic. Ungraded.

Price Range: $10.00

SPEAK AND SPELL

Curriculum Associates

A talking, visual learning aid. Uses 200 of the most problematic spelling and reading words. Students hear the word, key-in the spelling and see the word displayed. Speak and Spell announces whether the word is right or wrong. Ungraded.

Price Range: $55.00

WRITE TO READ TYPING PROGRAM

Curriculum Associates

Teaches reading, writing, and spelling through the development of typing skills. Large student workbook (easel design), large activity cards for short vowels and 20 prerecorded cassettes housed in durable storage box. Ungraded.

Price Range: $40.00

Table 7-1 (cont.)

Math

CUISENAIRE RODS	Cuisenaire Company
1 box of rods each color having a number value. Ungraded.	of America
Price Range: $10.00	
DEVELOPMENT OF NUMBER READINESS	Milton Bradley
Felt figures, chips, dominoes, blocks, and pegs. Primary level.	
Price Range: $60.00	
DISTAR ARITHMETIC	S.R.A.
Three kits—I, II, and III. Basic arithmetic program. Includes student take-home books and hands-on materials. Teacher guide included. Grades K–3.	
Price Range: $150.00 per kit	
FINDING SHAPES IN PICTURES	Troll Associates
10 transparencies. Good for visual closure and math readiness. Primary level.	
Price Range: $30.00	
HOW TO SOLVE STORY PROBLEMS	DLM
200 activity cards in sturdy usable box. Sequential approach. Ungraded.	
Price Range: $25.00	
KEY MATH: DIAGNOSTIC ARITHMETIC TEST	American Guidance Service, Inc.
Preschool–grade 6.	
Price Range: $25.00 for kit	
MATH FACT GAMES	Milton Bradley
6-game set dealing with addition and subtraction facts.	
5-game set dealing with multiplication and division. Ungraded.	
Price Range: $20.00	
MATH RESOURCE FILE FOR INDIVIDUALIZATION	Wayne Township Board of Education
Activity cards—resource file for individualization. Skills and concepts checklist, retrieval system, teacher ideas file, diagnostic test, answer sheets, and materials source list.	
Price Range: Primary level—$12.00 (ages 6–8) Intermediate level—$12.00 (ages 8–12)	

MATHEMATICS WORK-A-TEXT

Cambridge (The Basic Skills Company)

Combination workbook and teaching text. A simplified step-by-step approach to mathematics. Easy-to-read. Not too much on each page. Levels 1–6.

Price Range: Work-A-Text $2.50–$3.50 (depending on level)

MERRILL MATHEMATICS SKILL TAPES

Charles E. Merrill

A diagnostic prescriptive and instructional multimedia program—cassettes, booklets, diagnostic tests.

Price Range: $15.00 each tape
$ 6.00 student booklet

MILTON BRADLEY FLASH CARDS

Milton Bradley

4 basic operations. 80 cards per set. Primary.

Price Range: $2.50

MOVING UP IN NUMBERS

DLM

Sequential activity cards to reinforce basic operation skills. Sturdy usable box. Ungraded.

Price Range: $25.00

MOVING UP IN STORY PROBLEMS

DLM

Activity cards to help develop problem attack skills. Primary level.

Price Range: $25.00

MOVING UP IN TIME

DLM

Activity cards on time concepts. Sequentially presented from seasons of the year to time on a clock. Grades K–3.

Price Range: $25.00

PROGRAMMED MATH by Sullivan

McGraw-Hill

Individual self-correcting self-taught skill books. Limited words to read. Stresses basic math skills. Grades 1–6.

Price Range: Varies according to item

SET UP A MATH LEARNING CENTER

Wayne Township Board of Education

61 task cards—bright and easy to use. Primary and intermediate levels.

Price Range: $12.00

STERNS STRUCTURAL ARITHMETIC STARTER SETS

Houghton Mifflin

Hands-on multisensory approach to number values. Math program with rods and manuals. Primary and intermediate. Workbooks also available. Ungraded.

Price Range: $45.00 each set

Table 7-1 (cont.)

S.R.A. MATH PROGRAM	S.R.A.

Basal math program on easy-to-read texts. Presented in the context of the child's world. Consumable pupil text books and practice workbooks. Placement tests and reinforcement ditto masters available.

Price Range: Text $4.00–$8.00 (depending on level)
Workbook $1.50–$2.00
Teacher's Guide $11.00

STUDENT ACTIVITY CARDS FOR CUISENAIRE RODS	Cuisenaire Company of America

130 task cards for use with cuisenaire rods. Primary-secondary.

Price Range: $15.00

USEFUL ARITHMETIC	Frank E. Richards Publishing Co.

Math workbooks designed for the slow learner. Limited reading, slow sequential steps of practical skills. Vol. I, II, and III.

Price Range: $1.75 per book

USING THE CUISENAIRE RODS	Cuisenaire Company of America

A photo/text guide showing teachers how to use the rods for concrete teaching.

Price Range: $10.00

VISUAL APPROACH TO MATHEMATICS	S.R.A.

Each set contains one volume and visuals with over-lays.
Level I—Volumes 1–7
Level II—Volumes 1–7
Level III—Volumes 1–7

Price Range: $60.00 per set

Handwriting

ALPHABET WALL CARDS	Milton Bradley

Oak tag wall cards for hanging. Available in manuscript and cursive.

Price Range: $2.00

DUBNOFF PROGRAM	Teaching Resources, Inc.

Level I: Sequential perception-motor exercises.
Level II: Experimental perceptual-motor exercises.
Level III: Prewriting perceptual exercises.
Each level contains 3 student books with acetate and crayons.

Price Range: $35.00 each level.

KINESTHETIC SCRIPT LETTERS

Individual letters of the alphabet with tactile element. Ungraded.

Price Range: $40.00

Child Guidance Products

LETTER FORMS

Felt shapes to form letters on cards. Primary.

Price Range: $10.00

Milton Bradley

MAKE A SHAPE

Wipe-off cards for forming shapes.

Price Range: $10.00

Milton Bradley

MAKE A WORD

Wipe-off cards for forming words. Ungraded.

Price Range: $10.00

Milton Bradley

MANUSCRIPT ANIMATED ALPHABET

Teacher's guide, machine, and transparencies. Projects animated letters in direction of correct formation. Small letters and capital letters.

Price Range: $200.00

Photo-Motion Corp.

SLANT BOARD

Fiberboard on metal holder. Slants paper for better handwriting.

Price Range: $10.00

DLM

THE LEFT-RIGHT DISCRIMINATION PROGRAM

Program for helping to encourage laterality.

Price Range: $40.00

Mafex Associates, Inc.

THE NEW HANDWRITING SERIES

Developmental stroke sequence of letter formation in workbook format. Primary–8th grade.

Price Range: $1.25 each

Bowmar Noble Publishing, Inc.

VANGUARD SCHOOL HANDWRITING

Cursive writing is taught to establish words as unified wholes with a continuous flow of strokes. Tutoring kit has one teacher's guide, worksheets, and handwriting evaluation forms.

Price Range: Approximately $6.00

Lectro Learn, Inc.

Table 7-1 (cont.)

Spelling

BASIC GOALS IN SPELLING	Webster, McGraw-Hill
Written by William Kottmeyer and Audrey Claus. Excellent sequential approach to phonic spelling and sound. Consumable text format. Grades 1-8.	
Price Range: Approximately $3.00 per workbook, $7.50 per teacher's guide	
BASIC SPELLING	J. B. Lippincott
Ten nongraded books with step-by-step sequencing which emphasizes phonics approach.	
Price Range: Workbook: $2.50, Text: $4.50, Teacher's Guide: $4.00	
DIAL 'N SPELL	Milton Bradley
Inexpensive reinforcement game in wheel format. Primary level.	
Price Range: $2.00	
DR. SPELLO	McGraw-Hill
William Kottmeyer and Kay Ware. An intermediate remediation workbook for spelling for the slow learner. Visual and auditory stressed. Workbook format.	
Price Range: $2.25 per workbook.	
GILLINGHAM REMEDIAL TRAINING FOR CHILDREN WITH SPECIFIC DISABILITY IN READING, SPELLING & PENMANSHIP	Educators Publishing Service
Text stories, phonetic cards, proficiency scales for remedial training. Primary–High School.	
Price Range: Varies	
KEY-LAB SELF CORRECTING PROGRAM	Houghton Mifflin
Self-correcting spelling program. Primary and intermediate levels.	
Price Range: $45.00	
KNOW IT ALL	Educational Insights
Primary Program. Individualized learning cardboard discs in plastic wheel case. Basic spelling concepts.	
Price Range: $8.00	
LEARNING WITH LAUGHTER SERIES	Scott Education Division
Each kit includes cassette, filmstrip, manipulatives, and other materials. Primary level.	
Price Range: $21.00 per set	

LISTEN, READ, SPEAK AND SPELL — DLM

A program for independent growth in basic reading and spelling skills. Cassettes and ditto masters. Grades 3 and up.
Price Range: $75.00

MICHIGAN LANGUAGE PROGRAM EXAMINATION KIT — Ann Arbor Publishing Co.

Booklets include letter discrimination, word discrimination, sight words, sounding fluency, space discrimination, cursive writing, attending to words, and advanced listening skills. Ungraded.
Price Range: $25.00

SOUND FOUNDATION PROGRAM — DLM

Sequential, phonetic approach. Color-coded activity cards. Student works at own pace. 5 activities for each level. Usable storage box. Levels I and II. Grades 1–6.
Price Range: $20.00

SPELLEX WORD FINDER — Curriculum Associates

Student reference book containing a list of words most frequently used in writing. Not a dictionary, but a spelling source. Ungraded.
Price Range: $10.95 set of five

SPELLING B — Curriculum Associates

A new electronic learning aid that uses a highly individualized approach to make progress easy. Word-picture association. Grades K–5.
Price Range: $30.00

SPELLING GAMES — Milton Bradley

Kit consists of five games to reinforce spelling skills. Ungraded.
Price Range: $25.00

SPELLMASTER INDIVIDUALIZED SPELLING KIT — Curriculum Associates

20 spelling anthology kit booklets, 1000 punched pupil word cards, 1 set spelling activity cards, 20 card rings, and teacher's guide. Grades 3–8.
Price Range: Class set $30.00

SPILL AND SPELL — Parker Bros.

Spelling cube game. Primary–High School.
Price Range: $4.00

WORD BUILDING BOX — J. A. Preston Corp.

Box of word-building activities.
Price Range: $10.00

Table 7-1 (cont.)

WORKING WORDS IN SPELLING   Curriculum Associates

Skillbooks following a carefully researched design to teach spelling. Well-prepared and attractively presented. Levels A–G Available. Ten-pack and teacher's guide. Grades 1–8.

Price Range: $30.00

WRITE TO SPELL   Curriculum Associates

Eighty activity cards, two classroom posters, four spirit masters, and teacher's guide housed in a sturdy usable box. Grades 5–9.

Price Range: $20.00

Perception

AUDITORY PERCEPTION TRAINING   DLM

Sequential reinforcement of auditory perception skills. Developmental cassette tapes with spirit masters. Auditory memory, auditory motor, figure ground, auditory discrimination, auditory imagery.

Price Range: Total Program $300.00
                Can be purchased separately.

COLOR SHAPE MEMORY GAME   DLM

Recognition, matching, and memory skills.

Price Range: $20.00

DUAL PANEL/BUZZER/LIGHT MESSAGE UNIT   DLM

Develops auditory, visual discrimination, and memory skills.

Price Range: $20.00

EYE-HAND INTEGRATION EXERCISES   DLM

Visual motor integration—plastic coated cards with overlays and pencils.

Price Range: $8.00

PARQUETRY BLOCKS   DLM

Reinforces organization, spatial relationships, visual sequencing, matching, etc.

Price Range: Blocks: $8.00
                Designs: $4.00
                Insert Boards: $5.00

PEG BOARDS & PEGS   DLM

Muscle control and visual motor coordination skills.

Price Range: Board: $2.00
                      Pegs: $4.00
                      Design Cards to Copy: $12.00

PERCEPTION TASK CARDS   Milton Bradley

A set of 4 aids to enrich perception of shape, pattern,
and dimensionality. Task Cards—self-correcting.

Price Range: $20.00

S.R.A. LISTENING LANGUAGE LAB SERIES   S.R.A.

Vocabulary development, word understanding and
listening comprehension. 24 tape cassettes, 48 activity
page ditto masters and one teacher's guide. Grades
1–3.

Price Range: $300.00

SUPER EARS   Lowell & Lynwood Ltd.

Auditory Perception—gamelike technique. Record or
cassette. Primary readiness level.

Price Range: $15.00

TACTILE DRAWING BOARD   DLM

Frame holds flexo-film sheets on top of rubber pads.
Students use ballpoint pen to produce 3-dimensional
impressions.

Price Range: $11.00

Emotional Growth

DLM's PROGRAM OF AFFECTIVE LEARNING   DLM
(featuring *Mummenschanz*)

5 films plus a teacher's guide. Feelings, values, and
relationships are explored *non*verbally.

Price Range: $225.00

DEVELOPING UNDERSTANDING OF   American Guidance
SELF & OTHERS (DUSO)   Service

Stories, posters, puppets, tapes, and records. Focuses
on self-development utilizing moral issues and situations. Kit I—grades K–2, Kit II—grades 2–4.

Price Range: $125.00

PROJECT ME   Bowmar

Deals with concepts in early learning; body image,
visual perception, feelings, cause and effect, size, discrimination, form perception, and directionality.
Primary–3.

Price Range: $70.00–$100.00 each kit.

THE T.A. FOR EVERYBODY SERIES
Cleverly illustrated books about transactional analysis.
Builds self-esteem in children and teens.
Price Range: $135.00

Opportunities
for Learning

TOWARD AFFECTIVE DEVELOPMENT
Activities to explore feelings, understanding motiva-
tion, and participation. 190 lessons, filmstrips, casset-
tes, puppets, pictures, career folders, and manuals.
Grades 3–6.
Price Range: $110.00

American Guidance
Service

PUBLISHERS

Ann Arbor Publishing Company
P.O. Box 1446-611
Church Street
Ann Arbor, MI 48104

American Guidance Service, Inc.
Publisher's Building
Circle Pines, MN 55014

Barnell Loft
958 Church Street
Baldwin, NY 11510

Barnell Loft Ltd.
111 South Central Avenue
Rockville Centre, NY 11571

Book-Lab, Inc.
1449 37th Street
Brooklyn, NY 11218

Bowmar Noble Publishing, Inc.
4563 Colorado Blvd.
Los Angeles, CA 90039

Bowmar Publishers
622 Radier Drive
Glendale, CA 91201

Bowmar Publishing Corporation
4563 Colorado Blvd.
Los Angeles, CA 90039

Calloway House, Inc.
451 Richardson Drive
Lancaster, PA 17603

Cambridge (The Basic Skills
Company)
488 Madison Avenue
New York, NY 10022

Charles E. Merrill Publishing Co.
1300 Alum Creek Drive
Columbus, OH 43216

Child Guidance Products
Bronx, NY 10472

Continental Press
Elizabethtown, PA 17022

Cuisenaire Company of America
12 Church Street
New Rochelle, NY 10805

Curriculum Associates, Inc.
8 Henshaw Street
Woburn, MA 01801

Developmental Learning Materials
(DLM)
440 Nutchez Avenue
Niles, IL 60648

Dexter Westbrook Ltd.
958 Church Street
Baldwin, NY 11150

Educational Development Laboratories
(A Division of McGraw-Hill Book Co.)
1221 Avenue of the Americas
New York, NY 10020

Educational Insights Inc.
423 South Hendry Avenue
Inglewood, CA 90301

Educators Publishing Service, Inc.
75 Moulton Street
Cambridge, MA 02138

Enrichment Reading Corporation
of America
(ERCA)
Iron Ridge, WI 53035

Field Educational Publications
686 Forest Road, N. E.
Atlanta, GA 30312

Films Inc.
1144 Wilmette Ave.
Wilmette, IL 60091

Frank E. Richards Publishing
Company
330 First Street, Box 370
Liverpool, NY 13088

Frank Shaefer
266616 Indian Peak Road
Dept. 27 M
Rancho Palos Verdes, CA 90274

Ginn and Company
P.O. Box 2649
1250 Fairwood Avenue
Columbus, OH 43216

Harcourt Brace Jovanovich, Inc.
757 Third Avenue
New York, NY 10017

Houghton Mifflin Company
53 West 43rd Street
New York, NY 10017

Ideal School Supply Company
8312 South Birkhoff Avenue
Chicago, IL 60620

Instructo Corporation
11 Cedar Hollow Road
Paoli, PA 19301

J. A. Preston Corporation
71 Fifth Avenue
New York, NY 10003

Lectro Learn Inc.
Box 127
Berwyn, PA 19312

J.B. Lippincott
Educational Publishing Division
East Washington Square
Philadelphia, PA 19106

Love Publishing Company
6635 East Villanova Place
Denver, CO 80222

Lowell & Lynwood Ltd.
958 Church Street
Baldwin, NY 11150

McGraw-Hill Book Company
1221 Avenue of the Americas
New York, NY 10020

Mafex Associates, Inc.
111 Barron Avenue
Johnstown, PA 15907

Media Materials Inc.
2936 Remington Avenue
Baltimore, MD 21211

Milton Bradley
Springfield, MA 01100

Modern Curriculum Press
13900 Prospect Road
Cleveland, OH 44136

Open Court Publishing Company
Box 399
La Salle, IL 61301

Opportunities for Learning
8950 Lucline Avenue
Department 86
Chatsworth, CA 91311

Parker Brothers
Salem, MA 01970

Perma Bound
Vandalia Road
Jacksonville, IL 62650

Photo-Motion Corporation
Morrison Building
King of Prussia, PA 19406

Prentice-Hall, Inc.
Englewood Cliffs, NJ 07632

Scholastic Book Services, Inc.
904 Sylvan Avenue
Englewood, NJ 07632

Science Research Associates (S.R.A.)
College Division
1540 Page Mill Road
Palo Alto, CA 94304

Scott Education Division
Scott Graphics
Holyoke, MA 01040

Scott, Foresman & Company
1900 East Lake Avenue
Glenview, IL 60025

Teaching Resources Corporation
100 Boyleston Street
Boston, MA 02116

Troll Associates
320 Route 17
Mahwah, NJ 07430

Task Master
Division of Instructional Fair, Inc.
P.O. Box 1650
Grand Rapids, MI 49501

Wayne Township Board of
Education
Project: Open Classroom
P.O. Box 1110
Wayne, NJ 07410

Webster Division
McGraw-Hill Book Company
1221 Avenue of the Americas
New York, NY 10020

The following Resource Checklist was designed with the purpose of showing what items companies produce and what services are available through various organizations. In addition to the Materials List in which "tried and true" materials were described, the Resource Checklist presents invaluable aids to those responsible for choosing and purchasing materials for a wide variety of resource room programs.

Table 7-2 Resource Checklist

Companies & Organizations	Educational Assessment	Ongoing/Classroom Assessment	Communication Methods	PreVoc./Voc. Skills	Parent	Interagency Cooperation	Medical Assessment	Humanizing Environment	Service Delivery Rural	Behavioral Management	Teacher Training & Resources	Other Services	Other	Affective	Deaf	Blind	Visual Perception	Motor Skills	Self Help	Media
																	Instructional Materials Focus			
ACI Productions	X										X							X		X
Academic Therapy Pub.		X									X		X			X	X	X		X
American Seating Co.													X							
American Thermoform Corp.																X	X	X		X
Bardeens Inc.	X												X		X	X	X	X		X
Beckley-Cardy		X											X	X			X			X
Bowmar													X		X		X			X
Robert Brady Co.		X									X		X			X	X	X		X
Childcraft Education Corp.		X											X		X			X		
Consulting Psychologists Press	X	X											X		X					
Creative Playthings											X				X	X	X	X		X
A. Daigger & Co.															X	X	X	X	X	X
DLM	X										X		X		X	X	X	X		
ESP, Inc.		X									X		X		X		X	X		
Edmark Asso.					X													X	X	
Educational Development Corp.											X									X
Education R&D Information Office											X							X		
Educational Research Council of America	X	X								X	X		X			X	X	X		X
Educational Testing Service	X	X									X		X			X	X	X		X

Encyclopedia Britannica Education Corp.
Field Educational Pub., Inc.
Harvard Educational Review
Hubbard Scientific Co.
Ideal School Supply Co.
Instructional Appraisal Services
JS^2, Inc.
Language Resource Assn.
Learning Concepts
McGraw-Hill Book Co.
Northwest Regional Educational Lab.
Northwestern University Press
Perceptual Development Laboratories
Pickwick Company
Prentice-Hall
Primm Consultants LTD
Precision Acoustics Corp.
Psychodiagnostic Test Co.
Psychological Corp.
Remediation Assn., Inc.
Research Press
Royce International
SEMDC
Science for the Blind
Silver Burdett Co.
Speech & Language Materials Inc.
Teaching Resources Corp.
University of Utah Educational Media Center
Vocational Films
Alexander Graham Bell Assn. for the Deaf, Inc.

Table 7-2 (cont.)

The column group **Instructional Materials Focus** covers the columns *Media*, *Self Help*, *Motor Skills*, and *Visual Perception*.

Companies & Organizations	Media	Self Help	Motor Skills	Visual Perception	Blind	Deaf	Affective	Other	Other Services	Teacher Training & Resources	Behavioral Management	Rural Service Delivery	Humanizing Environment	Medical Assessment	Interagency Cooperation	Parent	PreVoc./Voc. Skills	Communication Methods	Ongoing/Classroom Assessment	Educational Assessment
American Assn. of Special Educators					X					X										
American Assn. of Workers for the Blind	X		X		X					X										
American Assn. on Mental Deficiency									X	X										
American Foundation for the Blind	X		X		X					X										
American Institute for Research in the Behavioral Sciences																				
American Medical Assn.														X						
American Printing House for the Blind					X															
Assn. for Children with Learning Disabilities										X										
American Assn. for the Education of the Severely/Profoundly Handicapped									X							X		X		
Center for the Study of Evaluation																			X	X
Epilepsy Foundation of America									X	X										
Learning Research & Development Center																			X	X
National Assn. for Retarded Citizens									X	X										
National Assn. of the Deaf						X			X	X										
National Braille Assn.					X				X	X										
National Easter Seal Society									X	X										
National Society for Autistic Children									X	X										
State Federal Information Clearinghouse for Exceptional Children										X						X				
United Cerebral Palsy Assn.									X	X										

Adapted from a list compiled by The Northeast Regional Resource Center, Hightstown, New Jersey.

```
A CHECKLIST FOR EVALUATING MATERIALS FOR AN INDIVIDUALIZED EDUCATION PROGRAM

Title _____

Author _____ Publisher _____

Evaluation _____ Evaluator _____
_____

Evaluated for use by _____ Type of learning problem _____
```

Flexibility   YES   NO
   1. Can this material be used:
         a. only as a complete program?   ____   ____
         b. in small units or modules?   ____   ____
   2. Can the material be used for:
         a. group instruction?   ____   ____
         b. individualized instruction?   ____   ____
         c. both?   ____   ____
   3. Are supplementary materials (A-V, manipulatives, etc.)
      provided or suggested?   ____   ____
   4. Are supplementary activities (classroom, individualized,
      field trips, etc.) provided or suggested?   ____   ____
   5. Is this material useful for:
         a. a variety of learning problems?   ____   ____
         b. a specific learning problem?   ____   ____
      (list (a) or (b) areas if desired)

_____

_____

Content

   1. Is the content appropriate to the:
         a. chronological age of the student?   ____   ____
         b. mental age of the student?   ____   ____
   2. Is the content appropriate for the cultural
      and social background of the student?   ____   ____
   3. Will the content provide real-life, self-help skills? ____   ____
   4. Is the material appropriately paced?   ____   ____
   5. Is there adequate reinforcement?   ____   ____
   6. Does the material provide motivation?   ____   ____
   7. Is there provision for assessment?   ____   ____

Practicality
   1. Does the Teacher's Manual provide:
         a. background information?   ____   ____
         b. suggestions for reinforcement or extension? ____   ____
         c. classroom management help?   ____   ____
   2. Is the Teacher's Manual well-organized,
      with clear instructions and/or suggestions?   ____   ____
   3. Is the student's material:
         a. durable?   ____   ____
         b. easy to store?   ____   ____
         c. safe?   ____   ____

Comments, if desired _____

_____

FORM 7-1 (Webster McGraw-Hill has designed this checklist for your use and it may be reproduced for educational material evaluation.)

ADDRESSES OF COMPANIES

ACI Productions
35 West 45th Street
New York, NY 10036

Academic Therapy Publications
1539 Fourth Street
San Rafael, CA 94901

American Seating Company
P.O. Box 1141
Syracuse, NY 13201

American Thermoform Corp.
8640 East Slauson Avenue
P.O. Box 125
Pico Rivera, CA 90660

Bardeens, Inc.
Fisher Road
East Syracuse, NY 13057

Beckley-Cardy
1900 North Narragansett Avenue
Chicago, IL 60639

Bowmar Publishers
622 Rodier Drive
Glendale, CA 91201

Robert Brady Co.
Bowie, MD 20715

Childcraft Education Corp.
150 East 58th Street
New York, NY 10022

Consulting Psychologists Press
577 College Avenue
Palo Alto, CA 94306

Creative Playthings
Princeton, NJ 08540

A. Daigger & Co.
159 West Kinzie Street
Chicago, IL 60610

Developmental Learning Materials
7440 North Natchez Avenue
Niles, IL 60648

ESP, Inc.
2304 East Johnson
Jonesboro, AR 72401

Edmark Associates
13249 Northrup Way
Bellevue, WA 98005

Educational Development Corp.
202 Lake Miriam Drive
Lakeland, FL 33803

Education R & D Information Office
775 Lincoln Tower
1860 Lincoln Street
Denver, CO 80203

Educational Research Council
of America
Rockefeller Building
W. 6th and Superior
Cleveland, OH 44113

Educational Testing Service
Princeton, NJ 08541

Encyclopedia Britannica Educational
Corp.
425 North Michigan Avenue
Chicago, IL 60611

Field Educational Publications, Inc.
2400 Hanover Street
Palo Alto, CA 94304

Harvard Educational Review
13 Appian Way
Cambridge, MA 02138

Hubbard Scientific Co.
2855 Shermer Road
Northbrook, IL 60062

Ideal School Supply Co.
Oak Lawn, IL 60453

Instructional Appraisal Services
Box 24821
Los Angeles, CA 90024

JS², Inc.
P.O. Box 182
Corinda, CA 94563

Language Research Associates
175 East Delaware Place
Chicago, IL 60611

Learning Concepts
2501 North Lamar
Austin, TX 78705

McGraw-Hill Book Co.
1221 Avenue of the Americas
New York, NY 10020

Northwest Regional Educational Lab.
710 S.W. Second Avenue
500 Lindsay Building
Portland, OR 79204

Northwestern University Press
1735 Benson Avenue
Evanston, IL 60201

Perceptual Development Laboratories
P.O. Box 1911
Big Spring, TX 79720

Pickwick Company
1120 Glass Road N.E.
Cedar Rapids, IA 52406

Primm Consultants LTD
85 Sparks Street, Suite 211
Ottawa 4, Ontario, Canada

Precision Acoustics Corp.
55 W. 42d Street
New York, NY 10036

Prentice-Hall, Inc.
Englewood Cliffs, N.J.

Psychodiagnostic Test Co.
Box 859
East Lansing, MI 48823

Psychological Corp.
757 Third Avenue
New York, NY 10017

Remediation Assn., Inc.
Box 318
Linden, NJ 07036

Research Press
Box 31775
Champaign, IL 61820

Royce International
4345 South Santa Fe Drive
P.O. Box 1337
Englewood, CO 80110

Special Education Materials
Development Center (SEMDC)
5401 Westbard Avenue
Washington, DC 20016

Science for the Blind
221 Rock Hill Road
Bala-Cynwyd, PA 19004

Silver Burdett Co.
Dept. LAPM, 250 James Street
Morristown, NJ 07960

Speech and Language Materials, Inc.
P.O. Box 721
Tulsa, OK 74101

Teaching Resources Corp.
100 Boylston Street
Boston, MA 02116

University of Utah
Educational Media Center
207 Bennion Hall
Salt Lake City, UT 84109

Vocational Films
111 Euclid Avenue
Park Ridge, IL 60068

REFERENCES

A Checklist for Evaluating Materials for An Individualized Education Program, Inside Front Cover—Materials Catalogue. New York, N.Y.: Webster Division, McGraw-Hill Book Company, 1978.

Bibliography of Selected Available Resources. Northeast Regional Resource Center, Hightstown, New Jersey, 1976.

sharing a day
in the life
of a resource room
teacher

8

This chapter contains the actual diary of a day spent in a resource room. It is written to give a realistic picture of what can happen on any given day.

8:00   I arrive at the front office and sign in. Greetings are exchanged with the school secretary. I peruse the bulletin board to see if any staff meetings have been scheduled. Oh-oh, there's a staff meeting this afternoon. If I would only remember to check the board more often. "May I use the phone?" I call my daughter who hasn't left for school yet to tell her to walk to her piano lesson after school, as I will be at a staff meeting.

8:05   Walking to my classroom I run into Miss Schmidt, a second grade teacher. She has some concerns about Carol, a resource room child, who is having difficult with reading comprehension. Although Carol can decode words on grade level, she rarely understands what she has read. After discussing yesterday's lesson with the teacher, we agree to increase Carol's time in the resource room for the next few days so she can take advantage of some additional comprehension learning stations. I make a mental note to concentrate more on comprehension during Carol's group time. (I must remember to write that in my plan book as soon as I get to my room.)

8:15   I remember the note I need to make about Carol and write it down as soon as my coat is hung up. I also make sure I note that she will be staying for an extra half hour for the next few days. I check Carol's clipboard which holds her weekly plan and add the comprehension stations. I also write a memo to Mr. Jones, the principal, and to the director of special services, Miss Kratz, informing them of Carol's change in schedule. I have learned that a memo sent to the administrators keeps them informed and me out of hot water.

8:45   I see that I have approximately fifteen minutes until the first students arrive. This gives me time to put the chairs in order, set out my lesson plans, and double-check the stations. I add pencils, crayons, and additional paper as they are needed at the stations. I write a direction card to replace a missing one from the spelling station. It never ceases to amaze me that a student would find a direction card valuable. I review my lesson plan for the first group, get out the necessary booklets and pencils. I'm running out of pencils again. If I could only stop pencils from leaving the room!

9:00   The first group of children arrive. Although six are scheduled from one classroom, by 9:00 only three have arrived. These children get their clipboards where their first assignment is listed. One child goes to the group table while the two others go to different stations. I make a fast "cruise" by the two occupied stations and make sure the children have chosen the station to which they were assigned. I also check the worksheet and the cassette they are using to make sure they match. Occasionally a student will waste valuable time listening to a cassette and trying to coordinate the wrong worksheet only to discover that fact too late. Parent volunteers come in handy for these chores.

9:05   I go to the wall intercom and buzz Miss Wilcox. "Did you forget?" As soon as she hears my voice she replies, "They're on their way—sorry." Just as I put the receiver down, in walk the missing three. They quickly get their clipboards and scurry to their assigned places. Two come up to the group table, and one goes to the Language Master station.

9:06   I join the three at the group table. After a quick discussion of how everyone feels this morning, we open our reading books to a story about a frog jumping contest. After looking at the pictures, each child takes a guess as to what the story will be about. Then they take turns reading, and so do I. My reading gives the children a chance to hear a reading model and also to hear expression used with oral reading. Jeremy, a second grader, is having difficulty hearing the difference between short vowels. I refer to the Slingerland picture-cued short vowel chart on the wall. We begin telling the story of the vowels: A apple /a/, E egg /e/, I indian /i/, O octopus /o/, U umbrella /u/. As we resume reading, I refer to the chart by pointing when Jeremy is stuck on a vowel. After the vowel drill we talk about how to tell if the word he just read is wrong. This is to help him by using context clues.

Jeremy read, "The frog hipped."
"Jeremy, how can a frog hip?" (giggles)
"Does that make sense? When you read a sentence and it sounds silly and doesn't make sense, what does that tell you?"
Annette answers, "You should read it again because maybe you read wrong."
"That's right, what do frogs do?"
Jeremy answers, "They make funny noises."
"Yes they sure do," I answer, "but how do they move around?"
Jeremy says, "They hop."
"Yes Jeremy, they hop. Come write hop on the board."

After writing hop correctly on the board I ask Jeremy to resume reading. He reads, "The frog hopped." Now we can move on.

9:25   Sara, Annette, and Jeremy go to their assigned stations, and the three children who were at stations come up to the group table. Before we begin the group lesson, I look at each child's station work. Using prepared answer sheets, which I keep in a folder in my plan book, we check the answers on their worksheets. Grace got 100 percent correct on the DLM Read, Speak, Spell, and Write programmed spelling lesson. Grace and I decide together that tomorrow she can go on to another level. She seems very pleased. Douglas missed four out of twenty answers on a doubling the consonant and adding "ing" task. After questioning him, he appears to understand the rule, but he was in a hurry and made careless mistakes. Douglas would like to use the Language Master tomorrow. We compromise—if he will use the twenty double consonant words at the language master station, he can go there tomorrow. He agrees—we are both satisfied. David hasn't finished his assigned station. He read the short story but didn't have time to answer the comprehension questions afterwards. He agrees to finish this station tomorrow.

9:30   Greg, a third grader, comes in, gets his clipboard and goes to his assigned station. This group is working on following written and verbal directions. We take out a "Following Directions" workbook and begin the first activity. The first task is to look through the workbook and underline all the direction words before starting. The children volunteer direction words as I write them on the board. After compiling a list of several of these words, they proceed to search for them in the workbook and underline the ones they find. Michael, who has been taking Rytalin (medication used to calm down hyperactive children) with much success, seems to be having a difficult time concentrating today. I suspect that something is wrong. Either he wasn't given his medication in the morning, or something is troubling him. After careful questioning, I discover that Michael's older brother was ill. His brother became ill during the night and had to be taken to a hospital by ambulance. A traumatic experience indeed for a young boy. I let Michael verbalize his feelings and concerns. I offer to call his home to check on his brother's progress. He would like that very much. I assure him that I will let him know when I find out any news. We continue the lesson on following directions which is now much more productive for Michael.

9:55   I call up the three people who are at assigned stations and quickly check over their station work. We decide together, based on their completed work, which station they will attend tomorrow. After returning their clipboards, the six children are sent back to their home rooms.

10:00   I have a planning period. I quickly go to the office and place a phone call to Michael's home. His mother is there and explains that Michael's older brother is responding well in the hospital. He has regained consciousness and will probably be returning home in a day or two. She knew Michael was upset by what happened and sent him a message that "everything is fine." I suggested that if Michael's brother has a phone in his room at the hospital, it might be reassuring to Michael to be able to talk to his brother. After hanging up, I go to Michael's classroom. I briefly tell Mrs. Wilcox what has happened and call Michael out in the hall to give him the good news. He is obviously relieved.

10:30   Time to make a classroom observation. I go directly to a fifth grade classroom where there are three resource room students. I enter the room quietly and go to the back and try to be as unobtrusive as possible. Experience has led me to believe that the less eye contact on the teacher the better. It is somehow more convincing that you are evaluating the students rather than the teacher. I notice that Tommy is not being very attentive. He has looked out the window, played with a pencil eraser, poked the back of the boy in front of him, and played with saliva bubbles in his mouth—all in the first five minutes that I am there. Norman seems to be paying attention but hasn't volunteered to answer a question. Penny is really trying to be involved. She seems to be listening and even asked a question. Three cheers for Penny. The fifth grade teacher, Mr. Young, is giving a lesson on the metric system. Not using concrete visuals can be a problem for Tommy and Norman. I make a mental note to try to reinforce this lesson when they come in this afternoon. I also must make a note on my conference sheet to suggest the use of visual aids to Mr. Young. This will be a sensitive area, and I must word this suggestion carefully so he doesn't think I'm being critical of his teaching. I leave a note on his desk.

Dear Mr. Young,

Tommy sure seems restless today. I loved the question Penny asked, didn't you? I look forward to discussing more at our conference on Friday. See you soon.

Natalie

11:00   After writing some quick notes on the classroom observation and putting them in the file, the next group of children arrive. There are seven in all. After a little discussion and a quick check in the plan book, we determine that five of them will go to individual stations and two are slotted for the group table. The two at the table are fifth graders who need help with study strategies and following directions. They are doing a lesson on synonyms. From a short story (one and one-half paragraphs long), they are to replace the underlined words with a list of given words. They must choose the correct word to use. Norman begins looking up each of the given words he does not know and writing a few key words from the definition above them. I think to myself, "Good for you, Norman. Last year at this time you would probably have guessed at the correct choice and gotten most wrong." What a good feeling it is to see children begin to realize what they really can do. Penny is writing out the paragraphs first and leaving room for the new words. Later she will go back and fill in with the words she is sure of. Both of these strategies are acceptable and will allow each of the children to be successful with the assignment.

11:25   Penny and Norman go to their assigned stations. Five other fifth graders come up to the group table for a reading lesson. We are working in *Palo Alto Sequential Reading Series,* Book 21. Before we begin I ask to check their station work. George was at a comprehension station. He had to read a series of three paragraphs and then answer questions about the details of these paragraphs. He answered half of the questions wrong. Paul is capable of understanding but because of his halting reading style is always in a rush to compensate for lost time. Consequently, he doesn't read thoroughly and does a lot of guessing. He is aware of this problem. Before I can even comment he responds with "I know I read too fast and didn't take time to understand, I'll do it over tomorrow." I agree with his decision and he is given his assignment for tomorrow. The other three have "two-day" stations. After checking over their preliminary work we all agree they can continue these stations tomorrow. We begin reading a story together, each one taking a turn. They are reading well today and their inflections are improving.

11:45   The intercom buzzes. The office secretary has called to inform me that I have lunch duty today. This means I eat between 12:00 and 12:30 and supervise the lunch room from 12:30 to 1:00. I put the receiver down and see a parent at the window of the door. I tell the group at the table to read silently while I go to the door. It is Mrs. Gibbons who has come to give her daughter Beth some cough medicine. I am ambivalent about this, knowing full well that Mrs. Gibbons tends to overprotect Beth, and the medicine should have been left with the nurse in the office. I suggest that she take Beth in the back of the room today but explain to her that it is a school policy for medicine to be given by the school nurse only. She mumbles an agreement but insists that it is too much trouble and easier for her just to come in and give the medicine. I sympathize with her but insist that I must follow the policies set down by the administration.

11:50   I return to the reading group at the table. I ask Jennifer to give a quick summary of the story. She has difficulty telling the story from the beginning in sequence. I give her the opening sentence of the story and structure her answers with appropriate questions to give her the experience of telling the story in its proper order. I glance up at the clock. It is time to check the stations of the two children still there. I direct the five at the table to begin a workbook page for the next five minutes. I go to the two stations and check the children's work. We agree together which stations they will attend tomorrow.

12:00   Everyone is dismissed for lunch. I straighten up the stations and put out the materials for the enrichment group which is scheduled for 1:00.

12:07   I arrive in the teacher's room. Several primary teachers are already eating their lunch. I say hello to everyone and find an empty seat at the table to eat my yogurt. (It's Monday which means a new diet begins.) I listen to Miss Ryan tell about her skiing weekend with interest. Two second grade teachers are discussing a resource room child. He is indeed a discipline problem and needs additional time and attention. I'm always uncomfortable when I hear a child being discussed in the teacher's room. I realize that when teachers get together they are bound to discuss their students, but nevertheless, I find it unfair to the child. Many "problem" youngsters are "tagged" in the teacher's room and are prejudged before a new teacher can get to know them. Knowing that expressing this point of view at this time would not win friends for me or the resource room program, I say nothing.

12:20   It is time to be on duty in the lunch room. I excuse myself and head downstairs to the lunch room. On the way I run into Miss Kratz. She reminds me of a staffing meeting at 2:00 on a youngster who has been causing a lot of upheaval in the regular classroom. I assure her that I'll be there.

12:30   The lunch room is noisy. I go to the microphone and request that talking be done in whispers only. The rest of the period is spent reinforcing and restating that request. There must be a better way for kids to spend a lunch period. I decide to bring it up at the next staff meeting. Perhaps by brainstorming, we can come up with something better.

1:00   The first grade enrichment group is due to arrive. There are ten children from the three first grades who have been recommended by their classroom teachers. They have displayed exceptional ability or talent in some area. This group seems to be science-oriented and has chosen to do a unit on rocks and minerals. Mr. Jonas, a geologist from the community, has already arrived and is busy setting up his rock collection. He is slated to give a talk on rocks and minerals. The children arrive in groups of twos and threes. They are fascinated by the rocks that they see being displayed on the table. They are bubbling over with questions. After getting them seated and quiet, Mr. Jonas begins his talk. Thankfully he has geared it toward their age level, and they are fascinated. When he has finished, he allows time for questions. Several of the children are interested in volcanoes. Each child is invited to give a theory on what causes a volcano to erupt. The imagination of these children is extraordinary. The session ends with each child handling and looking at the rocks on display. They are obviously motivated, and this turned out to be an excellent lesson to begin the unit on rocks and minerals.

1:30 I have a planning period for twenty minutes. I decide to change a station. The station I have already set up for vowel discrimination has been used by all those who were assigned. I decide to add a comprehension activity there instead. I set up a Dukane viewer, which automatically runs a filmstrip and cassette tape with a program on whales. It is a primary level film and has adequate material about which to ask comprehension questions. I preview the film while I jot down comprehension questions on a ditto master. I place the ditto on my desk with a note to myself to run off twenty copies after school.

1:50 I gather up the materials and the file on George, the child to be discussed at the staffing meeting. I take his test scores from the beginning of the year, the notes from conferences with his teacher, as well as notes on classroom observations. I scurry up to the child study team office where the staffing meeting will be held.

2:00 Already seated at the meeting are the psychologist, social worker, learning consultant, and classroom teacher. At my arrival the meeting begins. The classroom teacher, Miss Caviar, speaks first since she has requested the staffing. She explains that George, a fourth grade boy who attends the resource room for an hour a day, is creating a lot of distraction in the classroom. She reports that he often talks out, disturbing the others, and is generally a discipline problem. He seems to enjoy the attention he gets for misbehaving. His classroom work is barely acceptable. He does however enjoy reading and is showing improvement in that area. I report that in a small group situation George is not such a problem. However, he does seem to be more rambunctious than usual. I ask Miss Caviar about his peer relationships in the classroom. She explains that he doesn't really have a special friend in the classroom and always seems to be on the outside trying to get into unstructured group activities.

The social worker reviews his home situation with us. He is a youngster who is left alone a great deal. His history has been one of difficult peer relationships and an unstable home life. We all agree that a home visit from the social worker would be helpful. Perhaps some change in George's home life is causing this excessive need for attention.

The psychologist suggests that as much positive reinforcement as possible be given to George. Miss Caviar is encouraged to ignore as much negative behavior as possible. The ideal would be to have George strive for positive strokes rather than the negative. Miss Caviar says she'll try but would like the psychologist to come into the classroom to observe. He agrees to do that. An acceptable time is set up.

The learning consultant reviews George's learning patterns with us.

Another meeting will be scheduled when the social worker has something to report. The psychologist will send me a copy of his classroom observations of George.

2:30   I dash down to my room where three fourth graders are waiting—not a good situation for the principal to observe. One of these fourth graders is George. We all sit down at the group table where we are working on a map skills assignment sent by Miss Caviar. The children have great trouble spotting details on the map. This is a difficult lesson for them. By using index cards I help block out extraneous information and concentrate on small blocks. This seems helpful. We laboriously go through the lesson—finding cities and locating directions and bodies of water. At 2:50 the bell rings signaling the end of the day. I notice that George has been totally engrossed in the map skills lesson—an interesting phenomenon since there were no children at this particular group that he needed to impress. Perhaps the psychologist was right about his need for peer attention.

3:00   I write a memo to the psychologist reporting my observation about George's behavior. Hopefully this will give him more to go on concerning George's problem in the classroom.

3:05   After placing the chairs on their desks so the janitor can sweep the floor, I leave for the afternoon staff meeting.

3:10   I arrive just as state testing is being discussed. Our school did very well. As I look around the room, each teacher and specialist appears to be very pleased. All of us know that we had a part in preparing the children for these tests—results speak for themselves. The handful of children who scored below the minimum level are all receiving help in the resource room. This really is a feather in our caps since the proper children obviously have been identified. This is one of the rewards for a teacher. We must keep in mind that the results won't always be this positive, but for right now, it sure does feel good!

Next, Mr. Jones reports that there are several teachers who have expressed concern over the children leaving the classroom so much for special help. I squirm in my chair knowing full well that I will be called upon to justify my program. Mrs. Smith, a third grade teacher, speaks up. She feels that when the children leave the classroom to go to a specialist they lose out on lessons being taught in her class. Mr. Jones calls on me. I tactfully try to explain that it is unfortunate when the resource room children have to miss anything but that there are just so many hours in a teaching day. Our hope is that we can schedule around the essential teaching lessons like math and reading, but these are learning disabled children and they do need remedial help. I offer to review the present scheduling with any teacher and rearrange the child's time in the resource room if I possibly can. This seems to satisfy Mrs. Smith for now. I suspect that this question will come up again. It is a real problem. I sympathize with the classroom teacher who feels the responsibility for the educational program of an entire class of children. It is difficult to convince a teacher that she won't be "blamed" for a child not achieving in her room. Hopefully time and experience will solve this problem.

After several other administrative issues are discussed, the meeting is adjourned.

It is now 4:30. Mrs. Stanley, the resource room teacher, now becomes wife and mother and must rush home for the next part of a busy day.

developing
good
public relations

9

STAFF MEETING

Once the resource room concept is thoroughly understood by the special education staff and administration, a solid selling job must be done for the rest of the staff. One way this can be achieved is by scheduling a general staff meeting including the head of special services, the principal, and the resource room teacher. The principal or head of special services should introduce the program. This makes it official. The first description of the program will go a long way in influencing the regular staff. Here are some suggestions to help make a positive impression when first "selling" the resource room.

1. Stress the necessary compliance with federal legislation. The resource room fulfills the requirements of PL 94-142. (See Chapter 1.)
2. Be positive about the benefits of such a program to the children receiving the services.
3. Acknowledge the concerns the teachers have about classroom disruptions, scheduling, and missed classwork. Many teachers express concern over assignments missed in class. Do not belittle the importance of these assignments. Explain that every effort will be made to schedule the student at a time the teacher feels is best. Acknowledge that it is unfortunate when a student has to miss anything, but it is important to develop priorities based on the individual student's needs. Concentrating help on areas of weakness will help the student succeed in regular class subjects.
4. Admit that many unforeseen problems will occur as the program progresses. A statement such as "With all of us working together, we will be able to deal with these difficulties" promotes acceptance to a new and possibly threatening change in their established programs.
5. Explain that the priorities of the resource room program will differ with each child and will be established with input from teachers, parents, and specialists as well as the child if that is appropriate at an IEP meeting (see Chapter 3). For many children, the work done in the resource room will concentrate on the remediation of basic skills. This may include assignments from the regular class when it is appropriate. Many times regular classwork may need to be modified so that the student can be maintained in the regular class. (See Chapter 10.)

The Resource Room Teacher Speaks

Part of the job of the resource room teacher is to maintain good relations with other staff members. Here are some suggestions for selling the resource room and yourself at that first meeting.

1. Offer assistance to teachers in adapting their program for special education students. Let them know that you want to be "their resource." Discuss times that you will be available for informal conferences as well as regularly scheduled teacher–resource room teacher conferences.

2. Always use "we" rather than "I" when discussing the program. This reinforces the idea that the entire staff is working together.

3. Refer to the consultants (for example, the school psychologist) as an integral part of the program. They share the responsibility with you. They are *your* resource.

4. Explain that you will be making informal classroom visits from time to time. This may be threatening to some teachers, and it is best to discuss it openly in a group meeting. Stress that it is the child's behavior you are interested in, not the teacher's. Tell them that you will be looking at how the child is paying attention, staying on task, interacting with other students, or completing assignments. (Be sure while observing to do just that. Keep your eye contact as much on the children as possible.) Regardless of the activity taking place in the classroom, you will profit from the observation; therefore, assure the teacher that he/she does not have to begin an academic assignment if the class is doing an art project. Tell the staff that you will communicate your observations either through a note or at a later informal conference so that the information can be shared. By reassuring them of your interest in the student's behavior, these visitations will hopefully become less threatening.

Wrap-Up of the Staff Meeting

Close the staff meeting with the assurance that an in-service program in which teachers' concerns will be dealt with will be given in the near future. A question and answer period is a good idea. This is an opportunity to invite teachers who are new to the district to stay after the meeting is over and discuss additional problems or concerns.

DISCRETION AND CONFIDENTIALITY

The resource room teacher will be privy to many things that happen in classrooms as well as confidential information about the children and their families. It is your professional obligation not to break this trust. Be very aware of any references you make about what takes place in other classrooms. Nothing can destroy your credibility more than the knowledge that you repeat classroom happenings to other teachers. Make sure that information received and observations of other teachers remain confidential. Avoid talking about any staff member; rather, talk to them. Getting into the classrooms for observation and getting honest input on a child's performance from his/her teacher is essential to the success of your program. Do not jeopardize this by discouraging their confidence in you. It is clearly not worth the price.

GETTING ALONG WITH THE STAFF

Once the program is in operation, it is important for the resource room teacher to be accepted as a "regular" teacher. It is unrealistic to expect that basic interpersonal skills can be taught in a few paragraphs, a few pages, or even a few books. Each resource room teacher must self-evaluate how he/she is perceived by others. If the teacher has a problem in this area, running a resource room will be more difficult. Cooperation of the staff is a necessary part of the program. Some practical ways to encourage good rapport can be given but difficulties in interpersonal relationships must be dealt with by each individual in as honest a way as possible.

Some ways to encourage a good rapport with the staff are

1. Begin teaching on the first day of school.
2. Assume lunch duties, bus duties, and so on along with the regular staff.
3. Spend lunch times eating and socializing with the other teachers.
4. Volunteer to help on school committees.
5. Offer help in school plays and programs.
6. Attend evening programs that the children put on even if this is not required of you.
7. Try to become involved in teacher's extracurricular activities like staff volleyball teams or study groups.
8. Take a genuine interest in other teachers.
9. Be accessible to discuss children or teaching problems.
10. Try to attend to what each person is saying. Avoid letting your body language give off impatient vibes. A teacher who is listening just to be polite and is just waiting to "get away" conveys this to the listener.

HOW TO INVOLVE THE PARENTS

After briefing the staff, the parents need to be informed. This meeting is in addition to the classroom meeting with the child before school begins. Having a meeting where all the parents, the child study team, the school principal, and the resource room teacher are present is important. It is best for this meeting to take place before school starts. If not, have it as soon as possible thereafter. Parental fears have a way of multiplying when they are not dealt with. This meeting can allay many of these fears.

1. Hold the meeting in the resource room (if the room is large enough). Let the parents see the room set up for operation.
2. Prepare in advance an example of a hypothetical child's program. (Put it on a transparency for the overhead projector.)
3. Demonstrate a few of the materials that will be used. Have other materials, books, programs, and audiovisual equipment displayed around the room. A 3 x 5 card giving a brief explanation of the purpose of the material will give

parents information without them having to ask questions. (Refer to Materials List in Chapter 7.)

4. Explain how the children will be evaluated and in what form the parents will be receiving these evaluations (report cards, conferences, weekly notes or phone calls, or weekly plans sent home).

5. Explain the testing methods that will be used and what these tests show.

6. Be open to all questions from parents.

7. Do not discuss individual children or problems at this meeting. Schedule a private conference for this as soon as possible. If a parent asks a question about an individual child at the meeting you can tactfully say, "I'd really like to discuss that in depth with you. Let's schedule a conference time."

8. Circulate a list for parents who want a conference to go over any additional concerns they may have. Give an open invitation for them to visit the resource room. (Check with the building principal for school policies on parent visitations. Many schools require advance notice.)

9. Encourage parents to volunteer their time in the resource room. Involved parents are often supportive parents. Explain that volunteers are needed to help with

   a. Working with individual children
   b. Clerical work such as filing and running off dittos
   c. Creating or making new learning center materials
   d. Bulletin boards or art work
   e. Special talents they can share with a group of children
   f. Checking out materials to other staff members
   g. Any combination of the above

   Using volunteer parents has many benefits. It helps the parents to see many things for themselves.

   a. How their child compares to other learning disabled children.
   b. "Other children also have problems." Sometimes this is a real revelation.
   c. How the teacher works with their child. Hopefully this will have some carry-over at home.
   d. The variety of materials used to help their child.
   e. The kind of structure needed to provide a good environment for learning.
   f. "By God, maybe there's hope after all."

   It also helps the child to see
   a. Mother or Dad really care.
   b. The teacher and my parents talk to each other.
   c. A lot of people are working together to help me.
   d. "Maybe there's hope for me after all!"

10. Reemphasize your availability to parents. Any concerns they have in the future can be dealt with by a phone call to you.

11. Stress need for confidentiality for parent volunteers. Whatever happens in the resource room must not be discussed outside.

12. Tell parents how important it is to have their support in order for their children to be successful. Many times parents feel that school and home are separate phenomena. You really cannot succeed with their child without their support.

As a follow-up to the parents meeting, try to make a phone call to each family during the first few weeks of school. Call to tell them some positive happening concerning their child. For instance, "John seems to be making a fine adjustment. I just thought I'd call and let you know." This shows them that you are not only interested in their child but are looking for positives rather than negatives. Unfortunately many parents of resource room children have not received many positive calls about their child. Yours may be the first!

GETTING OFF TO A GOOD START
WITH THE CHILDREN

A new student to the resource room will need reassurance now. You will be dealing with many conflicting feelings. On one level the child knows he/she needs help and would like to improve academic skills; on another level no child likes to be singled out among his/her peers for special help. Your job will be to convince each child that the help received is well worth the trip.

1. Explain why the child is attending the resource room. Discuss the child's deficits and how you plan to help remediate them. For example, "you have an auditory deficit. This means you don't always understand what you hear. You do much better when you see what you are supposed to do or understand. Do you sometimes feel confused when Miss Jones gives directions to the class by talking?"

   This discussion can allay much of the personal anxiety the child may have. Suddenly the child does not have to hide or feel ashamed. He/she feels that the teacher understands the difficulties and knows a way to help make things better.

   Show the child some of the materials you will be using to strengthen his/her deficit modality. Show the child the materials you will be using to capitalize on his/her strength modality. Be optimistic and help the child to be positive about obtaining help.

2. Help the child to set realistic goals that he/she can expect to reach. Give explicit guidelines that will help the child achieve these goals. Encourage the child's input in developing these goals. (See Goals Checklist in Chapter 3.)

3. Children usually imagine they are worse than they really are. Sometimes, sharing test scores, when it is appropriate to do so, relieves anxiety rather than adds to it. Keeping secrets from the children concerning their abilities does not encourage their involvement in the learning process. This does not mean that you should be blatant or tactless. Refrain from using labels. You might say, "You may not learn as quickly as your friend in the classroom.

That's why you will come to the resource room—so we can work together to help you understand better." Giving the child an idea of what he/she *can* achieve will help the child become a participating member of the IEP process rather than a listener only.

4. Show the child the reading programs, spelling programs, and math programs that you may be using.

5. Ask the child what he/she has the most problems with. Write these down as the child talks. Dignify the child's opinions and ideas by honestly taking them into account.

6. Give the child practical ways to compensate for deficits in the classroom, for example: getting assignments in writing if he/she has an auditory deficit, or getting assignments on a tape recorder if he/she has a visual deficit. Explain that these compensating mechanisms can be useful throughout his/her life, not just this year.

7. Discuss openly the problems the child may have with other children. Do others call the child names? Does the child think he/she is stupid? When these problems are out in the open, you can begin reassuring the child and helping him/her to gain perspective. If you have plans to include the gifted in your program, this is a good time to share this information with the learning disabled child. At times the child will see the gifted and talented children leaving for the resource room just as he/she does. This should help modify his/her concerns.

8. Include the child in the parent–resource room teacher and teacher–resource room teacher conferences whenever possible. A conference held about a child without the child being there may make him/her feel that secret things are being said about him/her. (Consider including children in conferences from at least second or third grade and up.) Having a child in the conference reinforces the idea that you are making the child responsible for his/her own progress. During the conference speak *to* the child, not *about* the child. For example, "John, we went over your progress since last marking period the other day; now I would like to share it with your mother and father." (This approach goes against traditional parent–teacher conference practices, but there are so many benefits to including the child in the conference that it is recommended that you give it a try.)

9. Give an attitude survey questionnaire at the beginning of the year. (See Form 9-1.) Discuss with each child his/her feelings about the resource room. Involve the children in making changes in the resource room to fit their needs.

10. Keep rapport open between you and the child. Let the child know that you are approachable. Speak to the child as he/she walks down the hall. Tell the child personally if there is some schedule change. Encourage the child to express his/her feelings even if negative. An open dialogue between you and the child encourages wholesome learning attitudes.

HOW TO KEEP THE IMAGE POSITIVE

The attitude of the children who never use the resource room can influence the program. Their attitude is very important to the learning disabled child who attends. By eliciting the support of the non–resource room students you can make the transition easier for the resource room students.

Having the gifted children involved in the resource room will change the "aura" of the resource room. This alone however may not be enough.

```
                        NAME _____

                      ATTITUDE SURVEY

 1.  The resource room is a _____ place.

 2.  I feel _____ when it's time to go to the resource room.

 3.  The other children in my class think the resource room is _____

     _____.

 4.  The reasons I am coming to the resource room are:  _____

     _____

     _____.

 5.  My friends think I am coming to the resource room because _____

     _____.

 6.  If I could I would change school by _____

     _____.
```

FORM 9-1

Some things you may try are

1. Invite each class with the teacher to visit the resource room for an "open house." By making the room attractive and giving an enthusiastic explanation to the class, you can encourage positive feelings.
2. Ask for student volunteers to help with "peer-tutoring" on an ongoing or temporary basis.
3. Participate in team-teaching activities with regular classroom teachers whenever possible.
4. Talk to the children whenever you get a chance. Use your bus duty and lunchroom duty time to get to know all the students. *Your* general school image is important to the children who participate in the resource room program.

REPORTING TO PARENTS

Formal reporting is a tradition in most public schools. This is done by report cards and regularly scheduled conferences. Certainly the resource room teacher should be included in this reporting process.

Conferences

When school conferences are being held, it is important for the resource room teacher to schedule conferences with the parents (and hopefully the children) involved in the resource room. There are guidelines to follow to help make these conferences both positive and productive.

1. Arrange the seating for the conference in a semicircle if possible. Not having an obstruction such as a desk between the teacher and the parents promotes a more open feeling.
2. Have an outline of the important points you wish to discuss.
3. Have samples of the child's work ready to show the parents. (Keeping papers from the beginning of the year for a comparison is helpful.)
4. Refer to the objectives stated in the IEP and demonstrate how these are being implemented.
5. Begin the conference with as many positive points as possible. Even when the report of the child's progress or behavior is not a good one, some positives can always be found, for instance,

   - "John is usually so interested in the other children" or
   - "Gail seems to try very hard" or
   - "Evelyn can do good work when she tries" or
   - "Martha is excellent in outdoor activities" or
   - "Robert's handwriting shows improvement" or
   - "Tyrone has so many friends" or
   - "Ruth loves to retell her favorite T.V. show."

   There are always some positive things to say about a child. Some may take more thinking about than others, however.
6. When negative behavior is discussed it should be done in a productive fashion. Complaining about a child seldom promotes positive returns. It should be done with the attitude of "what can be done to make it better."
7. When suggestions are made by the teacher or the parent it is often helpful if these are written down to refer to later. Encourage the parents to take notes if they wish. (Have pencil and paper handy.)
8. At the close of the conference, a recap of what was discussed and decided helps to ensure that everyone in attendance will leave with the same impressions. It also emphasizes those things the parent, child, and teacher plan to do.
9. For those parents who appear dissatisfied or hostile, encourage a future meeting with the principal or head of special services. (Always leave a step higher than yourself to pursue.)
10. Try to promote an attitude of working together with the parents and child rather than the teacher having all the answers.
11. Elicit the suggestions of parents and the children when trying to work out problems.
12. Leave the parents with a specific time when you plan to be in touch with them again.
13. Encourage the parents to call or come in at any time to discuss problems or concerns.
14. Write a dated report about the conference to keep on file.
15. Be sure to act on any suggestions that you agreed to at the conference!

Report Cards

Resource room reports can be handled in many ways. They can be separate report cards that are given in addition to the regular class report card or they can be included in a space on the regular class report card. A resource room report can also be incorporated in the grades or remarks that the regular classroom teacher writes.

Separate resource room report cards included with the regular report card are an excellent way to evaluate a variety of categories. Sometimes the knowledge that a child will be held accountable for his/her progress by a report that goes home motivates better results. This method of reporting should be decided upon with the support of the administration before the program begins. When the resource room is introduced at the initial staff meeting, this issue should be discussed so that the classroom teacher knows which subjects taught in the resource room will be evaluated by the resource room teacher. It is also a good idea to confer with the regular classroom teacher on those grades or comments you will include in the resource room report. Making the report card as open as possible to incorporate the wide variety of areas taught in the resource room is a good idea. (See Form 9-2.)

The main point to keep in mind with any reporting procedure to parents is to keep the comments as positive as possible with an eye toward future progress and improvement. Try to keep the lines of communication as open as possible stressing the importance of a joint effort. Cooperation inspires success, and success comes from a positive attitude. That attitude must begin with and be transmitted by the resource room teacher.

```
                        RESOURCE ROOM REPORT
                                          DATE: _____

     NAME _____

     SUBJECTS _____

              _____

              _____

              _____


     COMMENTS:



     RESOURCE ROOM TEACHER _____

     PARENT'S SIGNATURE _____

     PARENT COMMENTS:
```

FORM 9-2

supporting
the classroom
teacher

10

A large part of the resource room teacher's job is the support of the regular classroom teacher who is working with the resource room children. This can be done in many ways.

I. REGULARLY SCHEDULED CONFERENCES WITH THE CLASSROOM TEACHER

If possible, these conferences should be held at least monthly. Scheduling them is not easy since classroom teachers are not pleased with conferences scheduled after school. Having the conference during a teacher's planning period is often the least imposing, but not complaint free. (Having a coffee pot available with cookies or doughnuts helps to soften the fact that they have given up their planning period for this conference.) Establishing a conference day where resource room students remain in the regular classroom and you schedule as many teachers as possible during their planning periods is most effective. If it is allowed in the budget, hiring a resource room substitute teacher for the conference day avoids a break in the routine for the children.

The teacher's conference should be structured to give the teacher the needed information on each child. Having a checklist with a carbon copy is useful since it keeps the conference on the right track, and the teacher leaves with a record of what was discussed. (See Form 10-1.) Keep these checklists on file to refer to at the next conference. They help to measure the child's progress and the effectiveness of the suggestions made at the last conference. This is also an acceptable way to make suggestions about modifying the classroom program for the mainstreamed youngster.

During the teacher conference, keep the focus of discussion on the child. When making suggestions to the teacher use tactful approaches such as: "When I worked with Susie, I found she really responded to visual clues such as writing directions on the board. If you can possibly do that in the classroom, it might help." Try to avoid pointing out things you saw in the class that you thought could be improved upon. This will not really effect change and can threaten the teacher and make you an unwelcome guest in his/her classroom. As trite as it may sound, tact is necessary at all times when dealing with the staff.

Some ways to help the teacher modify the classroom program when necessary are

1. Moving the child's desk closer to the teacher or away from other distractions
2. Simplifying worksheets (not including as much on a page)
3. Requiring less homework than is required of the others
4. Reading with the child individually rather than with a group
5. Structuring the child's time with a daily worksheet and schedule (see Weekly Plan, Chapter 5)

```
RESOURCE ROOM CONFERENCE

CHILD'S NAME _____

DATE: _____

TEACHERS PRESENT: _____


Reading _____
_____
_____


Math _____
_____
_____


Spelling _____
_____
_____


Handwriting _____
_____
_____


Social _____
_____
_____


Other _____
_____
_____


Modifications _____
_____
_____
```

FORM 10–1

6. Instituting a reward system for work completed correctly

7. Using an hour glass or egg timer to increase the child's attention span (for instance, "When the sand has gone out, you may get up and stretch")

8. Giving visual and auditory clues whenever possible (for example: writing directions on the board as you give them verbally)

9. Always stating things in positive terms—try to avoid using the word *if* when dealing with inappropriate behavior (for example, "As soon as you are quiet we will be able to go on," rather than "If you don't stop talking, we won't be able to go on")

10. Pointing out positive behavior rather than negative behavior (for example, "I see Johnny is sitting quietly and is ready to listen" rather than "George, you are talking and not listening")

11. Using supplemental materials like manipulative math programs and lower level materials

12. Writing a daily report to the parents about the child's behavior

13. Having the classroom teacher insist on an organized work space at the child's desk or table

14. Having the regular class assignment sent to the resource room to be taught and/or completed

15. Having the child take tests in the resource room.

Writing down the mutually agreed upon suggestions on a checklist such as Form 10-1 will help jog the teacher's memory and the suggestions will be taken more seriously. Ask for suggestions from the classroom teacher about how you can improve your techniques with the child. Let the teacher know that you value his/her input.

II. A REGULARLY SCHEDULED DAILY TIME WHEN A TEACHER CAN VISIT YOU IN THE RESOURCE ROOM

Post a regularly scheduled time on the bulletin board. Send out a notice at the beginning of the year inviting the teachers to visit you in the resource room at this fixed time for any current problems or to borrow materials. This is good public relations. Needless to say, be sure you are there at the posted time. If you should have to run out unexpectedly, leave a note on your door!

Being available for set times during the day gives the classroom teacher the assurance that you are there to support him/her as well as the child.

Have available materials attractively displayed and easy to find. Arranging materials according to subject and grade level is an effective way of organizing them. Even a file of ditto worksheets can be helpful to a classroom teacher trying to individualize a child's program.

Some useful materials to include for teachers to borrow are

Manipulative materials (DLM)
Individualized taped programs
Special education workbooks (Frostig)
Simplified textbooks
High interest–low reading level books
Pencil grip holders
Primary pencils
Wide-space writing paper
(Refer to Materials List, Chapter 7).

A teacher aide or a parent volunteer can organize a checkout system and supervise the materials library.

III. IN-SERVICE PROGRAMS

As soon as possible after the school year begins is the most beneficial time to present an in-service program. This should follow shortly after the general staff meeting during which the resource room program is introduced. (See Chapter 9.) Teachers who have not had handicapped children in their classroom before are understandably apprehensive. Therefore it is best to have an in-service meeting to give out information and to provide a forum for expressing anxieties. Have an agenda set up ahead of time and distribute it to the staff. A sample agenda might be

IN-SERVICE AGENDA

Welcome—Coffee and Refreshments
Introduction—Head of Special Services
Film—See Appendix D, In-Service Materials
Discussion Groups—Your Impression of the Film
Assembly—We Meet to Share
Lunch
Discussion Group—Problem Solving
Assembly—Wrap-up Presentations
Final Assembly—Questions and Answers and Materials Display

Choosing a Film

Organizations such as the Association for Children with Learning Disabilities (ACLD) can provide information on films available for rent or loan. (See Appendix E for addresses of special education organizations.)

Order the film well in advance of the scheduled meeting. Arrange to preview the film before showing it. (See Appendix D for in-service materials suggestions.)

Arranging the Discussion Groups

Before breaking down into groups, try to arrange it so that each discussion group includes a person who will be willing to assume a leadership role. Also try to have a mix of personalities that will include a few who would be willing to talk in front of the assembly. If the staff is new to you, elicit the aid of the principal to help make up the groups. A group of five to seven members should be the maximum number that allows everyone to have a chance for input. Tell the groups that their goal is to discuss the film in relation to problems they foresee in the classroom. Assign each group the task of appointing a leader to report to the assembly on their findings.

Making Up Group Tasks

While listening to each group's spokesperson, jot down main ideas. When pulling these ideas together, try to pick out those that have been mentioned most frequently. These will often reflect the underlying concerns of the group.

Sample:
Presented Problem (written on oak tag and posted at the front of the room)

Johnny, a mainstreamed youngster, is in a regular third grade class with twenty-seven other students. He frequently calls out of turn, does not follow verbal directions, wanders around the room, and is generally a nuisance. Miss Jones feels her frustrations building daily. She feels with twenty-seven other students she does not have adequate time to spend with Johnny.

Group Tasks (each group receives one)
Task #1   How to change the physical environment of the child in the classroom
Task #2   How to modify the academic environment
Task #3   How to modify inappropriate behavior of the child
Task #4   How to improve teacher-child relationship
Task #5   How to understand the teacher's reaction to the behavior of the child

Recap Suggestions

After each group presentation allow for group discussion. Encourage speakers to express their feelings as well as concrete suggestions to solve problem situations. Try to encourage teachers to deal with angry feelings they may have toward special education children in their classroom. We all have these feelings at times and the more avenues there are for expressing them, the healthier the environment will become.

Managing behavior of special education youngsters is an often expressed fear of regular teachers. Dealing with this problem in an open and honest fashion will encourage a good beginning for the teacher and the handicapped youngster.

Often, just acknowledging the presence of a problem is enough to make the teacher less fearful. It is usually when the regular classroom teacher feels that the child's problem is the result of his/her inadequacy that frustrations build.

At the end of the in-service program, it is imperative to put together the important points of the sessions and restate them to the group. Closure at this time helps the attendees to focus on the main issues and to leave feeling they gained something concrete.

It is also a good idea to end the meeting on an open-ended note. For instance, "We will be having more of these meetings in the future. Don't hesitate to bring any concerns or suggestions to the resource room teacher in the meantime." Reiterate that the resource room teacher will be having regularly scheduled conferences as well as a set daily time to discuss any matters that come up. Explain that an important part of the resource room teacher's job is to support classroom teachers in mainstreaming the handicapped youngsters.

Have reference books available for teachers to borrow at this time. (See reference books in Appendix C.) This is also a good opportunity to display materials that will be available to the teachers in the future for help in the classroom.

Having someone take minutes of the main sessions is a good idea. These minutes can be typed on a ditto and reproduced for distribution to staff.

All of the above techniques help to reinforce the importance of the resource room program as well as the idea that support will be available. The staff should leave feeling that the responsibility of the handicapped child mainstreamed in their classroom is a shared effort. This will lessen anxieties and promote a more positive attitude toward the program.

IV. FACULTY BULLETIN BOARD

A staff lounge is a good place to post articles and notices pertinent to the resource room program. Newspaper or magazine articles about learning disabilities or children's behavior are of interest to teachers and show that you are sharing current information with them. A heading on the bulletin board above the article saying "Please Read" or "Take a Look" helps to bring the articles to the teacher's attention.

Teachers will also become accustomed to checking this spot for notices of a coming resource room conference day or in-service meeting. Any local or state special education seminars about which you receive notice should be displayed on the bulletin board as well.

V. EVALUATING THE PROGRAM

Allowing the regular classroom teachers the opportunity to evaluate the effectiveness of the resource room program is most helpful. This not only gives the resource room teacher good input on how the program is perceived by the others but allows the classroom teachers an opportunity to vent their feelings and know that their opinions count. Many problems can be solved at these meetings where an open forum exists. Often problems which seem unsolvable are remedied when brainstorming can take place.

Having a general staff meeting mid-year to discuss any problems (along with the regularly scheduled monthly conference meetings) and an end-of-year evaluation meeting usually is sufficient. The composition of some districts may require these meetings more frequently. This really is a matter of judgment.

Many teachers who have opinions to share about the program will be more comfortable expressing these opinions in writing rather than at an open meeting. Therefore it is a good idea to provide in advance an evaluation form for the teachers to fill out and return to you via interoffice mail. (See Evaluation Form 10-2.)

There are those who prefer not to sign this sheet so that they may be more candid. If this is not acceptable to those receiving the evaluations, by all means request that signatures be included.

Review the returned evaluation forms ahead of time. Using a blank form, recap the main ideas. At the evaluation meeting project the evaluation form with the composite of the staff's comments on a transparency with an overhead projector or write the summary on a poster board. This is a convenient format for conveying the information in general terms. Encourage comments from the others with remarks such as "Are there any ideas I left out?" or "Can you think of any others?" or "Any new thoughts on this one?"

When the teachers respond, be attentive and accepting of their answers. Everyone needs to feel that what he/she says is important. Do not discount anyone's ideas. Leave the impression that all ideas and suggestions will be considered, and do consider them. Some of the seemingly "far out" ideas can become successful solutions.

Do not hesitate to tell someone at a later date that you tried an idea and then positively describe how it worked. Let the teachers you work with know that their cooperation and suggestions are vital to the success of a resource room program. Try to make the resource room program an integral part of the entire school program. Include everyone.

RESOURCE ROOM QUESTIONNAIRE

1. How do the children feel about attending the resource room? What feelings and reactions have you observed with regard to their participation?

----

2. How do the children who are not attending the resource room feel? What have been their feelings and reactions?

----

3. Do you feel the resource room scheduling is efficient, and do you think the amount of time is adequate? Why?

----

4. Is there enough communication between you and the resource room teacher? Do you think it would be a good idea to set up "regularly scheduled conference times" between the two teachers? How often?

FORM 10–2 (Warren Township Dept. of Special Services, Warren, N.J.)

5. Do you see carryover with what the child is doing in the resource
    room and in your classroom? As far as you are able to judge, are the
    children attending the resource room able to apply the skills they
    have been learning in your classroom?

---

6. What are your feelings about the enrichment program and what suggest-
    ions do you have for next year?

---

7. Do you have any ideas or suggestions that could be helpful to the
    resource room program for next year?

FORM 10–2 (cont.)

solving problems
in the resource room

11

Every teacher knows that some days in the classroom are better than others. Problems in teaching cannot be avoided. They are confronted on a daily basis. Some problems are more serious than others. This chapter has taken some of the more frequently expressed problems and attempted to give many possible solutions. As a resource room teacher you undoubtedly will recognize some of these situations. If this is your first resource room experience, this chapter may give you some insight into what to expect. The important thing to remember is that problems usually have more than one acceptable solution. You have to find the right one for you.

Problem: Johnny is using profanity in the classroom. His classroom teacher does not know how to handle this.

POSSIBLE SOLUTIONS:

1. Talk to Johnny. Give him a time limit to improve before you call his parents.
2. Call the parents and ask for support at home about this problem. Set up a daily reporting system with them.
3. Ignore profanity and reinforce positive language.
4. Tabulate the number of times profanity is used daily. Compare results with the child to chart progress.
5. Let Johnny know you are keeping an anecdotal record of when the profanity occurs.

Problem: Nina speaks out in class without raising her hand. This is disruptive to the others. What can be done?

POSSIBLE SOLUTIONS:

1. Discuss the problem with Nina in private. Ask her for possible solutions.
2. With the group's help, draw up behavioral guidelines for everyone on a large chart. Post it in the classroom.
3. Keep a record of the number of times Nina talks without raising her hand.
4. Chart her improvement.
5. Send home a daily report.
6. Ignore talking out and praise her lavishly when she raises her hand.
7. Call attention to others who raise their hands.

Problem: Sammy is fighting at the bus line and threatening the younger children. The principal has asked you to intervene. What do you do?

POSSIBLE SOLUTIONS:

1. Check out the story by talking to the children involved.
2. Have each child present his/her story in an accepting environment. Ask the children for possible solutions.

3. Write these solutions on the blackboard. Have each child copy the solutions on paper and sign his/her name at the bottom. Explain that you will send these copies to the principal for approval.
4. Follow up by checking with the children involved.

Problem: Greg is not bringing in his homework.

POSSIBLE SOLUTIONS:

1. Have a meeting with Greg and his classroom teacher.
2. Be sure the assignments are appropriate for his functioning level. If not, they need to be modified.
3. Have Greg keep a daily assignment sheet. This sheet must be signed daily by his classroom teacher when all assignments are written down and by his parents when they are completed.
4. Have his parents in for a conference to discuss a good study environment for homework (no T.V., quiet study place, working in short time periods).
5. Set up procedure to stay after school to make up finished work.
6. Consider the fact that Greg may be balking for emotional reasons. Watch for indications of this. A talk with the school psychologist may be in order.

Problem: Gail has been crying in class because other students have been calling her "retard." How do you handle this?

POSSIBLE SOLUTIONS:

1. Listen to Gail. Let her know you understand her feelings. Find out who the children are who have been calling her names.
2. Inform Gail's classroom teacher about the problem so that he/she can watch for this in the classroom.
3. Suggest an in-service film for the children in the building. (See film list in Appendix D.)
4. Call in the children who have been name-calling. Have an open discussion with them. If you feel Gail is mature enough, let her be present at the meeting.
5. Encourage Gail to tell the others how their name-calling makes her feel.
6. Write on the blackboard a list of suggestions to remedy the situation.
7. Have each child write out a contract about how he/she plans to modify his/her behavior.
8. If all else fails, elicit the support of the principal and possibly the parents of the name-callers.
9. Help Gail understand who she is and why she attends the resource room. Sometimes bolstering the child's ego helps the child to overcome sensitivity to name-calling.
10. Keep up with what is going on. Check with Gail from time to time to make sure the problem is under control.

Problem: Mrs. Jones, a classroom parent volunteer, is causing her child obvious distress when she is in the resource room. It is apparent that she can not work well with her own child. She is most enthusiastic and tells you each time she comes how much volunteering means to her. What do you do?

POSSIBLE SOLUTION:

1. Schedule a conference with Mrs. Jones. Tell her what a fine job she is doing. Let her know that you noticed how well she works with the other children. Tell Mrs. Jones that her child seems "distracted" when she is in the room. Assure her that this is a common happening when parents volunteer. Explain that because she is so enthusiastic, you would like to schedule her for a time when her child is not in the resource room. Working with other children will give her an opportunity to see how others work and how you work with other children. Be positive and encourage her to change her schedule. Often a parent volunteer who does not work well with his/her own child has much more success with others.

Problem: Mrs. Oakridge, a third-grade teacher, is very resentful of two children leaving her classroom to go to the resource room for an hour each day. She feels that they are "missing out" on important learning. She is freely expressing these concerns to the rest of the staff. What do you do?

POSSIBLE SOLUTIONS:

1. Schedule a conference with Mrs. Oakridge. Discuss the scheduling of the children leaving her room. If possible, rearrange the schedule.
2. Convey the message that the children's presence in the resource room is for the purpose of remediating skills to help them function better in the classroom. Ask for her suggestions.
3. Offer to teach these children some of the material they miss when they leave her room. You may be able to work on the necessary skills via the classroom subject matter.
4. Refer to the child's IEP for the most important goals and objectives. Stress that with all of you working together the children can achieve these objectives.
5. Try to have Mrs. Oakridge leave with the feeling that her input and cooperation are essential to your program. Also try to convey that she will not be "blamed" if the resource room children in her room do not make the expected amount of progress. (Refer to PL 94-142, Appendix B.) You could say, "Mrs. Oakridge, as you know John and Sue are classified as learning disabled youngsters and really aren't expected to be on grade level in science and social studies. Let's review their IEPs and see what their goals are for the year."
6. Most public schools have group scores and achievement test scores for handicapped students separated from those of the regular children. Knowing this may relieve a test-score–conscious teacher.

Problem: Mr. Stone, the school principal, has done an analysis of student-teacher contact time. He has discovered that you have forty minutes more planning time per week than the regular teachers. He sends you a memo asking you to justify your schedule. How do you handle this?

POSSIBLE SOLUTIONS:

1. Check a copy of the state law on special education. Some states specify a minimum time for planning per week. See if you are exceeding this minimum.

2. If you have extra time in your schedule that is not being well utilized, schedule children for additional one-to-one time or add another period for the enrichment group.

3. Once your schedule is justifiable send a detailed copy of each time slot to the principal. For instance:

9:00 to 10:00	Two learning disability reading groups (fourth grade)
10:00 to 10:30	Planning period, observe mainstreamed students, parent telephone conference
10:30 to 11:00	Remedial math group (third grade)
11:00 to 12:00	Emotionality workshop (fifth and sixth grade)
12:00 to 12:30	Lunch
12:30 to 1:00	Lunch duty
1:00 to 1:30	Teacher conference/materials workshop
1:30 to 2:00	Enrichment group
2:00 to 3:00	First grade readiness

   For each planning period slot, be sure to put in what you actually plan to do.

4. Ask for a conference with the principal. Discuss your schedule with Mr. Stone. Be sure to stress how parent and staff contact are an important part of your program.

5. Ask if he has suggestions for rearranging this time. If these suggestions are not workable, try explaining in a nondefensive, logical fashion, why not.

6. If all else fails, you may have to alter your schedule. Try to work with this for awhile. If the change is detrimental to the program, have another conference with Mr. Stone to explain. Flexibility is the key.

Problem: You come to observe in Miss Smith's first grade class. She meets you at the door and says, "You can't come in—you have no right." What do you do?

POSSIBLE SOLUTIONS:

1. Assure Miss Smith that of course you will not come in. Be pleasant and say, "We'll discuss a more convenient time at a later date." Then leave.

2. Send a note to Miss Smith that says,

   Dear Miss Smith,

   Sorry to have disturbed your class at an inconvenient time this morning. I hope that tomorrow at 10:30 will be better. Gerald has been coming to the resource room since September, and I must have a classroom observation on file.

   If another time would be better, please let me know when.

   Thanks,
   Natalie

3. When you are allowed in the classroom, be sure to keep your eye contact on the children only.
4. Leave a note when you leave commenting on Gerald's behvaior. Example:

Miss Smith,

Gerald really seemed to enjoy the lesson on toads. I'll try to follow up with his resource room work. Any suggestions?

Thanks,
Natalie

5. At the next teacher conference, be sure to mention the visit and prepare Miss Smith for future visitations.
6. Sometimes rather than antagonize a fellow teacher it is best to postpone classroom observations in their room until they are less anxious. Observations can also be made in gym, art, or music classes.

Problem: Mrs. Frees has phoned the office questioning why her child has not been included in the fourth-grade enrichment group. Now what?

POSSIBLE SOLUTIONS:

1. Check with John Frees's classroom teacher as to why he was not recommended. Be sure he just was not overlooked.
2. Inform the principal either by memo or a conference that Mrs. Frees has called and why.
3. Check John's cumulative folder to see if he has shown gifted tendencies in the past either by teacher comments or test scores.
4. Call Mrs. Frees. Explain to her the following:
    a. Children enter the program by classroom teacher recommendation (or test scores).
    b. The children are considered on the basis of classroom achievement and any evidence of particular talent or interest.
    c. Generally children are recommended by subject area. For instance, three children seem to excel in science so the teacher will recommend these three for this time segment. Those talented in other areas will probably be recommended at another time.
    d. Ask why she feels John should be included. If her reasons are valid, schedule a conference with Mrs. Frees, the classroom teacher, and yourself.
    e. Try to decide if the enrichment group would be an appropriate activity for John. If so, schedule him. Often, parents have insight into talents that a teacher can sometimes miss.
    f. If it is decided that John would be hindered by time taken from the regular program, explain that to Mrs. Frees.

Problem: Mrs. Grapevine frequently "pops into" the resource room. She is also a parent volunteer at a regularly scheduled time. It has come to your attention that Mrs. Grapevine is repeating stories about the children and their families to other parents. How do you handle this?

POSSIBLE SOLUTIONS:

1. Have a parent volunteers meeting. Go over general policies and procedures. At this time state very strongly the necessity for discretion. Stress the select position they are all in and how they must honor this.
2. Decrease Mrs. Grapevine's volunteer time per week. Tell her that other mothers also need time to be included in the volunteer program.
3. Discourage the spontaneous "drop-ins" by saying, "I'm awfully sorry but there is really no time now. I must be teaching."
4. Have an honest talk with Mrs. Grapevine. Tell her that some incidents have been repeated and the repercussions from this. Be as tactful as possible.

Problem: Mr. Rider, a second-grade teacher, wants to retain Philip, a resource room child. You feel that this would have a detrimental effect on Philip, who has a learning disability. What do you do?

POSSIBLE SOLUTIONS:

1. Have a meeting with the learning consultant and review Philip's learning profile. Be sure of your opinion.
2. Schedule a teacher conference with Mr. Rider. Discuss the following items:
   a. Philip's learning problems
   b. The progress he has made to date
   c. How retaining him will not make the learning disability go away.
   d. How Philip's poor image of himself from being retained may deter learning even further
   e. How the resource room program can continue to give support next year
   f. Ask for Mr. Rider's suggestions.
3. Schedule a meeting with Mr. Rider and Philip's parents. Discuss the issue. See what their views are.
4. Have a meeting with the IEP group to review Philip's plan. Determine whether or not Philip's goals are being met according to the plan.
5. Whatever the final decision, whether Philip is retained or not, adjust accordingly. If he is retained, allot time for morale boosting next year.

Problem: At a general staff meeting, the question, "Who grades the resource room children?" comes up. How do you respond?

POSSIBLE SOLUTIONS:

1. Ask for suggestions from the staff.
2. Explain that resource room grading can be done in different ways (refer to Chapter 9).
3. Suggest that grading be worked out between you and each teacher.
4. Ask the principal and special education supervisor what their positions are.

including the gifted
and talented

12

Offering a gifted and talented program in the resource room has many concomitant benefits.

Most special education teachers have had experience in dealing with a negative attitude attached to special education programs. This stigma often makes children attending these programs embarrassed and not eager to be seen involved with them. Needless to say, the attitudes of the students are not as positive and motivated as they should be for good learning.

The resource room offers an excellent vehicle for including other programs which will help to take this stigma away. The inclusion of a gifted and talented program is one excellent choice, for the following reasons:

1. The brightest and most talented children in the school have an opportunity to benefit from the resource room program.
2. The learning-disabled children are grouped with the more proficient children who go to the resource room from their classroom.
3. The reasons for children leaving their classrooms to use the resource room are not so clearly defined in the eyes of the other children. It is not always because a child is struggling with academics.
4. Unusual resource room gifted and talented projects can be done and shared with all the children in the school.
5. It gives the resource room teacher the opportunity to interact with the regular classroom teacher on another level.
6. It provides a needed service for the gifted and talented and helps the classroom teacher to enrich the regular program.
7. It allows parents of the gifted and talented population to become involved in the resource room program.
8. It is an opportunity for positive publicity about the school to be sent to the community via newspaper and word of mouth. This not only enhances the individual school but special services as well.
9. It gives the resource room teacher the opportunity to interact with more of the school population.
10. The resource room teacher enriches his/her teaching experience and is often stimulated by working with another curriculum.
11. The resource room becomes a place where all the children in the school want to have a turn to visit.
12. The learning disabled child basks in the positive aura of the resource room and attends with more enthusiasm and pride.

HOW TO BEGIN

It is best if the inclusion of the gifted and talented program is decided upon when the entire resource room project is organized. Initial planning should include scheduling, buying materials, general outline of the program, and public relations for the gifted and talented aspect of the program.

At the initial staff meeting where the resource room is presented, the guidelines for the gifted and talented program should be discussed. Teachers can be given a general outline of the program.

⚹ I. Length of Program

The children can be seen in four- to six-week blocks of time. This can be done by grade level. For instance,

1st graders—September 1–October 15
2nd graders—October 16–December 7 (holiday week)
3rd graders—December 8–January 31 (holiday week)
4th graders—February 1–March 15
5th graders—March 15–April 30
6th graders—May 1–June 15

The time slots will have to be arranged and modified to each district's calendar. Generally six weeks is an adequate amount of time to complete a short-term project. Occasionally a group will run over its allotted time. Leave some flexibility in your schedule to allow for this. Explain at the initial introduction meeting that the schedule is tentative and will undoubtedly have to be modified throughout the year.

⚹ II. How Many in Each Group?

The number of classes that the resource room is servicing will determine how many children can be seen from each class. For instance, if you feel that sixteen children is a viable number to work with and there are four first grades, then you would suggest that each first-grade teacher recommend four children for the program. Sometimes smaller groups are preferable to a resource room teacher, and the ratio can be adjusted accordingly.

If you happen to be in a building that has only one class per grade level, you have several scheduling options.

1. Extend the length of time for each group.
2. See a larger number of children on each level.
3. Keep groups small (three–five) and extend the length of time.
4. Add a multigrade enrichment group at the end of the year for a four- to six-week session.

III. Who Is Eligible?

There are many acceptable ways to include children in a gifted and talented program. Since this program is not a formalized ongoing option for those recommended, the criteria for evaluating need not be as formal. Renzulli and Gallagher have written extensively on methods for identifying gifted and talented students for formal gifted programming. (See references at the end of this chapter.)

An effective way of identifying children for a resource room gifted project that does not entail extensive testing is simply by classroom teacher referral. By providing the teacher with a checklist of behaviors which might indicate giftedness, you can help the teacher to identify appropriate children in his/her classroom. Included are three checklists which may be helpful. (See Forms 12-1, 12-2, and 12-3.)

Using a teacher referral method can work efficiently with few repercussions from parents or students. Because the program is on a short-term basis and the children selected are not permanently placed so that others have a chance the next time around, few parents or children feel threatened or left out.

IV. Notifying Parents

Once the children have been chosen for the program, the parents must be notified.

A letter stating the nature of the program as well as the amount of time the child will be attending is adequate. (See Form 12-4, p. 197.) Often, an invitation to the parents to help with the project or just to visit is a good idea. This is also a good time to inquire about resource people for future projects.

V. What Are the Activities?

The activities in the gifted and talented program are as varied as the interests of the children. Currently more and more materials are becoming available for work with the more able student. Many materials that already exist in a school or home can be adapted. (See Materials List at the end of this chapter.) Some of the activities which can be mentioned to the teachers are

Microscope study	Rock and mineral study
Crystal growing	Set up a mini museum
Planting experiments	Film making
Magnet experiments	Tutoring program
Newspaper production	Make hands-on games for other grades
Skeleton assembly	Social studies projects
Computer building (kits available)	Poetry writing
Pinhole camera construction	Independent study projects
Photography	Research projects
Creative writing	

CHECKLIST #1

SCALE FOR RATING BEHAVIORAL CHARACTERISTICS OF SUPERIOR STUDENTS

Joseph S. Renzulli/Robert K. Hartman

Name _____ School _____ Date _____

Part I: Learning Characteristics   1*   2   3   4

1. Has unusually advanced vocabulary for age
    or grade level; uses terms in a meaningful
    way; has verbal behavior characterized by
    "richness" of expression, elaboration, and
    fluency.   ___ ___ ___ ___

2. Possesses a large storehouse of information
    about a variety of topics (beyond the usual
    interest of youngsters his age).   ___ ___ ___ ___

3. Has quick mastery and recall of factual
    information.   ___ ___ ___ ___

4. Has rapid insight into cause-effect
    relationships; tries to discover the how
    and why of things; asks many provocative
    questions (as distinct from informational
    or factual questions); wants to know what
    makes things (or people) "tick."   ___ ___ ___ ___

5. Has a ready grasp of underlying principles
    and can quickly make valid generalizations
    about events, people, or things; looks for
    similarities and differences in events,
    people, and things.   ___ ___ ___ ___

6. Is a keen and alert observer; usually
    "sees more" or "gets more" out of a
    story, film, etc. than others.   ___ ___ ___ ___

7. Reads a great deal on his own; usually
    prefers adult level books; does not avoid
    difficult material; may show a preference
    for biography, autobiography, encyclopedias,
    and atlases.   ___ ___ ___ ___

8. Tries to understand complicated material by
    separating it into its respective parts;
    reasons things out for himself; sees logical
    and common sense answers.   ___ ___ ___ ___

                          Column Total   ___ ___ ___ ___

                               Weight   ___ ___ ___ ___
1* - Seldom or never
2 - Occasionally   Weighted Column Total ___ ___ ___ ___
3 - Considerably
4 - Almost always   Total   ___ ___ ___ ___

FORM 12-1 (J. S. Renzulli and R. K. Hartman, "Scale for Rating Behavioral Characteristics of Superior Students," *Exceptional Children of Superior Standing* [November 1971]. ©1971 The Council for Exceptional Children. Reprinted by permission of The Council for Exceptional Children.)

```
Part II:  Motivational Characteristics          1*    2    3    4

1.  Becomes absorbed and truly involved in
    certain topics or problems; is persistent
    in seeking task completion.  (It is some-
    times difficult to get him to move on to
    another topic.)                             ___  ___  ___  ___

2.  Is easily bored with routine tasks.         ___  ___  ___  ___

3.  Needs little external motivation to follow
    through in work that initially excites him. ___  ___  ___  ___

4.  Strives toward perfection; is self-critical;
    is not easily satisfied with his own spᵢed
    or products.                                ___  ___  ___  ___

5.  Prefers to work independently; requires
    little direction from teachers.             ___  ___  ___  ___

6.  Is interested in many "adult" problems such
    as religion, politics, sex, race--more than
    usual for age level.                        ___  ___  ___  ___

7.  Often is self-assertive (sometimes even
    aggressive); stubborn in his beliefs.       ___  ___  ___  ___

8.  Likes to organize and bring structure to
    things, people, and situations.             ___  ___  ___  ___

9.  Is quite concerned with right and wrong,
    good and bad; often evaluates and passes
    judgment on events, people, and things.     ___  ___  ___  ___

                           Column Total  ___  ___  ___  ___

                                 Weight  ___  ___  ___  ___
1* - Seldom or never
2  - Occasionally       Weighted Column Total  ___  ___  ___  ___
3  - Considerably
4  - Almost always                      Total  ___  ___  ___  ___
```

FORM 12-1   (cont.)

Part III: Creativity Characteristics   1*   2   3   4

1. Displays a great deal of curiosity about
    many things; is constantly asking questions
    about anything and everything.   ___ ___ ___ ___

2. Generates a large number of ideas or
    solutions to problems and questions; often
    offers unusual ("way out"), unique, clever
    responses.   ___ ___ ___ ___

3. Is uninhibited in expressions of opinion; is
    sometimes radical and spirited in disagree-
    ment; is tenacious.   ___ ___ ___ ___

4. Is a high risk taker; is adventurous and
    speculative.   ___ ___ ___ ___

5. Displays a good deal of intellectual play-
    fulness; fantasizes; imagines ("I wonder
    what would happen if..."); manipulates ideas
    (i.e., changes, elaborates upon them); is
    often concerned with adapting, improving,
    and modifying institutions, objects, and
    systems.   ___ ___ ___ ___

6. Displays a keen sense of humor in situations
    that may not appear to be humorous to others. ___ ___ ___ ___

7. Is unusually aware of his impulses and more
    open to the irrational in himself (free
    expression of feminine interest for boys,
    greater than usual amount of independence
    for girls); shows emotional sensitivity.   ___ ___ ___ ___

8. Is sensitive to beauty; attends to aesthetic
    characteristics of things.   ___ ___ ___ ___

9. Is nonconforming; accepts disorder; is not
    interested in details; is individualistic;
    does not fear being different.   ___ ___ ___ ___

10. Criticizes constructively; is unwilling to
    accept authoritarian pronouncements without
    critical examination.   ___ ___ ___ ___

                           Column Total   ___ ___ ___ ___

                                   Weight   ___ ___ ___ ___
1* - Seldom or never
2 - Occasionally   Weighted Column Total   ___ ___ ___ ___
3 - Considerably
4 - Almost always   Total   ___ ___ ___ ___

FORM 12-1   (cont.)

Part IV: Leadership Characteristics   1*   2   3   4

1. Carries responsibility well; can be counted
   on to do what he has promised and usually
   does it well.   ___ ___ ___ ___

2. Is self-confident with children his own age
   as well as adults; seems comfortable when
   asked to show his work to the class.   ___ ___ ___ ___

3. Seems to be well liked by his classmates.   ___ ___ ___ ___

4. Is cooperative with teacher and classmates;
   tends to avoid bickering and is generally
   easy to get along with.   ___ ___ ___ ___

5. Can express himself well; has good verbal
   facility and is usually well understood.   ___ ___ ___ ___

6. Adapts readily to new situations; is flexible in thought and action and does not
   seem disturbed when normal routine is
   changed.   ___ ___ ___ ___

7. Seems to enjoy being around other people;
   is sociable and prefers not to be alone.   ___ ___ ___ ___

8. Tends to dominate others when they are
   around; generally directs the activity in
   which he is involved.   ___ ___ ___ ___

9. Participates in most social activities
   connected with the school; can be counted
   on to be there if anyone is.   ___ ___ ___ ___

10. Excels in athletic activities; is well
    coordinated and enjoys all sorts of athletic
    games.   ___ ___ ___ ___

                            Column Total   ___ ___ ___ ___

                                  Weight   ___ ___ ___ ___
1* - Seldom or never
2 - Occasionally   Weighted Column Total   ___ ___ ___ ___
3 - Considerably
4 - Almost always   Total   ___ ___ ___ ___

FORM 12-1   (cont.)

```
                          CHECKLIST #2

                 SAN FRANCISCO UNIFIED SCHOOL DISTRICT
                 Programs for Mentally Gifted Minors

                    WILLIAM B. CUMMINGS, Supervisor


_____     _____     _____  _____
Student's Name            School              Grade   Room

_____
Teacher's Name

To the Teachers:

We need your help.  We're looking for children in your classroom who you
feel might be a lot smarter than their test scores indicate.  The follow-
ing list of characteristics, while by no means all inclusive, represents
traits found in gifted and creative children.  If any student in your
class is described by at least twelve (12) of the items on this list, you
may want to watch him more carefully for possible inclusion in the gifted
program.  Those items which are most applicable should be double checked.
Will you help us by responding to the following checklist for the top
students in your class.  This checklist should be sent to the building
principal who will then forward it to the Gifted Program Office.  Support-
ing information and comments should be written on the back of this form.

_____   1.  Is an avid reader

_____   2.  Has received an award in science, art, literature

_____   3.  Has avid interest in science or literature

_____   4.  Very alert, rapid answers

_____   5.  Is outstanding in math

_____   6.  Has a wide range of interests

_____   7.  Is very secure emotionally

_____   8.  Is venturesome, anxious to do new things

_____   9.  Tends to dominate peers or situations

_____  10.  Readily makes money on various projects or activities--is an
             entrepreneur

_____  11.  Individualistic--likes to work by self

_____  12.  Is sensitive to feelings of others--or to situations

_____  13.  Has confidence in self

_____  14.  Needs little outside control--disciplines self

_____  15.  Adept at visual art expression
```

FORM 12-2 (Cummings, William B., *Cummings Checklist of Characteristics of Gifted and Talented Children.* San Francisco Unified School District, Program for Mentally Gifted Minors, 1974.)

_____ 16. Resourceful--can solve problems by ingenious methods

_____ 17. Creative in thoughts, new ideas, seeing associations, innovations, etc. (not artistically)

_____ 18. Body or facial gestures very expressive

_____ 19. Impatient--quick to anger or anxious to complete a task

_____ 20. Great desire to excel even to the point of cheating

_____ 21. Colorful verbal expressions

_____ 22. Tells very imaginative stories

_____ 23. Frequently interrupts others when they are talking

_____ 24. Frank in appraisal of adults

_____ 25. Has mature sense of humor (puns, associations, etc.)

_____ 26. Is inquisitive

_____ 27. Takes a close look at things

_____ 28. Is eager to tell others about discoveries

_____ 29. Can show relationships among apparently unrelated ideas

_____ 30. Shows excitement in voice about discoveries

_____ 31. Has a tendency to lose awareness of time

FORM 12-2   (cont.)

CHECKLIST #3

LOS ANGELES UNIFIED SCHOOL DISTRICT
DIVISION OF EDUCATIONAL SUPPORT SERVICES
Counseling and Psychological Services Branch

CHARACTERISTICS OF ABLE DISADVANTAGED PUPILS

Name _____ Date _____

School _____ Grade _____ Age _____

Able disadvantaged pupils evidence superior ability in one or more of the
five areas listed below. No pupil is expected to demonstrate ability in
all areas, but an analysis of strengths may indicate potential. It is
important to note that these characteristics can be evidenced in both
positive and negative ways and either manifestation is an indicator of
strength. Examples of negative indicators have been enclosed in
parenthesis.

The classroom teacher who works daily with pupils is best qualified to
make these observations. Place an X on the line beside each statement
which BEST describes this pupil. If the behavior has not been observed,
leave the line blank.

LEARNING CHARACTERISTICS   YES   NO

Demonstrates verbal proficiency in small group problem-
solving tasks.   _____ _____

Has unusually advanced vocabulary for age or grade level. _____ _____

Has verbal behavior characterized by "richness" of expression, imagery, elaboration, and fluency in any
language, including nonstandard English. (Sometimes
rambles on and on.)   _____ _____

Possesses a large storehouse of information about a
variety of topics beyond the usual interests of age
peers.   _____ _____

Has rapid insight into cause-effect relationships;
tries to discover the how and why of things; asks
provocative questions; wants to know what makes things
or people "tick." (Can be an annoyance in persisting to
ask questions.)   _____ _____

Has a ready grasp of underlying principles; can quickly
make valid generalizations about events, people, or
things. (Sometimes skeptical.)   _____ _____

Looks for similarities and differences.   _____ _____

Reads independently; does not avoid difficult material.   _____ _____

Tries to understand complicated material by separating
it into its respective parts; reasons things out and sees
logical and common sense answers.   _____ _____

FORM 12-3 (Permission to reprint granted by the Los Angeles Unified School District.)

	YES	NO

Catches on quickly; retains and uses new ideas and information. _____ _____

Has a facility for learning English if bilingual. _____ _____

Is a keen and alert observer; usually "sees more" or "gets more" out of a story, film, etc. than others. _____ _____

MOTIVATION CHARACTERISTICS

Evidences power of concentration. _____ _____

Prefers to work independently with minimal directions from teachers. (Resists directions.) _____ _____

Has tendency to organize people, things, and situations. (Resists opinions of others; wants own way.) _____ _____

Is concerned with right and wrong, good and bad. (Makes decisions with little tolerance for shades of "grey.") _____ _____

Takes advantage of opportunities to learn and enjoys challenge. _____ _____

Is self-critical and strives for perfection. (Sometimes critical of others and not self.) _____ _____

Often is self-assertive. (Can be stubbornly set in ideas.) _____ _____

Requires little drill to grasp concepts; seeks other than routine tasks. (Needs to know reason for activity.) _____ _____

Becomes absorbed and involved in topics or problems of great personal interest. _____ _____

Is persistent in task completion. (Sometimes unwilling to change tasks.) _____ _____

Likes structure and order, but not static procedures. (Is frustrated by lack of progress.) _____ _____

Is motivated by sports, music, and concrete subjects. _____ _____

LEADERSHIP CHARACTERISTICS

Accepts and carries responsibility; follows through with tasks and usually does them well. _____ _____

Is self-confident with age peers; is usually well understood by them. (Can be assertive and dominant.) _____ _____

Seems well liked by classmates and is looked upon as a leader. (Needs peer approval and acceptance.) _____ _____

Shows developing understanding in how to relate to teachers and classmates. (Sometimes has a rebellious attitude.) _____ _____

FORM 12–3 (cont.)

	YES	NO

Tends to dominate others and generally organizes and directs activities when involved in a group. ____ ____

Adapts readily to new situations; is flexible in thought and actions and is not disturbed when normal routine is changed. ____ ____

Seems to enjoy being with other people; is sociable and prefers not to be alone. (Sometimes is a loner.) ____ ____

Takes initiative and shows independence of action. ____ ____

Is a social leader on playground and off campus. ____ ____

CREATIVITY CHARACTERISTICS

Displays intellectual playfulness; fantasizes; imagines; manipulates ideas by elaboration or modification. ____ ____

Is a high risk taker; is adventurous and speculative. (Has different criteria for success.) ____ ____

Displays a keen sense of humor reflective of own cultural background. ____ ____

Is individualistic; does not fear being different. (Departs from peer norm in action and behavior.) ____ ____

Makes predictions based on present information. ____ ____

Displays a curiosity about many things; has many hobbies. ____ ____

Generates a large number of ideas or solutions to problems and questions. ____ ____

Responds emotionally to stories, events, and needs of others. ____ ____

Shows ability in oral expression. ____ ____

Demonstrates exceptional ability in written expression; creates stories, plays, etc. ____ ____

Is sensitive to color, design, arrangement, and other qualities showing artistic appreciation and understanding. ____ ____

Is sensitive to melody, rhythm, form tonal coloring, mood and other qualities showing music appreciation. ____ ____

Demonstrates exceptional ability in one of the fine arts (underline area of strength): dancing, painting/drawing, sculpturing, clay modeling, instrumental or vocal music, role playing, drama. ____ ____

Demonstrates unusual ability in one of the practical arts (underline area of strength): handicrafts, wood, metal, print, design, mechanics. ____ ____

FORM 12-3 (cont.)

	YES	NO
Demonstrates exceptional skill and ability in physical coordination activities.	_____	_____
Shows interest in unconventional careers.	_____	_____
Improvises with commonplace materials.	_____	_____

ADAPTABILITY CHARACTERISTICS

	YES	NO
Handles outside responsibilities and meets school demands.	_____	_____
Learns through experience and is flexible and resourceful in solving day to day problems.	_____	_____
Deals effectively with deprivations, problems, frustrations, or obstacles caused by the complexities of living conditions.	_____	_____
Overcomes lack of environmental structure and direction. (Needs emotional support and sympathetic attitude.)	_____	_____
Displays high degree of social reasoning and/or behavior and shows ability to distinguish and select what is appropriate.	_____	_____
Uses limited resources to make meaningful products.	_____	_____
Displays maturity of judgment and reasoning beyond age level.	_____	_____
Is knowledgeable about things of which others are unaware.	_____	_____
Can transfer learning from one situation to another.	_____	_____

FORM 12-3 (cont.)

Criteria to consider when choosing a project with each group include

1. Can it be started and completed in a four- to six-week session?
2. Are the materials or equipment available to implement the project?
3. Is it actually an enrichment activity which will supplement a regular program?
4. Can the project chosen culminate in an activity that can be shared with others? (This is in keeping with Renzulli's theory of the child being a "producer.")
5. Will the project be acceptable to the staff and the administration?

VI. How Are the Activities Chosen?

Allowing the children to choose the project they are most interested in working on is usually successful. If possible, an inventory of each child's interests should be taken. This can be done informally by group discussion and/or teacher-made questionnaire or formally by the use of a commercial questionnaire. (See Materials List.) The exercise of each child declaring his/her interests either verbally or in writing not only educates the teacher but helps each child to crystalize his/her own opinions. This tends to make the group discussion much livelier and more productive.

It is helpful if the resource room teacher has several projects in mind and some materials on display to narrow down the list of alternatives from which to choose. This also informs the children about those projects for which materials and equipment are available. It is pointless to spend time discussing and choosing projects which are impossible to implement.

December, 1980

Mr. and Mrs. John Smith
100 Paradise Lane
Long Beach, New Hampshire

Dear Mr. and Mrs. Smith,

Your son Hans has been selected to participate in the Resource Room

Enrichment Program with Mrs. Jane Lafky. His schedule will consist of two

one-half hours, 11:00 to 11:30 A.M., on Wednesdays and Thursdays beginning

this week and continuing for about five weeks. Please feel free to visit

the resource room or to contact either of us if you have any further

questions.

Sincerely,

Mrs. Jones
Mrs. Jones
Director of Special Services

Jane Lafky
Jane Lafky
Resource Room Teacher

FORM 12-4 (Gifted Notification Letter to Parents)

VII. Culminating Activities

If the approach taken is one in which the gifted and talented not only learn by doing and studying but by sharing with others, many exciting activities can take place. For example,

1. Presentation at school assembly
2. Presentation in classroom
3. Presentation to adult group of similar interests, such as the Photography Club
4. Showing of a film made
5. Developing school or class newspaper
6. Display of materials made or labelled collection in hallway, e.g. rocks and minerals
7. Donation of original story books or poetry books to other classrooms, school library, or local hospital
8. Donation of handmade games or activities to other classrooms, school library, or local hospital
9. Radio program presented on school intercom
10. Donation of tapes or records made by the children to the school library or local hospital
11. Development of a mini museum to be visited by the school population and/or other schools in the district.

A FINAL WORD

The gifted and talented program has many positive benefits when included in a resource room program. In most states funds for gifted and talented programs are not provided by the same state and federal agencies that fund programs for handicapped students. The main point to remember, however, is that this type of program does not *take the place of* a full, ongoing, separately financed program for the gifted and talented. Although it can benefit those students involved in a very positive way, its original intent was to improve the "aura" of the resource room.

The one drawback to this type of program is that because of its existence in a school some administrators may feel that they are fulfilling their obligation to enrich the education of the gifted and talented. You as a resource room teacher must stress (perhaps more than once) that this type of programming was never meant to be the answer to providing adequate enrichment for the gifted and talented. It is important for all involved to understand that a resource room gifted and talented program can work hand in hand with an additional full- or part-time gifted and talented program in any school setting.

BIBLIOGRAPHY

The following bibliography was compiled by Woodbridge Township New Jersey School District Program for the Gifted and Talented.

Professional Books

Abraham, Willard, *Common Sense About Gifted Children*. New York: Harper & Row, Publishers, Inc., 1958.

Barbe, Walter B. (ed.), *Psychology and Education of the Gifted: Selected Readings*. Englewood Cliffs, N.J.: Prentice-Hall, Inc., 1965.

Boston, Bruce O. (ed.), *A Resource Manual of Information on Education of the Gifted and Talented*. Reston, Va.: Council for Exceptional Children, 1975.

Coffey, Kay. and others, *Parents Speak on Gifted and Talented Children*. Ventura, Calif.: Ventura County Superintendent of Schools Office, 1976.

Cutts, Norma E. and Nicholas Moseky, *Teaching the Bright and Gifted*. Englewood Cliffs, N.J.: Prentice-Hall, Inc., 1957.

Delp, Jeanne L. and Ruth A. Martinson, *The Gifted and Talented: A Handbook for Parents*. Ventura, Calif.: Ventura County Superintendent of Schools. 1975.

Drews, Elizabeth M. (ed.), *Guidance for the Academically Talented Student*. Washington, D.C.: National Education Association, 1961.

Education of Mentally Gifted Minors—K–12. Sacramento, Calif.: California State Department of Education, 1971.

Education of the Gifted and Talented. Washington, D.C.: U.S. Government Printing Office, 1972.

Ehrlich, Virginia Z., Dr., *The Astor Program Progress Report*. New York: Gifted Child Studies, 1974.

Fine, Benjamin, *Stretching Their Minds*. New York: Dutton, 1964.

Fliegler, L. A., *Curriculum Planning for the Gifted*. Englewood Cliffs, N.J.: Prentice-Hall, 1961.

Gallagher, James J., *Research Summary on Gifted Child Education*. Springfield, Illinois: Department for Exceptional Children: Gifted Program, 1966.

———. *Teaching the Gifted Child*. Boston: Allyn & Bacon, Inc., 1975.

———. *The Gifted Child in the Elementary School*. Washington, D.C.: National Education Association, 1959.

Goertzel, Victor and Mildred G. Goertzel, *Cradles of Eminence*. Boston: Little, Brown & Co., 1962.

Gold, M. J., *Education of the Intellectually Gifted*. Columbus, Ohio: Charles E. Merrill, 1965.

Gourley, Theodore J., *Programs for Gifted Students: A National Survey*. Pitman, N.J.: Educational Improvement Center, 1975.

Gowan, John C. and George D. Penos, *The Education and Guidance of the Ablest*. Springfield, Ill.: Charles C. Thomas, 1964.

Gowan, John Curtis and Paul E. Torrance (eds.), *Educating the Ablest*. Itasca, Ill.: F. E. Peacock Publishers, 1971.

Grost, A., *Genius in Residence*. Englewood Cliffs, N.J.: Prentice-Hall, Inc., 1970.

Grove, Richard, *Proceedings from the National Conference on Arts and Humanities–Gifted and Talented*. Spearfish, S. Dak.: 1974.

Hauck, Barbara B. and Maurice F. Freehill, *The Gifted Case Studies*. Dubuque, Iowa: Wm. C. Brown Company, Publishers, 1972.

Hildreth, Gertrude H., *Introduction to Gifted Children*. New York: McGraw-Hill Book Co., 1966.

Hoyt, Kenneth B. and Jean R. Hebeler, *Career Education for Gifted and Talented Students*. Salt Lake City: Olympus Publishing Company, 1974.

Keating, Daniel P. (ed.), *Intellectual Talent-Research and Development*. Baltimore: The Johns Hopkins University Press, 1976.

Labuda, Michael, *Creative Reading for Gifted Learners: A Design for Excellence*. Newark, Delaware: International Reading Association, 1974.

Lawless, Ruth F., *A Guide for Educating A Gifted Child In Your Classroom*. New York: D. O. K. Publishers, 1976.

Maker, June, *Training Teachers for the Gifted and Talented: A Comparison of Models*. Reston, Va.: The Council for Exceptional Children, 1975.

Martinson, Ruth A. and May V. Seagoe, *The Abilities of Young Children*. Reston, Va.: Council for Exceptional Children, 1967.

Martinson, Ruth A. and Jean Wiener, *The Improvement of Teaching Procedures with Gifted Elementary and Secondary School Students*. Washington, D.C.: Department of Health, Education and Welfare, 1968.

Martinson, Ruth A., *Curriculum Enrichment for the Gifted in the Primary Grades*. Englewood Cliffs, N.J.: Prentice-Hall, Inc., 1968.

———. *The Identification of the Gifted and Talented*. Ventura, Calif.: Ventura County Office of Superintendent of Schools, 1974.

———. *A Guide Toward Better Teaching of the Gifted*. Ventura, Calif.: Ventura County Superintendent of Schools Office, 1976.

Mentally Gifted Children and Youth. Harrisburg, Pa.: Pennsylvania Department of Education, 1973.

McElroy, John L. (ed.), *Handbook for Principals and Teachers of Secondary Programs for the Gifted*. San Diego, Calif.: San Diego City Schools, 1973.

McKay, Ralph H., *Handbook for Principals and Teachers of Elementary Programs for the Gifted*. San Diego, Calif.: San Diego City Schools, 1973.

Miley, James F. and others (comp.), *Promising Practices: Teaching the Disadvantaged Gifted*. Ventura, Calif.: Ventura County Superintendent of Schools Office, 1975.

New Directions for Gifted Education. Los Angeles: National/State Leadership Training Institute on the Gifted and the Talented, 1976.

Olivero, James L. and Irving S. Sato, *P. A. B. Conference Report and Follow-Up*. Ventura, Calif.: Office of the Ventura County Superintendent of Schools, 1974.

Osborn, Alex, *Applied Imagination*. New York: Charles Scribner's Sons, 1962.

Parnes, Sidney J., *AHA! Insights into Creative Behavior*. New York: D. O. K. Publishers, Inc., 1975.

———. *Creativity: Unlocking Human Potential*. New York: D. O. K. Publishers, Inc., 1972.

Renzulli, Joseph S. *A Guidebook for Evaluating Programs for the Gifted and Talented.* California: Office of Ventura County Superintendent of Schools, 1975.

———. *Program Evaluation in the Perspective of Theory.* Reston, Va.: The Council for Exceptional Children, 1968.

———. *The Enrichment Triad Model.* Withersfield, Conn.: Creative Learning Press, 1977.

Renzulli, Joseph S. and Assoc., *Scales for Rating the Behavior/Characteristics of Superior Students.* Withersfield, Conn.: Creative Learning Press, 1976.

Reynold, Maynard C. (ed.), *Early School Admission for Mentally Advanced Children.* Reston,Va.: Council for Exceptional Children, 1962.

Rice, Joseph P., *The Gifted Developing Total Talent.* Springfield, Ill.: Charles C Thomas, 1970.

Sato, Irving S., *Developing A Written Plan for the Education of Gifted and Talented Students.* Ventura, Calif.: Office of the Ventura County Superintendent of Schools, 1974.

Smith, Donald C., *Personal and Social Adjustments of Gifted Adolescents.* Reston, Va.: Council for Exceptional Cihldren, 1962.

Syphers, Dorothy F., *Gifted and Talented Children: Practical Programming for Teachers and Principals.* Reston, Va.: Council for Exceptional Children, 1972.

Terman, Louis M. and Melita H. Oden, *The Gifted Child Grows Up.* Vol. IV of the Genetic Studies of Genius Series, ed. Louis M. Terman. Stanford, Calif.: Stanford University Press, 1947.

———. *The Gifted Group at Mid-life.* Vol. V of the Genetic Studies of Genius Series, ed. Louis M. Terman. Stanford, Calif.: Stanford University Press, 1959.

Terman, Louis M. and others, *Mental and Physical Traits of a Thousand Gifted Children.* Vol. I of the Genetic Studies of Genius Series, ed. Louis M. Terman. Stanford, Calif.: Stanford University Press, 1926.

Torrance, Paul E., *Gifted Children in the Classroom.* New York: Macmillan, Inc., 1965.

Treffinger, Donald J. and Clifford D. Curl, *Self-Directed Study on Education of the Gifted and the Talented.* Ventura, Calif.: Ventura County Superintendent of Schools Office, 1976.

Ward, Virgil S., *Educating the Gifted: An Axiomatic Approach.* Charles E. Merrill Publishing Co., 1961.

Watson, Odell A. and Cornelia Tongue (eds.), *Suggestions for Identification of Gifted and Talented Students.* Raleigh, N.C.: State Department of Public Instruction, 1975.

Idea Books

Attea, Mary, *Turning Children on through Creative Writing.* New York: D. O. K. Publishers, Inc., 1973.

Challenging the Able Learner Revised. Cincinnati: Cincinnati Public Schools, 1964. (Intermediate Grades)

Challenging the Able Learner Revised. Cincinnati: Cincinnati Public Schools, 1964. (Primary Grades)

Creative Thinking Techniques for Stimulating Original Ideas in Students. Madison, Wis.: Tag Bonus Publications, n.d.

Creativity and Reinforcement of Basics. New York: D. O. K. Publishers, Inc., 1976.

DiPego, Gerald, under the direction of Professor Gary A. Davis, *Imagination Express.* New York: D. O. K. Publishers, Inc., 1970

East Whittier City School District. *Creative Prescription's Unlimited, Grades 1–2.* East Whittier, Calif.

Fixx, James F., *Games for the Super-Intelligent.* New York: Popular Library, 1972.

Gellis, Marilyn J. *Thinkisthenics.* Palm Springs, Calif.: Thinkisthenics, 1971.

Grimm, Gary and Don Mitchell, *The Good Apple Creative Writing Books.* Carthage, Ill.: Good Apple, Inc., 1976

Heafford, Philip, *The Math Entertainer.* New York: Harrow Books, 1959.

Hewitt-Buell, P., *A Child-Centered Language Arts Program.* Newton, Mass. Curriculum Associates, Inc., 1973.

The Instructional Fair. Birmingham, Mich.: The Instructional Fair Inc., 1973.

Judd Wallace, *Games, Tricks and Puzzles for a Hand Calculator.* Menlo Park, Calif.: Dymaxi, 1974.

Kaplan, Sandra Nine, and Sheila Kunishima Madsen, *Think-INS An Approach to Relevant Curriculum Stressing Creative Thinking and Problem Solving.* California: Creative Teaching Press, 1969–1974.

Lettaw, John H., *A-Maze-ing Number Puzzles.* Englewood Cliffs, N.J.: Prentice-Hall Learning Systems, Inc., 1975.

Longley-Cook, L. H., *Fun with Puzzles.* Greenwich, Conn.: Fawcett Books, 1965.

Markey, Connie, *I Wonder Whatever Happened to Amelia Pickett and Other Reasons for Writing.* Newton, Mass.: Curriculum Associates, Inc., 1976.

Metzner, Seymour, Richard M. Sharp, and Vicki F. Sharp, *Ready-in-a-Minute Math Games.* Englewood Cliffs, N.J.: Prentice-Hall Learning Systems Inc., 1975.

Mira, Julio A., *Mathematical Teasers.* New York: Harper & Row Publishers, Inc., 1970.

Mott-Smith, George, *Mathematical Puzzles.* New York: Dover Publications, Inc., 1954.

Peterson, Homer M., *Big Book of Pencil Games.* Garden City, N.Y.: Doubleday & Co., Inc., 1962.

Ranucci, Ernest R. and Wilma E. Rollins, *Brain Drain.* Fresno, Calif.: Creative Teaching Associates, Inc., 1975.

7 Search Visuals, Critical Thinking Skills. New York: Scholastic Search Magazine and Scholastic Book Services, 1975.

Schaffer, Frank, *Secret Codes for Fun.* Palos Verdes Peninsula, Calif.: Frank Schaffer, 1973.

Uraneck, William O. Dr. (ed.), *Young Thinkers Bk. 1.* Lexington, Mass.: Dr. W. O. Uraneck, 1974.

Wayman, Joe, *The Gifted and Talented.* Englewood, Colo.: Consulting Associates, Inc., n.d.

Why Doesn't an Igloo Melt Inside? A Handbook for Teachers of the Academically Gifted Talented. Memphis, Tenn.: Memphis City School System, 1973.

Williams, Frank E., *Classroom Ideas for Encouraging Thinking and Feeling.* New York: D. O. K. Publishers, Inc., 1970.

Williams, Frank E., *Classroom Ideas for Developing Productive-Divegent Thinking.* St. Paul, Minn.: National Schools Project, 1966.

REFERENCES

Characteristics of Able Disadvantaged Pupils. Los Angeles, Calif.: Los Angeles Unified School District, n.d.

Cummings, William B., *Cummings Checklist of Characteristics of Gifted and Talented Children.* San Francisco, Calif.: San Francisco Unified School District, Programs for Mentally Gifted Minors, 1974.

Gallagher, James J., *Teaching the Gifted Child* (2nd ed.). Boston: Allyn & Bacon, Inc., 1975.

Renzulli, Joseph S., *Enrichment Triad Model: A Guide for Developing Defensible Programs for the Gifted and Talented.* Withersfield, Conn.: Creative Learning Press, 1977.

Renzulli, Joseph S. and Robert K. Hartman, *Exceptional Children,* 38, no. 3 (November 1971), 211–214, 243–258.

Syphers, Dorothy F., *Gifted and Talented Children: Practical Programming for Teachers and Principals.* Reston, Va.: The Council for Exceptional Children, 1972.

implementing
a secondary level
resource room

13

WHY HAVE A RESOURCE ROOM
AT THE SECONDARY LEVEL?

The resource room can offer an acceptable option for the older student with learning handicaps. Many learning-disabled secondary level students have the social and physical skills to blend into the regular school program. A self-contained program may be necessary for those students with more severe handicaps.

The resource room offers the flexibility to meet the needs of secondary students with learning handicaps by providing remedial instruction in reading and math as well as providing modified programs in social studies and science. A resource room teacher can provide needed support to regular teachers to help ensure successful mainstreaming. This type of program can also provide a crisis intervention center, a place where handicapped students can come to study, take tests, or just relax. Often in a junior or senior high school, the resource room teacher functions as the student's advocate to peers, parents, other teachers, and school authorities.

HOW DO YOU SET UP A SECONDARY LEVEL
RESOURCE ROOM?

Placement of the Room.   The location of the room is important. Often special education programs at this level are received with negative feelings. The challenge is to modify this as much as possible. These negative feelings may emanate from the special education students themselves rather than from the regular students. One way to reduce this is to make the resource room as desirable a place to be as possible. Locating the room near other academic classrooms rather than completely separated or grouped with other special education classrooms is important. Since the students will be going to some regular classes, they will have to be able to get to and from the resource room easily.

Name of the Room.   Either *resource room* or *learning lab* might be an appropriate name. See Chapter 1 for more suggestions.

Physical Set-Up.   As much as possible, make the resource room look like any other classroom. Continue to use multimedia materials to help the secondary learning-disabled students to learn. Display these materials in a manner that will be accepted by teenagers. Low-level materials such as an alphabet can be placed inconspicuously in the classroom rather than above the chalkboard. Library-style study carrels provide quiet places for work, study, or relaxation. Learning centers may be assigned similarly to the elementary format, but if the materials are stored in file folders in a filing cabinet, they may be more acceptable to the secondary student. Sensitivity to the embarrassment of the learning-disabled adolescent is important.

Obtain as much audiovisual equipment as possible. Learning filmstrips, tapes, and records are quite acceptable to secondary students.

Set aside one area where students can read magazines, listen to music, or "rap." Some of these students may have difficulty socializing in the larger school environment, and the resource room can be a relaxed social setting for their free periods.

Scheduling.   This is one of the most challenging aspects of organizing a resource room at the secondary level. It will probably be necessary to hand schedule rather than computer schedule to ensure the correct class composition, teacher selection, and course selection. The amount of time spent in the resource room will be determined at the IEP meeting. This should be based on the time needed for remedial work as well as the number of courses the student can handle in the mainstream.

When choosing regular classes for students, consider the following factors:

1. Composition of the classes: If classes are hetereogeneously grouped, this will make the scheduling more difficult.
2. Teaching style of the teacher: Some students respond well to a highly structured approach; others do better when given more choice.
3. Number of special education students within each class: No more than three or four L.D. students per class is recommended.
4. Requirements of the course: Can the student keep up with the normal requirements?
5. Can the requirements be modified or reduced?
6. How much will the teacher cooperate?

Public Relations.   The teacher and the administrators of the resource room program will have to "sell" the concept to the regular students, teachers, and the learning-disabled students. Here are some suggestions.

1. List the resource room courses in the school bulletin. Though students do not usually sign up for the resource room courses, a well-written course description along with a course number can aid in the acceptance of the program as part of the total school offerings.
2. Resource room teachers should assist in regular teaching responsibilities, such as homeroom, lunch duty, and after-school supervision. In this way, the resource room teacher becomes one of the regular teaching staff rather than an outsider. The contact with the entire school population also gives the resource room teacher a better perspective of the expectations for secondary students.
3. It is important to contact parents early in the school year. After years of living with a learning-disabled child, the parents are often discouraged about their child's learning.

Invite the parents to an informal visit to the resource room before school begins. Give them a specific time, and open the invitation to the students if they so desire. This visit is really for the parents. It is not wise to have parents drag an unwilling teenager along to shake hands with the new teacher.

This informal meeting allows the resource room teacher an opportunity to meet the parents and establish rapport. During the first week of school, call each parent to report on the child's progress. (Try to make this report a positive one.) This can establish the groundwork for a cooperative relationship between teacher and parents. Later on it may be necessary to call parents about school problems, but hopefully you have created a warm, caring image, and these situations will not seem as threatening.

If the student is involved in a serious behavioral or academic problem, you will want to ask the parents to come in immediately. It is usually beneficial to have a conference with everyone involved. For instance, a regular teacher, the student, parents, and resource room teacher may be involved in the meeting. It will be helpful to the student and parents if the resource room teacher can act as moderator during these meetings. Help those involved to avoid putting undue pressure on the student by dwelling on the wrongdoing and by focusing on alternative ways of solving the problem.

For example: A student is caught smoking marijuana in the restroom. The usual punishment is a two-week suspension. The parents are called in to meet with the principal, resource room teacher, and the student. A suspension would mean the student would be missing school for two weeks. An alternative solution might be an in-house suspension where he could continue the learning program. This could mean that he would not be allowed any social activities during school hours.

Parents need to know what is available to help them deal with their concerns about their learning-disabled child. Provide information on the local programs available to them and their youngsters, for example,

1. Local Association for Children with Learning Disabilities (A.C.L.D. chapters)
2. Local Council of Exceptional Children (C.E.C.)
3. Community family counseling services
4. Church groups
5. Social clubs for L.D. youngsters
6. Local sports programs
7. Local crafts programs

FOCUS OF THE SECONDARY LEVEL RESOURCE ROOM

During the elementary years, the major thrust of teaching many students with learning handicaps is to teach or remediate basic skills so that the student can cope with as much of the regular curriculum as possible.

Some learning disabled students still require remediation at the secondary level. To keep these children in the mainstream as much as possible is still the main focus. A specific structure set up in the resource room to deal with learning-disabled adolescents who have often had years of special education programming is indeed a challenge. Motivation is often lacking, so the presentation of lessons and materials in a fresh and inspiring format is essential. The following suggestions may help:

ACADEMIC

1. The teacher should have the opportunity to give input on the purchase of appropriate materials for the program. (See Materials List at the end of this chapter.)
2. The teacher needs an adequate amount of audiovisual equipment so that several students can work simultaneously. The equipment may be purchased or borrowed for the year from the school library or audiovisual center.
3. The resource room teacher will need to devise an efficient method of assigning students to centers, tutoring sessions, independent assignments, and evaluation meetings by use of
   a. Weekly assignment sheets in file folder (see Chapter 5)
   b. Boxes containing assignments
   c. Rotating charts
   d. Individualized cassette tapes with assignments
4. The resource room teacher should create lessons in the content areas that are self-directing. To facilitate record keeping and evaluation of the student's progress, it is helpful if these lessons are self-contained each day. They should include the presentation of a few important ideas and a body of work that can be completed within the period.
5. The resource room teacher should devise a backup system to deal with behavioral problems. This may be a fellow teacher, dean of students, psychologist, counselor, or principal. The choice will depend on the resources available in the school. Even if the only available backup is a quiet corner in the school office, it is important for the resource room teacher to have support in dealing with difficult students.

EMOTIONAL

Due to the increased demands of independent assignments and greater reliance on reading skills at the secondary level, many L.D. secondary students experience feelings of inadequacy. Some may want to give up entirely since they are so acutely aware of their relative standing among their peers.

The resource room teacher must deal with these feelings. Each case is different, but here are some suggestions to consider in dealing with some of these sensitive problems.

1. Work on survival skills. They need to know how to read traffic signs and directions, write a check, fill out applications, and so on. Responding to these basic skill needs will often relieve many fears they have.
2. Expose them to a wide variety of career opportunities. Help students find out about the requirements, salaries, and satisfactions of many jobs within their ability levels.

✗ 3. Consider sharing with them their present reading and math skill levels. Some students believe their levels are lower than they really are. It is a delicate area, and each student should be told as much as will enhance his/her self-esteem.

4. Help them to accept their present functioning level. Many students will express the opinion that they can do much more difficult work than you give them. Accept this as a necessary defense. Comments such as, "You could handle many of the concepts in the social studies text, but the reading level is so difficult, we wouldn't expect you to be able to read words you haven't learned yet." This will help the student save face and be more realistic about his/her current functioning level.

   Older students are quick to recognize third-grade material even when updated for teenagers. Many times, you will want to use elementary materials that fit the skill level of the student. This can result in great resistance. Acknowledge to the student that you are aware the material is "baby stuff." Explain the reason you want to use the material, for instance, "This book deals with the /ai/ sound that you've been having difficulty with. Would you be willing to read through this even though it really is too childish for you?" If the student continues to resist, give up on the material. Find another way. Better to lose the material than the student.

5. Offer opportunities for students to talk about their concerns. This could be called class meeting, gripe session, or talk time. The format does not need to be complicated. Three basic rules should be adhered to, however. Encourage students to

   - a. Talk about personal experience
   - b. Not to attack others
   - c. Not to give advice.

   It would be beneficial if the school psychologist or social worker could lead the group on a regular basis. Since this person does not have to discipline or grade students, he/she is more likely to encourage openness.

   Make sure you have the support of the school and parents in conducting these rap sessions. A discussion about these meetings at a special-education parents gathering usually gains the support needed.

ALTERNATIVES TO ACADEMIC CLASSES

1. The student can serve as student aide in the cafeteria, office, or gym. Students can be supervised by the secretary, cafeteria personnel, or gym teacher. They can perform routine duties such as delivering messages, sorting mail, stacking trays, or putting away equipment. This alternative assignment offers students an opportunity to assist adults in a nonthreatening environment and fosters a good self-image.

2. The student can serve as a teacher assistant to a regular classroom teacher. Students can help with clerical duties, bulletin boards, or operating audiovisual equipment. They can be assigned to a willing classroom teacher for a specific period during each day for one marking period. The teacher can make a comment on the report card for that marking period about the student's reliability in serving as a teacher's assistant.

3. The student can audit a course. This removes much of the pressure from the student when the requirements are beyond his/her ability and allows the student to participate in some aspects of the course, such as classroom discussion, that he/she is able to handle. When the teacher knows that he/she is not responsible for the student's performance, there is less chance that the

teacher will make unreasonable demands on the child. Auditing a course does present some conflicts. For instance, the other students are aware that the L.D. child does not have to meet the same requirements that they do. If the learning-disabled student can deal with the peer pressure, auditing may be a beneficial alternative.

MAINSTREAMING AT THE SECONDARY LEVEL

The secondary student is involved with several teachers each grading period. These teachers may change every few weeks. Thus, there are many people to communicate with concerning the resource room students. Contrary to the elementary approach in which teachers remain constant throughout the year, the regular secondary teachers may work with over one hundred students during the day. They have limited opportunities to follow a particular student's progress beyond the one period. It is necessary for the resource room teacher to keep in touch with the student's total program. Here are some suggestions for doing this.

1. In-service and staff meetings.
    a. Inform the staff of the laws concerning the mainstreaming of special students. When the regular teachers realize this is part of their job, rather than a special request or favor, there will be easier acceptance of the students in their classroom.
    b. Impress on teachers that students who have incurred much failure may act out and appear not to care about learning. They care very much but often have experienced difficulty in meeting adult expectations. Solicit the support of the regular teacher in understanding these dynamics. Emphasize the fact that you will be available for consultation to help work out these problems.
    c. Explain how contracts for course requirements will be made among the regular teacher, students, and resource room teacher to help share the responsibilities in the learning process. Example:

    > Course—Social Studies 8th Grade
    > Teacher—Mr. Jones
    > Student—Sam B.
    > Sam will be able to attend class on time, take part in class discussions, and take an oral test covering the basic ideas of the material at the end of the marking period.
    >
    > Student Signature _____
    >
    > Teacher Signature _____

    Suggestions of what the student can handle should be made by the resource room teacher. Begin with slightly less than it appears the student can achieve. When the student succeeds at the assigned tasks he/she can go on to more difficult assignments.

2. Good communication with the regular teachers
    a. Every three weeks send a brief evaluation form to each teacher to be filled out. Example:

Date: _____

Dear Miss Smith:

In order for me to evaluate how Sam is doing in your class, please check the appropriate lines.

_____ 1. Work is completed

_____ 2. Work is not completed

_____ 3. Behavior is good

_____ 4. Behavior is not good

_____ 5. Comments _____

Thank you,

Resource Room Teacher

Sharing these evaluations with the student has many positive effects. It helps the student to monitor his/her own progress. It also gives the resource room teacher clues as to how to design the student's program from week to week. Serious problems can be handled via a conference with the student, regular teacher, or both.

b. Keep track of assignments in other classes. Some students respond well to a structured method of keeping an assignment sheet. The resource room teacher will have to determine which students will resent the intrusion and which really would welcome the assistance. A daily or weekly check on short- and long-term assignments helps some resource room students cope with the demands of regular classes. Example:

| | | | *Date* |
| *Date* | *Class* | *Assignment* | *Completed* |

INDIVIDUALIZING FOR SECONDARY STUDENTS

The resource room program at the secondary level requires a very individualized approach. Students are often functioning at a wide range of ability levels, and this may require that several subjects be given in the resource room. In order to meet these divergent needs, the program must be versatile. Here are some suggestions.

1. *Adapting Regular Materials.* Often it is necessary to adapt regular materials for the resource room students. Many students are able to handle the concepts presented in a social studies or science book but cannot read the materials for themselves. Several alternatives exist.

   a. Do not attempt to cover the entire book. Choose chapters or sections of the book that are most important. Have students read aloud, helping them with unfamiliar words.

   b. Do not read the text but pull important information from it and present it to the students. Outline these points simultaneously—the teacher writing on the board and the students copying on paper.

   c. Tape record important chapters or sections. Teacher's aides or parent volunteers can read the material into the tape recorder. After each section, have the reader recapitulate the main ideas.

      d. Rewrite chapters, simplifying the material. Type onto a ditto material that can be covered in twenty to thirty minutes. Have a follow-up activity for each lesson. This activity might be: three or four questions to answer from the text; drawings to label; words to define; or a concept to explain in their own words.

      e. Use filmstrips, movies, and the overhead projector to present new ideas for discussion.

      f. Do some research of the texts available in your district. Often easier reading texts exist which cover much of the same material. These can be purchased for use in the resource room.

      g. There are also many excellent special education materials that require a low reading level but cover secondary subjects. (See Secondary Materials List.)

2. *Teaching Reading.* "What, short vowels again?" The secondary resource room teacher has to be very creative in order to teach reading skills to students who are tired of learning. Here are some suggestions to help motivate these students.

      a. Use content areas to teach reading. Follow a history or biology lesson with an activity on unfamiliar terms. Break down the terms phonetically or look up pronunciations in the dictionary—the longer the word, the better. Students are impressed with long words, and you can review many phonetic skills in one word.

      b. Have students tape record easy reading books and write comprehension questions for elementary school children. Make sure you have an outlet for these materials and see if your student can visit the school and see younger children using them. The book-cassette package might be incorporated into the elementary school library, and for the students to see their names in an actual card catalogue can provide increased incentive and serve as an ego booster.

      c. Taped reading programs are reasonably successful. The students do not have to exhibit their reading skills to anyone and can progress at their own speed.

      d. Programmed and sequential individualized reading programs may be more acceptable to students than traditional reading programs. (Refer to Materials List.)

      e. Find alternatives to the traditional reading group lesson. Instead have a five-minute reading evaluation session with each student in which you ask the student to read orally, decode difficult words, or answer comprehension problems. Too often, the student has had years of failure experiences in traditional reading groups. An alternative to this inspires a better chance of success.

3. *Teaching Math.*

      a. Use teaching machines when possible to drill on basic facts.

      b. Programmed math approaches are useful except where students would prefer to get through as quickly as possible. Then, they become careless. A decision must be made based on each student's learning style.

      c. Teach students to use a calculator in order to do math more quickly and accurately.

      d. If computer facilities are available in your school, there are many excellent computer programs which individualize math instruction.

e.   Students enjoy the competition of math games such as math bingo (which can be handmade or purchased).

4. *Teaching Content Areas.* Whenever possible, students should be mainstreamed for subjects such as social studies and science. However, there will be cases when the program cannot accommodate these students or when the students would not benefit from being in these classes even with modifications. It will be necessary, therefore, for the resource room to offer the flexibility of programming in order for the students to receive instruction in these courses. (Refer to section on Adapting Regular Materials, p. 211.)

5. *Reviewing and Testing.* Your students will need frequent reviews in class in order to retain information. Having practice reviews and study sessions will teach the students *how* to study. A good way to review is to use a T.V. game show format, for example, *The Match Game:*

a.   Line up desks in equal rows.

b.   Provide students with scraps of paper and pencils.

c.   Ask questions that can be answered in one or two words.

d.   The game can be individualized by requiring correct spelling from those students who can be expected to answer accurately.

Test students frequently. Teach students how to study for the test by having a study session. Explain underlining key terms, relating a term with its meaning by association, memorizing a list of facts by making a mnemonic device (word made up of first letter of each word). Make students aware of different types of test strategies.

a.   Short answer questions—Do the ones you know immediately first, then go back and take time with the difficult ones.

b.   Long answer—Write down the main idea in a brief outline form. Then write the paragraph adding details.

c.   Multiple choice—Read all the choices carefully, then eliminate the obvious wrong choices first.

d.   True/False—If you are not sure, guess. There is a 50 percent chance of being correct.

Show the students how to be in the right psychological state for taking tests. They should study hard, get plenty of rest, and review briefly. It is probably beneficial to be a little nervous, but excessive nervousness can cause blocking. To prevent this, have them take deep breaths and tell themselves that they have done a good job preparing for the test, and they will do the best they can.

Give a practice test the day before; then give either the same test again or one with a similar format the next day. The rationale for this type of testing is not only to see what students have learned but also to teach them how to take a test and to review the material by actually taking the test.

GRADING SECONDARY STUDENTS

Grading students with learning difficulties on the secondary level presents many questions.

1. Should the teacher compare and grade the work of the L.D. student with that of the regular student?

2. Should the teacher compare and grade the work of the L.D. student only with other similar students?
3. Should L.D. students be graded only on their effort to perform?
4. Should L.D. students be graded only on their ability to perform?

No matter what method one chooses in order to grade the L.D. student, there will be drawbacks. First, the L.D. student knows that his/her grades are inflated if he/she cannot keep up with the regular classroom. Second, it is conceivable that an L.D. student who receives grades based on his/her performance among similar students will score such high grades as to give the impression he/she no longer needs remedial help. There are no easy answers to these grading conflicts. Here are some alternatives.

1. Grade students compared to other handicapped students. State on the report card or send an accompanying letter to parents explaining the basis for the grades.
2. Grade students based on individual progress only. State this on the report card.
3. Have a special attainment Dean's List where L.D. students can be recognized for making exceptional progress or effort.
4. Ask students to help you decide how they will be graded. Some students may want to be compared to the regular students.
5. Base grades on specific work to be completed. This should be decided on at the beginning of the term. If students want to earn an *A,* they will have to complete a set number of projects or assignments.

The key to success with any of the ideas chosen is to be honest both with the parents and the child and keep them both informed.

IEPs FOR OLDER STUDENTS

The format for planning and writing IEPs is the same for secondary students as for elementary students. (See Chapter 3.) The important difference is that students should be involved with all parts of the IEP. Older students may be resistant to adults making the decisions about their school program. Thus, when they are given the chance to help plan and implement their own Individual Educational Plan, the chances of success in meeting the goals is increased. Students may be apprehensive about actually participating in a meeting composed of all adults. As an alternative, many students will appreciate a pre-IEP meeting with the resource room teacher. During this meeting the student and teacher can discuss

1. Reasons for writing an IEP
2. Where the student is currently functioning
3. What the student's own goals are for the year—these may be quite different from what is important to the others at the meeting
4. Ways the student can meet these goals.

These suggestions can be incorporated into the IEP during the meeting. When the written IEP is completed, go over it with the student. Explain that these are guidelines for the year. They can be altered according to the student's needs as the year passes. Let the student know you are always available to discuss how he/she is progressing.

SECONDARY LEVEL MATERIALS LIST

Language Arts

Addison-Wesley Publishing Co., Inc.
Box 3220
Reading, MA 01867
> *Checkered Flag Series A:* (Price Range: $35.00 each)
> Includes: Filmstrips, records, tapes, books, teacher's guide.
> BEARCAT
> RIDDLER
> SMASHUP
> WHEELS
> *Checkered Flag Series B:*
> 500
> FLEA
> GRAND PRIX
> SCRAMBLE

Barnell-Loft Ltd.
958 Church Street
Baldwin, NY 11510
> *Specific Skills Series* (Price Range: $2.00 each)
> Using the Context, Levels C, D, E, F
> Getting the Facts, Levels C, D, E, F
> Getting the Main Idea, Levels C, D, E, F
> Drawing Conclusions, Levels C, D, E, F
> Teacher's Manual

Developmental Learning Materials
7440 Natchez
Niles, IL 60648
> *Sensitivity* (Price Range: $10.50)
> 46 humorous cards—presents problems of junior high and high school students.

Educators Publishing Service, Inc.
75 Moulton Street
Cambridge, MA 02138
> Exercises in English Grammar Books 1 & 2 (Price Range: $2.50)
> SLD Book 6 (Price Range: $3.00)
> Systematic Spelling (Price Range: $1.50)
> Reading Comprehension in Varied Subject Areas:
> Grade Levels 3–12
> Answer Keys Books 1–12 (no charge)
> Answer Keys Wordly Wise Books 1–3 (Price Range: $2.50–3.00 each)
> Wordly Wise (Vocabulary), grades 4–12 (Price Range: $2.50–3.00)

A Programmed Workbook Series to Introduce the Parts of Speech (Price Range: $2.50):
Words that Name
Words that Tell Action
Words that Describe
Words that Connect
Teacher's Guide (no charge)
Basic English Sentence Patterns (Price Range: $4.50)
Teacher's Manual (Price Range: $3.50)

Elementary Secondary Multi-Media Co.
180 East Sixth Street
St. Paul, MN 55101
Women Who Win Series (Price Range: $14.00 each)
Includes: teacher's guide, cassettes, books, skill sheets, activity cards
JANET LYNN, SHANE GOULD, OLGA KORBUT AND CHRIS EVERT
EVONNE GOOLAGONG—SMILES AND SMASHES
LAURA BRAUGH—GOLF'S GOLDEN GIRL
CATHY RIGBY—ON THE BEAM
WILMA RUDOLF—RUN FOR GLORY
ANNEMARIE PROELL: QUEEN OF THE MOUNTAIN
JOAN MOORE PRICE: THE OLYMPIC DREAM
MARY DECKER: SPEED RECORDS AND SPAGHETTI
ROSEMARY CASALS: THE REBEL ROSEBUD

Houghton Mifflin Co.
Pennington-Hopewell Road
Hopewell, NJ 08525
Discoveries Grades 4–12 (Price Range: $2.50–$4.00 each)
21 paper readers, individualized reading
High interest

Learning Resource Center
10655 S. W. Greenburg Road
P. O. Box 23077
Portland, OR 97223
Complete Power Building (Price Range: $45.00)
50 books and 5 Rec. Rdg. Series
Multi-Sensory Skill Development (Price Range: $5.00)

New Readers Press
1320 Jamesville Avenue
Box 131
Syracuse, NY 13210
Practice in Survival Skills (Price Range: $1.50)
Grades 4–12
Functional reading approach

Reader's Digest Services, Inc.
Educational Division
Pleasantville, NY 10570
Content Area Studies
Book 4 (reading level 4) (Price Range: $1.70)
Book 4 Duplicating Masters (Price Range: $4.00)
Book 5 (reading level 5) (Price Range: $3.50)

Book 5 Duplicating Masters (Price Range: $4.00)
Book 6 (reading level 6) (Price Range: $1.70)
Book 6 Duplicating Masters (Price Range: $4.00)

Frank E. Richards
P. O. Box 66
Phoenix, NY 13135
My Language Arts Book (Price Range: $2.00)

Scholastic Book Services
904 Sylvan Avenue
Englewood, NJ 07632
Action Library I (Price Range: $10.00 each)
Includes: High interest book with worksheets

THE '50 FORD
THE HOUSE THAT HALF-JACK BUILT
A NEW LIFE FOR SARITA
THE RATCATCHER OF WHITESTONE
SILVER DOLLAR MYSTERY

Action Library IA
THE CARNIVAL MYSTERY
THE CHASE
LANE FOUR
THAT FACE IN THE MIRROR
THE ZERO PEOPLE

Action Library II
CRASH AT SALTY BAY
THE GIRL WHO KNEW RULE ONE
NO GIRLS ALLOWED
ONE PUNCH AWAY
THE RACE DRIVER

Action Library IIA
BAG FULL OF TROUBLE
FOREST FIRE
MYSTERY OF THE CRYING CHILD
NOW IS NOW
STOP, THIEF

Action Library III
COP'S SON
RODEO ROAD
SKYJACKED
WADE'S PLACE
WITCHES GET EVERYTHING

Action Library IV
THE BREAK-IN

Action Magazine—Subscriptions: $3.00 each

Science Research Associates, Inc.
155 North Wacker Drive
Chicago, IL 60606
Cracking the Code (Price Range: $10.00)
Decoding Program 4–9, Word Attack Skills
Includes: Student Book and Workbook

Getting It Together (Price Range: $20.00)
A reading series about people—levels 1, 2, 3
The Job Ahead: A Career Reading Series

Math

Cambridge (The Basic Skills Company)
888 Seventh Avenue
New York, NY 10019
    Cambridge Math Program (7–8) (Price Range: Work-a-Text $4.50; Teacher's
Edition $4.50–$6.00)
These work-a-texts review the basic operations and introduce new, more
advanced math concepts.Focus on career development.

Learning Essentials
Learning Resource Center, Inc.
10655 S. W.Greenburg Road
P. O. Box 23077
Portland, OR 97223
    7UF Math Game (Price Range: $10.00)
    What Can I Do Now? (Price Range: $2.00)
    Good Time Math Event Cards (Price Range: $15.00)

Media Materials, Inc.
2936 Remington Avenue
Dept. G 765
Baltimore, MD 21211
    Basic Mathematics: (Price Range: $90.00)
Complete series—nine learning packages—cassette and worksheets.
    Naming and Identifying Fractions (Price Range: $10.00)
    Renaming Fractions (Price Range: $10.00)
    Follow That Sign (Price Range: $10.00)

Frank E. Richards
P. O. Box 66
Phoenix, NY 13135
    Reading for Math (Price Range: $2.50)
    Useful Arithmetic
    Useful Arithmetic (Teacher's Edition)
    Useful Arithmetic II
    Useful Arithmetic II (Teacher's Edition)
    Measuring the Metric Way
    Understanding the Metric System

Social Studies

Developmental Learning Materials
7440 Natchez
Niles, IL 60648
    Where I Am Set of 15 (Price Range: $9.00)
Includes map orientation, 32-page workbook, multiple activities, and projects
suggested. Guide included.

E.M.I.
Box 4272
Madison, WI 53711
    HELP (Price Range: $12.00)
    View Master (Price Range: $2.50)
    Entertainer View Master (Price Range: $12.00)
    View Master Reels (Price Range: $2.00 each)
    THE REVOLUTIONARY WAR
    FORGING OF A NATION
    WESTWARD EXPANSION
    20th CENTURY
    THE CIVIL WAR
    GRAND TOUR AFRICA
    GRAND TOUR CENTRAL AND SOUTH AMERICA
    GRAND TOUR EUROPE
    Can of Squirms (Price Range: $7.00)
    Social Studies Spirit Masters
    HISTORY OF OLD WORLD (Price Range: $5.50)
    GETTING ACQUAINTED WITH OUR WORLD (Price Range: $4.00)

E.S.P., Inc.
1201 East Johnson
P.O. Drawer 5037
Jonesboro, AR 72401
    Learning Safety First (grades 5–9) (Price Range: $4.00 ea.)
    Our Constitution and Government (Grades 5–Adult)
    The American Farmer (Grades 5–9)
    Travel and Transportation (Grades 5–9)
    Communication (Grades 5–9)
    Crime andPunishment (Grades 6–Adult)

Fearon Pitman Publishing, Inc.
6 Davis Drive
Belmont, CA 94002
    Building Safe Driving Skills (Price Range: $18.00)
    Includes: teacher's guide, student workbook, chapter tests

National Geographic Society
17 & M Streets, N.W.
Washington, DC 20036
    World Subscription (Price Range: $6.00)

Opportunitities for Learning
8950 Lurline Avenue, Dept. A979
Chatsworth, CA 91311
    American Government Spirit Masters (Price Range: $4.00 each)
    THE CONSTITUTION AND BILL OF RIGHTS
    AMENDMENTS TO THE CONSTITUTION
    3 BRANCHES OF GOVERNMENT
    Map Reading Set (Price Range: $8.00)

Reader's Digest Services, Inc.
Pleasantville, NY 10570
    U.S. History (Price Range: $5.75)
    Reading level 4: Book 5, includes duplicating masters

U.S. Modern History (Price Range: $5.75)
Reading level 6: Book 8, includes duplicating masters
The Non-Western World (Price Range: $5.75)
Reading level 6: Book 9, includes duplicating masters
Teacher's guide (Price Range: $.75)

New Readers Press
Box 131
Syracuse, NY 13210
    Signs Around Town (Price Range: $.50–$2.00 each)
    Your Daily Paper
    It's on the Map
    Drugs: Facts for Decisions
    Drugs: Exercises
    Alcohol: Facts for Decisions
    Alcohol: Exercises
    Can You Give First Aid
    This Is Your Body
    Studying for a Driver's License
    Puzzles from News for You
    News for You A&B
    How to Register and Vote
    Our United States
    Our United States Workbook
    Bound Set, Units 1–10 (Price Range: $13.00)
    Bound Set, Units 11–20

Frank E. Richards
P. O. Box 66
Phoenix, NY 13135
    Getting Ready for Payday (Price Range: $1.75 each) Includes Book 1, 2, 3
    Bank, Bldg. & Employment (Price Range: $2.00)
    How to Write Yourself Up (Price Range: $2.00)
    You (Price Range: $2.00)
    All About the Hall Family (Price Range: $4.00)
    The Bank Book (Price Range: $2.00)
    Your Government and You (Price Range: $2.00)
    Teacher's Guide (Price Range: $1.00)
    Finding Ourselves (Price Range: $2.00)

Steck Vaugh
807 Brazos
P. O. Box 2028
Austin, TX 78768
    Our Nation's Story (1&2) (Price Range: $1.30 each)
    Our Democracy (Price Range: $1.80)
    Our American Constitution (Price Range: $1.80)
    Our Government (Price Range: $1.80)

Science

E.M.I.
Box 4272
Madison, WI 53711
    Astronautics Conquest of Space (Price Range: $15.00)
    Astronomy Exploring the Universe (Price Range: $2.00)

Entomology—Insect World
Geology Planet Earth
Ichthyology—Fish Life
Ornithology—Birds of the World

E.S.P.
1201 East Johnson
P.O. Drawer 5037
Jonesboro, AR 72401
    Our Solar System (grade 7) (Price Range: $4.00 each)
    Systems of the Human Body (grades 5-9
    Pollution & Environment (grades 7-12)
    The Science World (grades 4-7)

McDonald's Systems
McDonald Plaza
Oak Brook, IL
    McDonald's Ecology and Energy Action Packs (Price Range: $2.00 each)
    McDonald's Nutrition Action Pack
    McDonald's Economic Action Pack

Opportunities for Learning
8950 Lurline Avenue, Dept. A979
Chatsworth, CA 91331
    Planet Science Kit (Price Range: $23.00)
    Leaves Alike and Not Alike (Price Range: $7.00)
    Science in Your World (Price Range: $60.00)
    Energy X (Price Range: $20.00)
    Crystal Radio Kit (Price Range: $6.00)
    Flying Machine Kit (Price Range: $6.00)
    Electric Motor Kit (Price Range: $6.00)
    Visual Flashlight Kit (Price Range: $3.00)

Frank E. Richards
P. O. Box 66
Phoenix, NY 13135
    What is Electricity? (Price Range: $1.25 each)
    Weather & U.S. Book 1&2
    Getting Ready to Drive (Price Range: $2.00)
    Useful Science
    The World Around Us
    The World Around Us Teacher's Edition (Price Range: $3.00)

School Masters
745 State Circle
Ann Arbor, MI 48104
    Electronics (Price Range: $13.00)
        100 Components with 40 experiments
    The Visible Pumping Heart (Price Range: $6.00)
    Anatomy Wall Charts (set of 14) (Price Range: $17.00)
    Brontosaurus (Price Range: $1.50 each)
    Corythosaurus
    Tyrannosaurus
    Dimetrodon
    Ankylosaurus
    Proctouranti
    Magnifier (Price Range: $6.50)

Magnetism (Price Range: $5.00)
Introductory Set (Price Range: $7.00)
Land Mass Relief Globe
   Cross Section of Earth (Price Range: $27.00)
Single Living Globe (Price Range: $13.00)
Environment Pollution Test Set (Price Range: $10.00)
Microscope Kit (Price Range: $20.00)
Solar Engine (Price Range: $3.50)
5 Senses (Price Range: $16.00)
Weather Forecaster (Price Range: $17.00)
Ecology (Price Range: $4.00 each)
Ecology Problems
The Science Experiments (Price Range: $6.00)
Science in Your World II
   6 color filmstrips with tapes (Price Range: $60.00)
Weather School (5–9) (Price Range: $8.00 each)
Earth Science (5–9)
Human Body (5–9)
Solar System & Space Travel
Social Studies and Activities w/a tape recorder
   (Price Range: $3.50)
Metric Thermometer
   (Farenheit & Celsius) (Price Range: $8.00)
Rocks, Minerals, Fossils (Price Range: $3.25)
Geological Demonstrating Kit (Price Range: $25.00)
Classroom Slides (144 slides) (Price Range: $35.00)
World of Triceratops (Price Range: $4.00 each)
World of Tyrannosaurus (Price Range: $4.00 each)
World of Stegosaurus (Price Range: $4.00 each)
Neanderthal Man (Price Range: $3.00 each)
Cro-Magnon Man (Price Range: $3.00 each)

SEE
Three Bridge Street
Newton, MA 02195
   Directional Compass (per dozen) (Price Range: $4.50)
   Student Planetarium (3–12) (Price Range: $8.00)
   Space Hop (Price Range: $13.00 each)
   Circulation Game
   Basic Electronics Kit (Price Range: $11.00)
   Simple Science Experiments
      Activity Cards—Electricity (Price Range: $4.50)
   The Reasons for Seasons (Price Range: $5.00 each)
   Miniature DC Motor (Price Range: $4.00)

Steck Vaughn
Box 2028
Austin, TX 78768
   Water Life (Price Range: $2.00 each)
   The Human Body
   The Earth and Beyond
   Land Animals

SECONDARY LEVEL PROGRAMS[1]

The following secondary level resource room programs are located throughout the country and can be contacted for further information.

Secondary ED/LD Programs

Child Service Demonstration Center   Director: James N. Riley
for Children with Learning Disabilities
El Dorado School District 15
700 Columbia Street
El Dorado, Arkansas 71730

(501) 863-3541   Resource Room Model

The project has been used successfully on a secondary level. It is a resource room model with some modification at the secondary level. There is in addition to teaching staff, a regular counselor and career education counselor available to help with future plans. Social as well as academic competencies are stressed. In addition it has a *strong parent program*. The proposal does not detail teacher training though it is an important component of the program.

The Engineered Classroom for   Director: Mr. Robert H. Ostdiek
Students Who Are Mentally Handicapped
and Behaviorally Maladjusted
Papillion-Lavista Public Schools
1217 Golden Gate Drive
Papillion, Nebraska 68046

(402) 339-3411   Resource Room Model

ESEA Title III Dissemination Project

It was designed for elementary mildly handicapped pupils. However, it is being tried on junior and senior-high level using the same basic design. Though used with EMR students, seems applicable to LD/ED students as well. Resource room approach—called Learning Center. Each center staffed by special education teacher plus aide. Center staff provide assistance both to pupils and their regular classroom teachers. Center provides supportive help to students in an individualized manner. Emphasis on instruction is on academic, self-concept, and behavioral areas. The amount of time, type of instruction, and goals are determined by a staffing team according to the child's needs. There is also strong support for parental involvement.

---

[1]Compiled by the Northeast Regional Educational Improvement Center, Hightstown, N.J.

Resource Room Program
Experimental Education Unit
Child Development and Mental
Retardation Center
University of Washington
Seattle, Washington 98195

Director: Norris Haring

Resource Room Program at
Elementary and Junior High
Levels

The program operated in both elementary and junior high schools and is being continued at the Mercer Island Junior High School. It focuses on teacher training with specific competencies detailed and taught. Though applied on a junior high level, it seems appropriate for resource teachers on a secondary level as well.

Program for Children with Specific
Learning Disabilities
Kanawha County Schools
200 Elizabeth Street
Charleston, West Virginia 25311
(304) 348-6640

Director: Mrs. Frances Fuller

DPT Model

This is a CSDC program. It has operated on K–12 levels indirectly through teacher training. It utilizes the diagnostic-prescriptive teaching model to develop in classroom teachers competencies in diagnosis, prescription, intervention, and consultation.

Child Service Demonstration
Center
Secondary Learning Disabilities
Kansas City Public Schools USD 500
625 Minnesota Avenue
Kansas City, Kansas 66101
(913) 621-3073

Director: Mr. Donald Lamb

Resource Room Model

This model is a resource room approach emphasizing three (3) areas:
1. Basic skills acquisition
2. Social emotional development
3. Career exploration and education

Project ECHO
Education Service Center
Region XII
401 Franklin Avenue
Waco, Texas 76701

Director: Mr. Donald Weston
and   Ms. Linda Scott

Resource Room Model

The project is serving 9–10th graders ages 15–16. The project has produced its own instructional materials (mini-modules) in the areas of language arts, math, and science. It uses a classroom management system with project teachers supporting regular teachers in a mainstreamed situation. At each site there are three teachers, one in each of the major disciplines—language arts, math, and science. Teachers from the resource room work in the students' regular classroom with the regular classroom teacher.

Learning Disabilities Child Service
Demonstration Program
Region V Educational Service Center
P.O. Box 1069
Lancaster, South Carolina

Director: Dr. Stuart Brown

Resource Room Program at
the Junior High Level

This project is at the junior-high-school level. Formerly it operated successfully at the elementary level and has produced a good basic manual for operating an elementary level resource room for LD children. It includes information relative to the administration of such a program as well as record-keeping, curriculum, and remedial techniques. A manual for the junior high program will be developed this year. The approval is a resource room in each junior high school for LD students with project staff giving in-service to resource room teachers, regular teachers, guidance, and administrators.

Ohio's Learning Disabilities
Child Service Demonstration Program
Ohio Division of Special Education
933 High Street
Worthington, Ohio 43085
(614) 294-3583

Director: Ms. Shirley Moorehead

Resource Room Model

Learning center approach for secondary LD students. Learning center teacher is primarily concerned with teaching those skills prerequisite to the mastery of the basic fundamental concepts taught in required high school courses. There is also a provision for the learning center teacher to serve as a consultant though the actual implementation of this role is not described. There are also a teacher training component and parent involvement program which are not described.

Alternative Learning Project

   ESEA Title III Dissemination Project

Year Program Established: 7/71

Target Population: Students of all abilities grades 9–12; can be a complete program or adapted to supplement an ongoing program. Students all have expressed dissatisfaction with the traditional educational system.

Approach: ALP is a community-based experimental high school that combines a strong basic skills program with site placement activities and continuous counseling. It operates with 125 students and 8 full-time staff. They seek to encourage parent and community participation. All ALP staff act as counselors as well as teachers. Emphasis is on individualized programming, student responsibility, and accountability. Another interesting feature is competency-based system used for awarding diplomas.

Contact: Ms. Barbara Tucker
Mr. Chuck Kenyon
ALP
180 Pine Street
Providence, Rhode Island 02903
(401) 272-2080

The New Model Me (Curriculum for Meeting Modern Problems)
Title III Dissemination
Year Established: 7/69

Target Population: It has been used with varying ability levels including ED/LD students on a secondary level. (The program also has separate curriculums for middle school and primary grades).

Approach: The program is affective in nature and content rather than dealing directly with academic areas. On a secondary level it aims to help students and teachers look at the underlying *causes* of behavior, understand the *consequences* of behavior and select viable *alternatives* to non-constructive behavior. The curriculum can be a separate course or integrated into other content areas. It contains units on Behavior, Controls, Real Self, Values, Response, and Change.

Contact: John R. Rowe
Project Director
Lakewood Board of Education
1470 Warren Road
Lakewood, Ohio 44107
(216) 579-4267

(P.A.L.) Pupils Advance in Learning
ESEA Title I Dissemination Project
Year Established: 7/65

Target Population: Has been used with students in grades 1–12 who are deficient in reading skills, self-image, and attitude. Has also been used with parents of these students, administrators, teachers, and aides.

Approach: The primary focus is on reading improvement with a secondary focus on improving attitudes toward school and self using diverse image-building activities. Parent involvement is also an important component and a *Parent Involvement Guide* included in the package provides techniques for involving parents for service and advice. Other materials from the project include an *Instructional Program Kit* which describes the educational program units and techniques and the *Program Management Manual* covering planning implementation, operation, evaluation and dissemination of P.A.L. as well as a *Staff Development Kit.*

Contact: Ms. Carolyn Tennant
Special Programs Consultant
Adams County School District #12
10280 N. Huron Street
Denver, Colorado 80221
(203) 451-1151

High School in the Community (HSC)
ESEA Title III Dissemination Project
Year Program Established: 8/70
Target Population: Disaffected secondary students of all ability levels. A range of students are accommodated by the program. The one similarity is that they have all had dissatisfactory experience with the traditional school.

Approach: It is an alternative high school approach designed to accommodate between 50–300 students. It strives to make the educational experience more personalized and suited to the goals of the individual students who have been turned off by the traditional system. Students plan their programs together with staff advisors including the option of the Community Orientation Program which places students with volunteer teachers in various community settings.

Contact: Mr. Edward Linehan
Dissemination Coordinator
High School in the Community
45 Nash Street
New Haven, Connecticut 06511
(203) 624-1357

administrating
a resource room

14

In reviewing the previous chapters of the book, it becomes apparent that a major aspect of a well-run resource room program is missing—the administration. Proper administrative procedures are essential to the success of a resource room program. Like a well-built house that stands on a sound foundation, the resource room must also be based on sound administrative practices which are established long before the actual program takes place.

This administrator's guide is an attempt to assist administrators of a new resource room program, beginning with "selling" the program to the board of education to the final evaluation of the resource room program at the end of the year.

WHO ARE THE ADMINISTRATORS OF A RESOURCE ROOM?

The organizational plan of each school district will determine who will administrate the resource room. The administrator might be a resource room coordinator, the building principal, the director of special services, a department chairman, a head teacher, or the superintendent of schools.

In some school districts, the responsibility for administration of special programs is shared by more than one person. For instance, some districts give the responsibility of the resource room to both the building principal and head of special services. Still others divide the responsibility among the head of special services, the building principal, and a resource room coordinator. It is best to decide beforehand which portion of the responsibility will be assumed by each administrator so that the program will not be over- or underadministered.

GETTING APPROVAL FROM THE BOARD

After determining the need for a resource room program, the special services department should request the addition of this program through the proper channels. An excellent case can be made for the financial and educational efficiency of the resource room.

A formula used by the New Providence, New Jersey School District from their Prescriptive Teaching Workshop Resource Manual is as follows:

1. Salary of Workshop Teacher	$8,880.00*
2. In-Service Teacher Training	1,000.00
3. Instructional Materials and Supplies	5,500.00
4. Equipment	4,500.00
5. Orientation of Parents	250.00
	$20,130.00

*Salary and costs are based on 1972–73 salary guide

Each learning disabled child is provided an average of two hours of instruction daily in the workshop. Prior to the workshop, the model district had provided two hours of supplemental instruction per child per day in order to remediate skills. For 15 children at $7.00 per hour, the cost for supplemental instruction was $1,050 per week or $39,000 per year. The cost of implementation of the workshop for the first year was $20,130. The average per pupil cost was reduced from $2,666 for supplemental instruction to $1,342 for the workshop. The total net savings to the district is shown below:

Cost of remediation without workshop:
Supplemental Instruction
15 children x 10 hrs/wk x 38 wks x $7–$39,900

Cost of implementation of workshop for first year:
1st year ————————————————————————————— –$20,130

Total Net Savings $19,770

Prior to enrollment in the workshop, two children, in addition to the above, were placed in a special class outside the district. The cost to the district was $3,800 per child per year. Although the change from supplemental instruction and out-of-district placement to workshop was not predicated on saving the district money, the end result was a more appropriate program with less cost to the district. Once the workshop is initially equipped, the recurring cost is no greater than the cost of a regular classroom.[1]

Although costs have risen drastically since the above formula was devised, the ratio can be adapted to fit any budget. It is important to keep in mind that both in-service costs and material costs will be drastically cut in subsequent years, making the cost feasibility of such a program even more economical.

HIRING A TEACHER

After board approval, the next step should be the hiring of a resource room teacher. The advertising of an opening for teachers can be done through local newspapers, professional journals, college bulletins, and special education department placement offices. Sometimes word of mouth is the most efficient method of reaching prospective teachers. Once applications begin arriving, initiate a screening process. Things to be considered include

1. *Educational Background.* Check your state requirements for special education teachers and resource room teachers in particular. The candidate should have the appropriate teaching license and fulfill all the educational requirements for that license. Request all candidates to send you copies of all transcripts and teaching certificates in addition to the application form and vita.

[1]*Prescriptive Teaching Workshop Resource Manual,* New Providence, New Jersey School District, pp. 62–63.

Even statements from previous employers can be requested at the outset to provide you with a total picture of the candidate.

There are more and more teachers with masters degrees in special education. Many states are requiring a masters degree as a prerequisite for certification. Look for candidates that either have an advanced degree or are in the process of getting one. Consider the variety of clinical experiences the candidate had in his/her college training. This is possibly one of the most valuable courses in the college curriculum for special education teachers.

2. *Work Experience.* The candidate should have varied work experience. A resource room program deals with a potpourri of special education children. The candidate should have experience not only with a variety of handicaps but also with a variety of age groups. Each handicap as well as each age group brings its own unique problems. Experience in dealing with these problems is important. Learning how to organize and run a resource room is time-consuming in itself. Knowledge of special education children and how to teach them should not have to be learned on the job.

The candidate should show an interest in keeping up with the field by past attendance at workshops, courses, and conferences. Any leadership role the candidate has assumed either in college or on the job is worth noting.

3. *Recommendations.* Letters of recommendation should be reviewed carefully. Unfortunately letters of recommendation can be so general as to give the wrong impression. Be wary of vague sounding statements. Sometimes these are negative feelings disguised in polite form and say very little. For example,

> Miss Jones taught in our district for one year. She taught in the first grade. Her attendance record was excellent.

The reference should reflect an ability to get along with the staff as well as an ability to establish rapport with children. Strong remediation skills are imperative, as well as success with interpersonal relationships and special skills in teaching learning-disabled children. Sometimes a phone call to a former employer may give you a more candid opinion than a written recommendation.

Interview

At an interview you have the opportunity to hear firsthand what the candidate has accomplished. This is important since one cannot include everything in a resume. The very thing you may or may not be looking for can come out during an interview. Be aware of

1. Does the candidate have the verbal skills to communicate an idea clearly and pleasantly?
2. Does the candidate have a pleasant personality?
3. Do you respond to the candidate in a friendly way?
4. Does the candidate express real caring for children?
5. How has the candidate handled problem situations in teaching?
6. Why is the candidate looking for a job?

Rely on your "gut" feeling about a candidate. No matter how good the credentials look, if you have negative feelings about a candidate, be very cautious. Administrators have been overheard to say, "If only I would have believed my instincts about that teacher . . ." If you get the feeling that the candidate is competent, personable, experienced, and most of all eager for the job, you have a viable candidate. Hiring a teacher with these qualities helps to ensure the success of your new resource room program.

GETTING THE PROGRAM STARTED

The Tentative Class List

Examine the population of the school in which the resource room will be established.

To determine what type of resource room is necessary, you will want to consider children who are

1. Newly referred by the Child Study Team
2. New to the district with a previous history of special education
3. Formerly in a self-contained special education class and mainstreamed for reading
4. Currently receiving supplemental instruction.

Categorize the list according to disability. For instance,

1. Perceptually impaired
2. Neurologically impaired
3. Emotionally disturbed
4. Communication handicapped
5. Physically handicapped
6. Socially maladjusted
7. Educationally retarded.

Also check to see if the majority of students will fall into an age group, such as lower or uppper elementary. Having a general idea of the types of disabilities and the age of the possible resource room students will help in making initial plans for the program. (Refer to Chapter 1—Types of Resource Rooms.)

Meet with the Teacher

The information to be shared with the teacher should include

1. The tentative class list and its breakdown (disabilities and age span)
2. The type of program planned
3. A basic plan for implementing the program (a copy of *The Resource Room Primer* can be helpful)

4. The budget allotment for the program for the entire year
5. Materials sources that may be unfamiliar (materials that can be shared, loaned, or requisitioned locally)
6. Suggestions for materials to be purchased—See Chapter 7
7. The amount of the budget that can be left to the discretion of the teacher, preferably to be used as needs arise rather than ordered all at once in the beginning of the year—many times new students enter the program and need specific materials. Having the right tool for the job can help in meeting the individual needs of all students.
8. Federal programs such as NISCEM where materials information for every possible disability is available—See Appendix C
9. The complete files on each child assigned to the resource room. A member of the Child Study Team, the psychologist, social worker, or learning consultant, should meet with the teacher to discuss each child. This will be helpful not only to familiarize the resource room teacher with the children but to prepare him/her to contribute to the IEP meeting which will be held shortly after school begins. Included in the child's folder should be complete testing results from each team discipline, a summary of these reports, and the Child Study Team conclusions and suggestions for teaching. A sample copy of this summary is included. (See Form 14-1.)

Arrange for the IEP Meeting

The Individual Education Program meeting should be coordinated by a Child Study Team member or administrator in charge of the program. (See Chapter 3.) This is often specifically defined in your state law. Be sure to check.

1. The meeting date must be scheduled. This must be coordinated with the classroom teacher, the resource room teacher, the building principal, the Child Study Team members, and the parents.
2. Set up the schedule for each conference. Generally thirty to forty-five minutes is a sufficient amount of time to set aside for each conference. Leaving a fifteen-minute gap between conferences is a good cushion in case you are running late.
3. Arrange to hire a "floating" substitute to cover the classrooms of the teachers who will be attending the conferences and a substitute teacher for the resource room teacher.
4. Send out letters to the parents confirming the time, date, and place of the IEP meeting. Include a general description of the purpose of the meeting. (See Form 3-7, p. 58.)
5. Send out notices to the resource room teacher, regular classroom teachers, speech therapist, and anyone else involved with each child's program. Include in this notice the schedule of conferences, who will be in attendance, and what their responsibilities will be at the meeting. (See Form 14-2, p. 238.)
6. Inform those children who will be included in the conference of the time, date, and place of the conference. Encourage the teacher to give them an idea of what will be happening in the meeting and offer suggestions as to how they can participate. (See Goals Checklist Form 3-8, p. 59). PL 94-142 states that children will attend these meetings when it is appropriate for them to do so.

DIAGNOSTIC WORKSHEET AND REPORT
(Keep in Pupil Folder)

Name: _____

Date: _____

Areas Assessed	Date Assessed	Results	Comments
I. Intellectual Group _____ (Name)		Verbal Perf. IQ	
Individual			
II. Auditory Perception Acuity			
Auditory Discrimination			

FORM 14–1

Areas Assessed	Date Assessed	Results	Comments
Auditory Memory			
III. Visual Perception Acuity			
Visual Discrimination			
Visual Memory			
IV. Visual-Auditory Learning			
V. Visual-Motor			

FORM 14–1 (cont.)

Areas Assessed	Date Assessed	Results	Comments
VI. Abstract Thinking			
VII. Academic Reading			
Arithmetic			
Spelling			
Listening			
Language Development			

FORM 14-1 (cont.)

Areas Assessed	Date Assessed	Results	Comments
VIII. Miscellaneous Handwriting			
IX. School Group Achievement Tests (list only if pertinent)			

FORM 14-1 (cont.)

Which children attend will be determined by their age and the extent of their handicap. Input by the resource room teacher and classroom teacher will help to make the decision.

7. Check with Chapter 3, Planning an IEP, Due Process, and Parents' Rights, to see how the meeting should be run. When the plan has been completed and signed, each teacher, parent, and team member should get a copy for his/her files.

8. Assign a Child Study Team member to monitor the implementation of the IEP. This is a requirement of PL 94-142.

Choose the Room

Room choice is important to the success of a resource room program. An oversized closet in the basement of the school will reflect a negative image of the resource room. A regular-size classroom located on the same corridor as other classes will give a positive image. Visibility of the resource room will help it become part of the entire school program. Good room placement does not guarantee a successful program, but it helps. Good lighting and enough electrical outlets are necessary to make use of the audiovisual equipment needed in a resource room.

```
Dear _____,

On ____(date)____, at _(time)_, your pupil, _____(name)_____,
is scheduled to have an IEP meeting.

In compliance with PL 94-142, this meeting will include the teachers, the
parents, the child study team, and, when possible, the child.

Please be prepared to share the goals and objectives which you feel are
important for this child.

If you have any questions, please feel free to contact me. Be advised
that books are available in the school library dealing with goals and
objectives.

                                          Sincerely,

                                          Administrator
```

FORM 14-2   (IEP Meeting Notification Form)

Lending Support to the Program

Devote one part of a staff meeting or a separate meeting to introducing the resource room to the entire staff. Other staff members will be curious about this new program. Deal with the questions at the outset. Plan the agenda for this introductory meeting with the resource room teacher. (See Chapter 9.) Topics to be covered include

1. The purpose of the program (Chapter 1)
2. The goals of the program
3. The responsibilities of the resource room teacher
4. The responsibilities of the regular classroom teacher
5. The mechanics of how the program will function
6. How children are referred for the program
7. Arrangement for monthly conferences
8. Question and answer session.

Become familiar with the state and federal rules and regulations concerning resource room programming and be alert to changes. This will influence future decisions and may clear up questions staff members have about the program. The resource room concept is an excellent alternative to self-contained classrooms for many learning-disabled children and also meets the requirements of PL 94-142. A reprint of PL 94-142 can be found in Appendix B.

Monthly Conferences

The administrator and resource room teacher should plan ahead of time a schedule and format for these meetings. Limit the meetings to the classroom teacher and the resource room teacher. This provides an intimate dialogue. Inform the classroom teachers in advance of the format so they can prepare. Any pertinent test information or work samples will be helpful during the conference. A sample format might be

1. The resource room teacher shows samples of work done in the resource room and the weekly plans.
2. The classroom teacher gives a review of the work the child is expected to do.
3. Problem areas are discussed by both.
4. A plan of action is set up and written (in triplicate) with copies given to both teachers and one set to the administrator. These plans can be reviewed at future meetings and evaluated. A compilation of these forms will be helpful at the end of the year IEP meeting. (See Form 10–1, p. 168.)
5. Date of the next conference is set.

In-Service Program

Future in-service meetings to discuss the resource room will probably be needed throughout the year. (See Chapter 10.) Scheduling them either before school or during the school day will be well received by the teachers. Most communication can be taken care of through the resource room teacher at the regularly scheduled teacher conferences. Inform the teachers that an end-of-the-year evaluation form and meeting will be available to help evaluate the success of the program.

Introductory Parents Meeting

Decide between two possible types of parent meetings. One method involves meeting with each set of parents privately to tell them more about the resource room. The other alternative would be holding a group meeting of all the parents. (This should occur in addition to the initial notification meeting where the child's enrollment in the resource room is discussed.) There are benefits to both types of meetings. It is more time-consuming to see each set of parents individually, but this method may be less threatening. The group meeting, however, can be supportive to wary parents. Hearing positive remarks from "veteran" parents can reassure new parents. Both types of meetings have advantages. Holding the meeting early in the school year is essential. Having parental support makes running a successful program much more likely. (Refer to Chapter 9 where the parents' meeting is discussed in detail.)

Monthly Parent Meetings

Regularly scheduled parent group meetings should continue throughout the year. Having speakers available at these meetings to talk on pertinent subjects usually yields a good turnout of parents. Appointing a special education teacher to coordinate these meetings and help line up speakers has worked successfully. Publicity sent out early enough for parents to be able to plan on attending is most important.

It is essential to allow time for questions and answers, group discussions, and socializing at these meetings. The more ways there are to involve parents constructively in special education programming, the more cooperation seems to exist. Some program ideas are

1. School psychologist to talk on behavior management in the home
2. State special education official to talk on parents' rights (see state addresses in Appendix A)
3. Physical eduation teacher to talk on motor development
4. Representative from ACLD to talk about organization (see Appendix E for address)
5. Local college special education personnel to talk about problems
6. Parent, teacher, psychologist panel to discuss improving school programming or behavior management at school
7. Nutritionist from local hospital to discuss nutrition and health
8. Representative from state vocational educational school to discuss future programming
9. County special education representative to discuss community resources.

EVALUATING THE PROGRAM

Using a checklist of things to be evaluated is efficient for the administrator and fair to the teacher. This checklist or evaluation form should be shared with the resource room teacher at the beginning of the school year. This will not only include him/her in the evaluating process but will help to encourage good organization and let the teacher know your expectations of the program. Evaluation Form 14–3 is a rating form evaluating the total program as it relates to the resource room teacher role. Evaluation Form 14 4, "The True Measure of Effectiveness of the Resource Room Plan and Operation" (Carroll 1974), is an analysis of the facilities, resources, and personnel and is an excellent guide for the resource room teacher and the administrator.

When the evaluation form is completed a conference to discuss the evaluation is helpful. This gives the teacher a chance to "defend" if necessary and to be "stroked" at the same time. Successful administrators achieve better results by pointing out positives as well as negatives. Taking a positive approach even while criticizing is possible. For instance,

> Miss Jones, how do you think we can improve the flow of children in the room?

By giving the teacher the opportunity to solve the problem with you, you dignify the teacher's abilities and at the same time let him/her know that there is a problem. Chances are the teacher is already aware that the problem exists and would welcome the opportunity to get some help in solving it.

EVALUATION FORM

EVALUATION AREAS	RATING	SUGGESTIONS
Room Design		
Flow of students		
Materials displayed		
Clear directions available		
Multiability materials available		
Scheduling		
Adequate time allotted		
Pupil contact time		
Observation time		
Conferencing		
Conflicts with classroom specials		
Pupils' understanding of schedule		
Student Programming		
Pretesting		
Progress evaluation		
Lesson plans		
Diagnostic teaching		
Individualized instruction		
Teacher Attitude		
Enthusiasm		
Flexibility		
Reliability		

FORM 14-3

FACILITY ANALYSIS

According to Carroll (1974), the following questions should be answered
about the facility (adapted with permission of the author and publisher):

1. Are facilities available to provide for large and small group
   interaction within the classroom? YES _____ NO _____

2. Are individual study areas available (i.e., portable bookshelves
   or bulletin boards that can be used to divide the areas)? YES _____
   NO _____

3. Are learning carrels available (i.e., portable desk top carrels)?
   YES _____ NO _____

4. Are activity centers available (i.e., communication centers, science
   centers, etc.)? YES _____ NO _____

5. Are book corners readily accessible to students? YES _____ NO _____

6. Does the student have his or her own desk or cupboard where he or
   she can store personal material? YES _____ NO _____

7. Are there facilities available in the room or in the school for
   crisis intervention (i.e., a time-out room)? YES _____ NO _____

8. Are there large areas available in the building or outside that can
   be used for play activities, drama presentations, etc.? YES _____
   NO _____

9. Is there an area around the building that can be used for exploration?
   YES _____ NO _____

10. Are small rooms available within the building for subdividing the
    class into subunits? YES _____ NO _____

PERSONAL ANALYSIS

1. What is the ratio of students to teachers? _____

FORM 14–4 (A. W. Carroll, "The Classroom as an Ecosystem," *Focus on Exceptional Children,* 4 [1974], 1–12.)

2. What personnel are available to help in the personalizing approach
   (i.e., within the classroom)? _____

   a. Community volunteers or senior citizens groups? YES _____
      NO _____

   b. Peers within the classroom for additional teaching? For example,
      intrapeer tutoring or older students to help younger students?
      YES _____ NO _____

   c. Paid aides? YES _____ NO _____

   d. College interns in preservice educational programs? YES _____
      NO _____

3. Interested parent groups? YES _____ NO _____

RESOURCE ANALYSIS

1. Building Resources
   What resources are available to the classroom teachers?

   a. Health resources--nurses, school physicians? YES _____ NO _____
      (specify)

   b. Psychological resources--psychologists, consulting psychiatrists,
      social workers? YES _____ NO _____ (specify)

   c. Parent involvement? YES _____ NO _____

   d. Instructional resource materials? YES _____ NO _____

   e. Resource Room? YES _____ NO _____

   f. Human resources available within the building--reading specialist,
      counselor, etc.? YES _____ NO _____ (specify)

2. District resources? YES _____ NO _____ (specify)

3. Community resources? YES _____ NO _____ (specify)

4. State resources? YES _____ NO _____ (specify)

5. National resources? YES _____ NO _____ (specify)

FORM 14-4 (cont.)

Be Available

The way an administrator conducts a parent-teacher conference when there is a problem gives an important message to the teacher. By supporting the teacher you let him/her know that you are behind him/her. This of course does not mean giving support in the face of blatant wrongdoing, but giving the teacher the benefit of the doubt while listening and supporting the parent as well is a delicate balance for which to strive.

The message from the administrator that says, "I am available," must be conveyed to the resource room teacher. Just knowing that a ready ear is available in case of a problem lends the teacher a great deal of support. Consult with the teacher on a regular basis to let him/her know that you are there and interested. Let the teacher know that you appreciate his/her efforts and are on his/her side.

REFERENCES

Carroll, A. W., "The Classroom as an Ecosystem." *Focus on Exceptional Children,* 4 (1974), 1–12.

Prescriptive Teaching Workshop Resource Manual, New Providence, N.J.: New Providence School District, 1972.

special education
state agencies
and addresses

appendix **A**

STATE SPECIAL EDUCATION DEPARTMENTS

ALABAMA
Exceptional Children and Youth
State Department of Education
868 State Office Building
Montgomery, AL 36130
(205) 832-3316

ALASKA
State of Alaska
Department of Education
Office for Exceptional Children
Special Education Programs
Pouch F 0500
Juneau, AK 99811
(907) 465-2970

ARIZONA
Division of Special Education
Arizona Department of Education
1535 W. Jefferson
Phoenix, AZ 85007
(602) 271-3183

ARKANSAS
Special Education Section
Department of Education
Arch Ford Building
Capitol Mall
Little Rock, AR 72201
(501) 371-2161

CALIFORNIA
California State Department
of Education
Office of Special Education
721 Capitol Mall
Rm. 614
Sacramento, CA 95814
(916) 445-4036

COLORADO
Colorado Department of Education
State Office Building
201 East Colfax
Denver, CO 80203
(303) 839-2727
ATTN: Special Education

CONNECTICUT
Bureau of Pupil Personnel and
Special Educational Services
State Department of Education
P.O. Box 2219
Hartford, CT 06115
(203) 566-3561

DELAWARE
Exceptional Children/
Special Programs Divison
State Department of Public Instruction
John G. Townsend Building
P.O. Box 1402
Dover, DE 19901
(302) 678-4667

DISTRICT OF COLUMBIA
Special Education
Division of Special Educational
Programs
Presidential Building
Room 602
415 12th Street, N.W.
Washington, D.C. 20004
(202) 724-4018

FLORIDA
Bureau of Education for Exceptional
Students
Florida Department of Education
204 Knott Building
Tallahassee, FL 32304
(904) 488-1570

GEORGIA
Program for Exceptional Children
Georgia Department of Education
State Office Building
Atlanta, GA 30334
(404) 656-2425

HAWAII
State Department of Education
Special Education Department
45-955 Kam Highway
Kaneohe, HI 96744
(808) 235-2443

IDAHO
Department of Education
Special Education Division
650 West State Street
Boise, ID 83720
(208) 384-2203

ILLINOIS
Department of Specialized
Educational Services
Illinois Office of Education
100 North First Street
Springfield, IL 62777
(217) 782-6601

INDIANA
Division of Special Education
Department of Public Instruction
229 State House
Indianapolis, IN 46204
(317) 927-0216

IOWA
State of Iowa
Department of Public Instruction
Special Education Division
Grimes State Office Building
Des Moines, IA 50319
(515) 281-3176

KANSAS
Special Education Administration
Section
Kansas State Department of Education
120 E. Tenth
Topeka, KS 66612
(913) 296-3866

KENTUCKY
Bureau for Education of Exceptional
Children
Capital Plaza Tower
8th Floor
Frankfort, KY 40601
(502) 564-4970

LOUISIANA
Division of Special Educational Services
State Department of Education
Capital Station
P.O. Box 44064
Baton Rouge, LA 70804
(504) 342-3631

MAINE
Division of Special Education
State Department of Educational &
Cultural Services
State House
Augusta, ME 04333
(207) 289-3451

MARYLAND
Division of Special Education
State Department of Education
P.O. Box 8717
Balt-Wash International Airport
Baltimore, MD 21240
(301) 796-8300 Ext. 245

MASSACHUSETTS
Division of Special Education
State Department of Education
Park Square Building
31 St. James Avenue
Boston, MA 02116
(617) 727-5700

MICHIGAN
Special Education Services
State Department of Education
P.O. Box 30008
Lansing, MI 48909
(517) 373-0923

MINNESOTA
Special Education Section
State Department of Education
Capitol Square Bldg.
550 Cedar Avenue
St. Paul, MN 55101
(612) 296-4163

MISSISSIPPI
Special Education Section
State Department of Education
P.O. Box 771
Jackson, MS 39205
(601) 354-6950

MISSOURI
Director of Special Education
P.O. Box 480
Jefferson City, MO 65101
(314) 751-3502

MONTANA
Special Education Unit
Office of Public Instruction
State Capitol
Room 106
Helena, MT 59601
(406) 449-5660

NEBRASKA
State Department of Education
Special Education Branch
301 Centennial Mall South
Lincoln, NE 68509
(402) 471-2295

NEVADA
Nevada Department of Education
Special Education Division
Capital Complex
400 West King Street
Carson City, NV 89710
(702) 885-5700 Ext. 214

NEW HAMPSHIRE
New Hampshire Department
of Education
Division of Vocational Rehabilitation
Special Education Section
105 Loudon Rd.
Concord, NH 03301
(603) 271-3741

NEW JERSEY
Division of Special Education
New Jersey Department of Education
Division of School Programs
Branch of Special Operations and
Pupil Personnel Services
Room 232
225 West State Street
Trenton, NJ 08625
(609) 292-4692

NEW MEXICO
Division of Special Education
State Department of Education
Education Building
300 Don Gaspar Avenue
Santa Fe, NM 87503
(505) 827-2793

NEW YORK
Office for the Education of Children
with Handicapping Conditions
State Education Department
55 Elk Street
Albany, NY 12234
(518) 474-5548

NORTH CAROLINA
Division for Exceptional Children
State Department of Public Instruction
Room 352, Educational Building
Raleigh, NC 27611
(919) 733-4258

NORTH DAKOTA
Division of Special Education
Department of Public Instruction
State Capitol
Bismarck, ND 58505
(701) 224-2277

OHIO
Division of Special Education
State Department of Education
933 High Street
Worthington, OH 43085
(614) 466-2650

OKLAHOMA
State Department of Education
Special Education Section
2500 N. Lincoln Blvd.
Room 263
Oliver Hodge Building
Oklahoma City, OK 73105
(405) 521-3351

OREGON
Special Education
Oregon Department of Education
942 Lancaster Drive, N.E.
Salem, OR 97310
(503) 378-3598

PENNSYLVANIA
Pennsylvania Department of Education
Bureau of Special and Compensatory
Education
P.O. Box 911
Harrisburg, PA 17126
(717) 783-1264

RHODE ISLAND
Rhode Island Department
of Education
Special Education Unit
234 Promenade Street
Providence, RI 02098
(401) 277-3505

SOUTH CAROLINA
Office of Programs for the
Handicapped
State Department of Education
Room 309, Rutledge Building
1429 Senate Street
Columbia, SC 29201
(803) 758-7432

SOUTH DAKOTA
Section for Special Education
Richard F. Kneipe Bldg.
Pierre, SD 57501
(605) 773-3678

TENNESSEE
Division for the Education of the
Handicapped
State Department of Education
103 Cordell Hull Building
Nashville, TN 37219
(615) 741-2851

TEXAS
Department of Special Education
Texas Education Agency
201 East 11th Street
Austin, TX 78701
(512) 475-3501

UTAH
Division of Staff Development
Utah State Board of Education
250 East Fifth South
Salt Lake City, UT 84111
(801) 533-5982

VERMONT
Special Educational and Pupil
Personnel Services
State Department of Education
Montpelier, VT 05602
(802) 828-3141

VIRGINIA
Division of Special Education
State Department of Education
1322-28 E. Grace
P.O. Box 6Q
Richmond, VA 23216
(804) 786-2673

WASHINGTON
Division of Special Services
Mail Stop FG 11
Old Capitol Bldg.
Olympia, WA 98504
(206) 753-6733

WEST VIRGINIA
Division of Special Education and
Student Support Systems
West Virginia Department
of Education
Capitol Complex, Room B-315
Charleston, WV 25305
(304) 348-8830

WISCONSIN
State Department of Public Instruction
Bureau for Crippled Children
126 Langdon Street
Madison, WI 53702
(608) 266-3726

WYOMING
Office of Exceptional Children
State Department of Education
Hathaway Bldg.
Cheyenne, WY 82002
(307) 777-7411

PL 94-142

appendix B

Public Law 94-142
94th Congress, S. 6
November 29, 1975

An Act

To amend the Education of the Handicapped Act to provide educational assistance
to all handicapped children, and for other purposes.

*Be it enacted by the Senate and House of Representatives of the
United States of America in Congress assembled,* That this Act may
be cited as the "Education for All Handicapped Children Act of 1975".

Education for
All Handicapped
Children Act of
1975.
20 USC 1401
note.

EXTENSION OF EXISTING LAW

SEC. 2. (a)(1)(A) Section 611(b)(2) of the Education of the
Handicapped Act (20 U.S.C. 1411(b)(2)) (hereinafter in this Act
referred to as the "Act"), as in effect during the fiscal years 1976 and
1977, is amended by striking out "the Commonwealth of Puerto Rico,".

(B) Section 611(c)(1) of the Act (20 U.S.C. 1411(c)(1)), as in
effect during the fiscal years 1976 and 1977, is amended by striking
out "the Commonwealth of Puerto Rico,".

(2) Section 611(c)(2) of the Act (20 U.S.C. 1411(c)(2)), as in
effect during the fiscal years 1976 and 1977, is amended by striking
out "year ending June 30, 1975" and inserting in lieu thereof the
following: "years ending June 30, 1975, and 1976, and for the fiscal
year ending September 30, 1977", and by striking out "2 per centum"
each place it appears therein and inserting in lieu thereof "1 per
centum".

(3) Section 611(d) of the Act (20 U.S.C. 1411(d)), as in effect during the fiscal years 1976 and 1977, is amended by striking out "year
ending June 30, 1975" and inserting in lieu thereof the following:
"years ending June 30, 1975, and 1976, and for the fiscal year ending
September 30, 1977".

(4) Section 612(a) of the Act (20 U.S.C. 1412(a)), as in effect
during the fiscal years 1976 and 1977, is amended—

(A) by striking out "year ending June 30, 1975" and inserting
in lieu thereof "years ending June 30, 1975, and 1976, for the
period beginning July 1, 1976, and ending September 30, 1976,
and for the fiscal year ending September 30, 1977"; and

(B) by striking out "fiscal year 1974" and inserting in lieu
thereof "preceding fiscal year".

(b)(1) Section 614(a) of the Education Amendments of 1974 (Public Law 93–380; 88 Stat. 580) is amended by striking out "fiscal year
1975" and inserting in lieu thereof the following: "the fiscal years
ending June 30, 1975, and 1976, for the period beginning July 1, 1976,
and ending September 30, 1976, and for the fiscal year ending September 30, 1977,".

20 USC 1411
note.

(2) Section 614(b) of the Education Amendments of 1974 (Public
Law 93–380; 88 Stat. 580) is amended by striking out "fiscal year 1974"
and inserting in lieu thereof the following: "the fiscal years ending
June 30, 1975, and 1976, for the period beginning July 1, 1976, and
ending September 30, 1976, and for the fiscal year ending September 30,
1977,".

20 USC 1411
note.

20 USC 1413
note.

(3) Section 614(c) of the Education Amendments of 1974 (Public
Law 93–380; 88 Stat. 580) is amended by striking out "fiscal year
1974" and inserting in lieu thereof the following: "the fiscal years ending June 30, 1975, and 1976, for the period beginning July 1, 1976, and
ending September 30, 1976, and for the fiscal year ending September 30, 1977,".

Ante, p. 773.

(c) Section 612(a) of the Act, as in effect during the fiscal years
1976 and 1977, and as amended by subsection (a)(4), is amended by
inserting immediately before the period at the end thereof the following: ", or $300,000, whichever is greater".

20 USC 1412.

(d) Section 612 of the Act (20 U.S.C. 1411), as in effect during
the fiscal years 1976 and 1977, is amended by adding at the end thereof
the following new subsection:

Publication in
Federal Regis-
ter.

"(d) The Commissioner shall, no later than one hundred twenty
days after the date of the enactment of the Education for All Handicapped Children Act of 1975, prescribe and publish in the Federal
Register such rules as he considers necessary to carry out the pro-

Ante, p. 773.
20 USC 1411
note.
visions of this section and section 611.".

(e) Notwithstanding the provisions of section 611 of the Act, as in effect during the fiscal years 1976 and 1977, there are authorized to be appropriated $100,000,000 for the fiscal year 1976, such sums as may be necessary for the period beginning July 1, 1976, and ending September 30, 1976, and $200,000,000 for the fiscal year 1977, to carry out the provisions of part B of the Act, as in effect during such fiscal years.

STATEMENT OF FINDINGS AND PURPOSE

20 USC 1401
note.
SEC. 3. (a) Section 601 of the Act (20 U.S.C. 1401) is amended by inserting "(a)" immediately before "This title" and by adding at the end thereof the following new subsections:

"(b) The Congress finds that—

"(1) there are more than eight million handicapped children in the United States today;

"(2) the special educational needs of such children are not being fully met;

"(3) more than half of the handicapped children in the United States do not receive appropriate educational services which would enable them to have full equality of opportunity;

"(4) one million of the handicapped children in the United States are excluded entirely from the public school system and will not go through the educational process with their peers;

"(5) there are many handicapped children throughout the United States participating in regular school programs whose handicaps prevent them from having a successful educational experience because their handicaps are undetected;

"(6) because of the lack of adequate services within the public school system, families are often forced to find services outside the public school system, often at great distance from their residence and at their own expense;

"(7) developments in the training of teachers and in diagnostic and instructional procedures and methods have advanced to the point that, given appropriate funding, State and local educational agencies can and will provide effective special education and related services to meet the needs of handicapped children;

"(8) State and local educational agencies have a responsibility to provide education for all handicapped children, but present financial resources are inadequate to meet the special educational needs of handicapped children; and

"(9) it is in the national interest that the Federal Government assist State and local efforts to provide programs to meet the educational needs of handicapped children in order to assure equal protection of the law.

"(c) It is the purpose of this Act to assure that all handicapped children have available to them, within the time periods specified in section 612(2)(B), a free appropriate public education which emphasizes special education and related services designed to meet their unique needs, to assure that the rights of handicapped children and their parents or guardians are protected, to assist States and localities to provide for the education of all handicapped children, and to assess and assure the effectiveness of efforts to educate handicapped children.".   Ante, p. 773.

(b) The heading for section 601 of the Act (20 U.S.C. 1401) is amended to read as follows:

"SHORT TITLE; STATEMENT OF FINDINGS AND PURPOSE".

DEFINITIONS

SEC. 4. (a) Section 602 of the Act (20 U.S.C. 1402) is amended—   20 USC 1401.

(1) in paragraph (1) thereof, by striking out "crippled" and inserting in lieu thereof "orthopedically impaired", and by inserting immediately after "impaired children" the following: ", or children with specific learning disabilities,";

(2) in paragraph (5) thereof, by inserting immediately after "instructional materials," the following: "telecommunications, sensory, and other technological aids and devices,";

(3) in the last sentence of paragraph (15) thereof, by inserting immediately after "environmental" the following: ", cultural, or economic"; and

(4) by adding at the end thereof the following new paragraphs:

"(16) The term 'special education' means specially designed instruction, at no cost to parents or guardians, to meet the unique needs of a handicapped child, including classroom instruction, instruction in physical education, home instruction, and instruction in hospitals and institutions.

"(17) The term 'related services' means transportation, and such developmental, corrective, and other supportive services (including speech pathology and audiology, psychological services, physical and occupational therapy, recreation, and medical and counseling services, except that such medical services shall be for diagnostic and evaluation purposes only) as may be required to assist a handicapped child to benefit from special education, and includes the early identification and assessment of handicapping conditions in children.

"(18) The term 'free appropriate public education' means special education and related services which (A) have been provided at public expense, under public supervision and direction, and without charge, (B) meet the standards of the State educational agency, (C) include an appropriate preschool, elementary, or secondary school education in the State involved, and (D) are provided in conformity with the individualized education program required under section 614(a)(5).

"(19) The term 'individualized education program' means a written statement for each handicapped child developed in any meeting by a representative of the local educational agency or an intermediate educational unit who shall be qualified to provide, or supervise the provision of, specially designed instruction to meet the unique needs of handicapped children, the teacher, the parents or guardian of such child, and, whenever appropriate, such child, which statement shall include (A) a statement of the present levels of educational performance of such child, (B) a statement of annual goals, including short-term instructional objectives, (C) a statement of the specific educational services to be provided to such child, and the extent to which such child will be able to participate in regular educational programs, (D) the projected date for initiation and anticipated duration of such services, and (E) appropriate objective criteria and evaluation procedures and schedules for determining, on at least an annual basis, whether instructional objectives are being achieved.

"(20) The term 'excess costs' means those costs which are in excess of the average annual per student expenditure in a local educational agency during the preceding school year for an elementary or secondary school student, as may be appropriate, and which shall be computed after deducting (A) amounts received under this part or under title I or title VII of the Elementary and Secondary Education Act of 1965, and (B) any State or local funds expended for programs which would qualify for assistance under this part or under such titles.

20 USC 241a note, 881.

"(21) The term 'native language' has the meaning given that term by section 703(a)(2) of the Bilingual Education Act (20 U.S.C. 880b–1(a)(2)).

"(22) The term 'intermediate educational unit' means any public authority, other than a local educational agency, which is under the general supervision of a State educational agency, which is established by State law for the purpose of providing free public education on a regional basis, and which provides special education and related services to handicapped children within that State.".

(b) The heading for section 602 of the Act (20 U.S.C. 1402) is amended to read as follows:

"DEFINITIONS".

ASSISTANCE FOR EDUCATION OF ALL HANDICAPPED CHILDREN

SEC. 5. (a) Part B of the Act (20 U.S.C. 1411 et seq.) is amended to read as follows:

"PART B—ASSISTANCE FOR EDUCATION OF ALL HANDICAPPED CHILDREN

"ENTITLEMENTS AND ALLOCATIONS

20 USC 1411.
Post, p. 793.

"SEC. 611. (a)(1) Except as provided in paragraph (3) and in section 619, the maximum amount of the grant to which a State is entitled under this part for any fiscal year shall be equal to—

"(A) the number of handicapped children aged three to twenty-one, inclusive, in such State who are receiving special education and related services;
multiplied by—
"(B)(i) 5 per centum, for the fiscal year ending September 30, 1978, of the average per pupil expenditure in public elementary and secondary schools in the United States;

"(ii) 10 per centum, for the fiscal year ending September 30, 1979, of the average per pupil expenditure in public elementary and secondary schools in the United States;
"(iii) 20 per centum, for the fiscal year ending September 30, 1980, of the average per pupil expenditure in public elementary and secondary schools in the United States;
"(iv) 30 per centum, for the fiscal year ending September 30, 1981, of the average per pupil expenditure in public elementary and secondary schools in the United States; and
"(v) 40 per centum, for the fiscal year ending September 30, 1982, and for each fiscal year thereafter, of the average per pupil expenditure in public elementary and secondary schools in the United States;
except that no State shall receive an amount which is less than the amount which such State received under this part for the fiscal year ending September 30, 1977.

"(2) For the purpose of this subsection and subsection (b) through subsection (e), the term 'State' does not include Guam, American Samoa, the Virgin Islands, and the Trust Territory of the Pacific Islands. "State."

"(3) The number of handicapped children receiving special education and related services in any fiscal year shall be equal to the average of the number of such children receiving special education and related services on October 1 and February 1 of the fiscal year preceding the fiscal year for which the determination is made.

"(4) For purposes of paragraph (1)(B), the term 'average per pupil expenditure', in the United States, means the aggregate current expenditures, during the second fiscal year preceding the fiscal year for which the computation is made (or, if satisfactory data for such year are not available at the time of computation, then during the most recent preceding fiscal year for which satisfactory data are available) of all local educational agencies in the United States (which, for purposes of this subsection, means the fifty States and the District of Columbia), as the case may be, plus any direct expenditures by the State for operation of such agencies (without regard to the source of funds from which either of such expenditures are made), divided by the aggregate number of children in average daily attendance to whom such agencies provided free public education during such preceding year. "Average per pupil expenditure."

"(5)(A) In determining the allotment of each State under paragraph (1), the Commissioner may not count—
"(i) handicapped children in such State under paragraph (1)(A) to the extent the number of such children is greater than 12 per centum of the number of all children aged five to seventeen, inclusive, in such State;
"(ii) as part of such percentage, children with specific learning disabilities to the extent the number of such children is greater than one-sixth of such percentage; and
"(iii) handicapped children who are counted under section 121 of the Elementary and Secondary Education Act of 1965. 20 USC 241c-1.
"(B) For purposes of subparagraph (A), the number of children aged five to seventeen, inclusive, in any State shall be determined by the Commissioner on the basis of the most recent satisfactory data available to him.

"(b)(1) Of the funds received under subsection (a) by any State for the fiscal year ending September 30, 1978—
"(A) 50 per centum of such funds may be used by such State in accordance with the provisions of paragraph (2); and
"(B) 50 per centum of such funds shall be distributed by such State pursuant to subsection (d) to local educational agencies and intermediate educational units in such State, for use in accordance with the priorities established under section 612(3).
"(2) Of the funds which any State may use under paragraph (1)

(A)—

"(A) an amount which is equal to the greater of—
  "(i) 5 per centum of the total amount of funds received under this part by such State; or
  "(ii) $200,000;
may be used by such State for administrative costs related to carrying out sections 612 and 613;
  "(B) the remainder shall be used by such State to provide support services and direct services, in accordance with the priorities established under section 612(3).
"(c)(1) Of the funds received under subsection (a) by any State for the fiscal year ending September 30, 1979, and for each fiscal year thereafter—
  "(A) 25 per centum of such funds may be used by such State in accordance with the provisions of paragraph (2); and
  "(B) except as provided in paragraph (3), 75 per centum of such funds shall be distributed by such State pursuant to subsection (d) to local educational agencies and intermediate educational units in such State, for use in accordance with priorities established under section 612(3).
"(2)(A) Subject to the provisions of subparagraph (B), of the funds which any State may use under paragraph (1)(A)—
  "(i) an amount which is equal to the greater of—
    "(I) 5 per centum of the total amount of funds received under this part by such State; or
    "(II) $200,000;
may be used by such State for administrative costs related to carrying out the provisions of sections 612 and 613; and
  "(ii) the remainder shall be used by such State to provide support services and direct services, in accordance with the priorities established under section 612(3).
  "(B) The amount expended by any State from the funds available to such State under paragraph (1)(A) in any fiscal year for the provision of support services or for the provision of direct services shall be matched on a program basis by such State, from funds other than Federal funds, for the provision of support services or for the provision of direct services for the fiscal year involved.
"(3) The provisions of section 613(a)(9) shall not apply with respect to amounts available for use by any State under paragraph (2).
"(4)(A) No funds shall be distributed by any State under this subsection in any fiscal year to any local educational agency or intermediate educational unit in such State if—
  "(i) such local educational agency or intermediate educational unit is entitled, under subsection (d), to less than $7,500 for such fiscal year; or
  "(ii) such local educational agency or intermediate educational unit has not submitted an application for such funds which meets the requirements of section 614.
"(B) Whenever the provisions of subparagraph (A) apply, the State involved shall use such funds to assure the provision of a free appropriate education to handicapped children residing in the area served by such local educational agency or such intermediate educational unit. The provisions of paragraph (2)(B) shall not apply to the use of such funds.
"(d) From the total amount of funds available to local educational agencies and intermediate educational units in any State under subsection (b)(1)(B) or subsection (c)(1)(B), as the case may be, each local educational agency or intermediate educational unit shall be entitled to an amount which bears the same ratio to the total amount available under subsection (b)(1)(B) or subsection (c)(1)(B), as the case may be, as the number of handicapped children aged three to twenty-one, inclusive, receiving special education and related services in such local educational agency or intermediate educational unit bears to the aggregate number of handicapped children aged three to twenty-one, inclusive, receiving special education and related services in all local educational agencies and intermediate educational units which apply to the State educational agency involved for funds under this part.
"(e)(1) The jurisdictions to which this subsection applies are Guam, American Samoa, the Virgin Islands, and the Trust Territory of the Pacific Islands.
"(2) Each jurisdiction to which this subsection applies shall be

entitled to a grant for the purposes set forth in section 601(c) in an <u>Ante</u>, p. 774. amount equal to an amount determined by the Commissioner in accordance with criteria based on respective needs, except that the aggregate of the amount to which such jurisdictions are so entitled for any fiscal year shall not exceed an amount equal to 1 per centum of the aggregate of the amounts available to all States under this part for that fiscal year. If the aggregate of the amounts, determined by the Commissioner pursuant to the preceding sentence, to be so needed for any fiscal year exceeds an amount equal to such 1 per centum limitation, the entitlement of each such jurisdiction shall be reduced proportionately until such aggregate does not exceed such 1 per centum limitation.

"(3) The amount expended for administration by each jurisdiction under this subsection shall not exceed 5 per centum of the amount allotted to such jurisdiction for any fiscal year, or $35,000, whichever is greater.

"(f)(1) The Commissioner is authorized to make payments to the Secretary of the Interior according to the need for such assistance for the education of handicapped children on reservations serviced by elementary and secondary schools operated for Indian children by the Department of the Interior. The amount of such payment for any fiscal year shall not exceed 1 per centum of the aggregate amounts available to all States under this part for that fiscal year.

"(2) The Secretary of the Interior may receive an allotment under this subsection only after submitting to the Commissioner an application which meets the applicable requirements of section 614(a) and which is approved by the Commissioner. The provisions of section 616 shall apply to any such application.

"(g)(1) If the sums appropriated for any fiscal year for making payments to States under this part are not sufficient to pay in full the total amounts which all States are entitled to receive under this part for such fiscal year, the maximum amounts which all States are entitled to receive under this part for such fiscal year shall be ratably reduced. In case additional funds become available for making such payments for any fiscal year during which the preceding sentence is applicable, such reduced amounts shall be increased on the same basis as they were reduced.

"(2) In the case of any fiscal year in which the maximum amounts for which States are eligible have been reduced under the first sentence of paragraph (1), and in which additional funds have not been made available to pay in full the total of such maximum amounts under the last sentence of such paragraph, the State educational agency shall fix dates before which each local educational agency or intermediate educational unit shall report to the State educational agency on the amount of funds available to the local educational agency or intermediate educational unit, under the provisions of subsection (d), which it estimates that it will expend in accordance with the provisions of this part. The amounts so available to any local educational agency or intermediate educational unit, or any amount which would be available to any other local educational agency or intermediate educational unit if it were to submit a program meeting the requirements of this part, which the State educational agency determines will not be used for the period of its availability, shall be available for allocation to those local educational agencies or intermediate educational units, in the manner provided by this section, which the State educational agency determines will need and be able to use additional funds to carry out approved programs.

"ELIGIBILITY

20 USC 1412.   "SEC. 612. In order to qualify for assistance under this part in any fiscal year, a State shall demonstrate to the Commissioner that the following conditions are met:

"(1) The State has in effect a policy that assures all handicapped children the right to a free appropriate public education.

"(2) The State has developed a plan pursuant to section 613(b) in effect prior to the date of the enactment of the Education for All Handicapped Children Act of 1975 and submitted not later than August 21, 1975, which will be amended so as to comply with the provisions of this paragraph. Each such amended plan shall set forth in detail the policies and procedures which the State will undertake or has undertaken in order to assure that—

"(A) there is established (i) a goal of providing full educational opportunity to all handicap, ₂d children, (ii) a detailed timetable for accomplishing such a goal, and (iii) a description of the kind and number of facilities, personnel, and services necessary throughout the State to meet such a goal;

"(B) a free appropriate public education will be available for all handicapped children between the ages of three and eighteen within the State not later than September 1, 1978, and for all handicapped children between the ages of three and twenty-one within the State not later than September 1, 1980, except that, with respect to handicapped children aged three to five and aged eighteen to twenty-one, inclusive, the requirements of this clause shall not be applied in any State if the application of such requirements would be inconsistent with State law or practice, or the order of any court, respecting public education within such age groups in the State;

"(C) all children residing in the State who are handicapped, regardless of the severity of their handicap, and who are in need of special education and related services are identified, located, and evaluated, and that a practical method is developed and implemented to determine which children are currently receiving needed special education and related services and which children are not currently receiving needed special education and related services;

"(D) policies and procedures are established in accordance with detailed criteria prescribed under section 617(c); and

"(E) the amendment to the plan submitted by the State required by this section shall be available to parents, guardians, and other members of the general public at least thirty days prior to the date of submission of the amendment to the Commissioner.

"(3) The State has established priorities for providing a free appropriate public education to all handicapped children, which priorities shall meet the timetables set forth in clause (B) of paragraph (2) of this section, first with respect to handicapped children who are not receiving an education, and second with respect to handicapped children, within each disability, with the most severe handicaps who are receiving an inadequate education, and has made adequate progress in meeting the timetables set forth in clause (B) of paragraph (2) of this section.

"(4) Each local educational agency in the State will maintain records of the individualized education program for each handicapped child, and such program shall be established, reviewed, and revised as provided in section 614(a)(5).

"(5) The State has established (A) procedural safeguards as required by section 615, (B) procedures to assure that, to the maximum extent appropriate, handicapped children, including children in public or private institutions or other care facilities, are educated with children who are not handicapped, and that special classes, separate schooling, or other removal of handicapped children from the regular educational environment occurs only when the nature or severity of the handicap is such that education in regular classes with the use of supplementary aids and services cannot be achieved satisfactorily, and (C) procedures to assure that testing and evaluation materials and procedures utilized for the purposes of evaluation and placement of handicapped children will be selected and administered so as not to be racially or culturally discriminatory. Such materials or procedures shall be provided and administered in the child's native language or mode of communication, unless it clearly is not feasible to do so, and no single procedure shall be the sole criterion for determining an appropriate educational program for a child.

"(6) The State educational agency shall be responsible for assuring that the requirements of this part are carried out and that all educational programs for handicapped children within the State, including all such programs administered by any other State or local agency, will be under the general supervision of the persons responsible for educational programs for handicapped children in the State educational agency and shall meet education standards of the State educational agency.

Administration.

"(7) The State shall assure that (A) in carrying out the requirements of this section procedures are established for consultation with individuals involved in or concerned with the education of handicapped children, including handicapped individuals and parents or guardians

Notice, hearings.

of handicapped children, and (B) there are public hearings, adequate notice of such hearings, and an opportunity for comment available to the general public prior to adoption of the policies, programs, and procedures required pursuant to the provisions of this section and section 613.

"STATE PLANS

20 USC 1413.

"SEC. 613. (a) Any State meeting the eligibility requirements set forth in section 612 and desiring to participate in the program under this part shall submit to the Commissioner, through its State educational agency, a State plan at such time, in such manner, and containing or accompanied by such information, as he deems necessary. Each such plan shall—

"(1) set forth policies and procedures designed to assure that funds paid to the State under this part will be expended in accordance with the provisions of this part, with particular attention given to the provisions of sections 611(b), 611(c), 611(d), 612(2), and 612(3) ;

"(2) provide that programs and procedures will be established to assure that funds received by the State or any of its political subdivisions under any other Federal program, including section 121 of the Elementary and Secondary Education Act of 1965 (20

20 USC 241c-1.

U.S.C. 241c-2), section 305(b)(8) of such Act (20 U.S.C. 844a (b)(8)) or its successor authority, and section 122(a)(4)(B) of the Vocational Education Act of 1963 (20 U.S.C. 1262(a)(4) (B)), under which there is specific authority for the provision of assistance for the education of handicapped children, will be utilized by the State, or any of its political subdivisions, only in a manner consistent with the goal of providing a free appropriate public education for all handicapped children, except that nothing in this clause shall be construed to limit the specific requirements of the laws governing such Federal programs;

"(3) set forth, consistent with the purposes of this Act, a description of programs and procedures for (A) the development and implementation of a comprehensive system of personnel development which shall include the inservice training of general and special educational instructional and support personnel, detailed procedures to assure that all personnel necessary to carry out the purposes of this Act are appropriately and adequately prepared and trained, and effective procedures for acquiring and disseminating to teachers and administrators of programs for handicapped children significant information derived from educational research, demonstration, and similar projects, and (B) adopting, where appropriate, promising educational practices and materials development through such projects;

"(4) set forth policies and procedures to assure—

"(A) that, to the extent consistent with the number and location of handicapped children in the State who are enrolled in private elementary and secondary schools, provision is made for the participation of such children in the program assisted or carried out under this part by providing for such children special education and related services; and

"(B) that (i) handicapped children in private schools and facilities will be provided special education and related services (in conformance with an individualized educational program as required by this part) at no cost to their parents or guardian, if such children are placed in or referred to such schools or facilities by the State or appropriate local educational agency as the means of carrying out the requirements of this part or any other applicable law requiring the provision of special education and related services to all handicapped children within such State, and (ii) in all such instances the State educational agency shall determine whether such schools and facilities meet standards that apply to State and local educational agencies and that children so served have all the rights they would have if served by such agencies;

"(5) set forth policies and procedures which assure that the State shall seek to recover any funds made available under this part for services to any child who is determined to be erroneously classified as eligible to be counted under section 611(a) or section 611(d) ;

"(6) provide satisfactory assurance that the control of funds provided under this part, and title to property derived therefrom, shall be in a public agency for the uses and purposes provided in this part, and that a public agency will administer such funds and property;

"(7) provide for (A) making such reports in such form and **Reports and** containing such information as the Commissioner may require **records.** to carry out his functions under this part, and (B) keeping such records and affording such access thereto as the Commissioner may find necessary to assure the correctness and verification of such reports and proper disbursement of Federal funds under this part;

"(8) provide procedures to assure that final action with respect **Notice,** to any application submitted by a local educational agency or **hearings.** an intermediate educational unit shall not be taken without first affording the local educational agency or intermediate educational unit involved reasonable notice and opportunity for a hearing;

"(9) provide satisfactory assurance that Federal funds made available under this part (A) will not be commingled with State funds, and (B) will be so used as to supplement and increase the level of State and local funds expended for the education of handicapped children and in no case to supplant such State and local funds, except that, where the State provides clear and convincing evidence that all handicapped children have available to them a free appropriate public education, the Commissioner may waive in part the requirement of this clause if he concurs with the evidence provided by the State;

"(10) provide, consistent with procedures prescribed pursuant to section 617(a)(2), satisfactory assurance that such fiscal control and fund accounting procedures will be adopted as may be necessary to assure proper disbursement of, and accounting for, Federal funds paid under this part to the State, including any such funds paid by the State to local educational agencies and intermediate educational units;

Evaluation. "(11) provide for procedures for evaluation at least annually of the effectiveness of programs in meeting the educational needs of handicapped children (including evaluation of individualized education programs), in accordance with such criteria that the Commissioner shall prescribe pursuant to section 617; and

State advisory "(12) provide that the State has an advisory panel, appointed **panel.** by the Governor or any other official authorized under State law to make such appointments, composed of individuals involved in or concerned with the education of handicapped children, including handicapped individuals, teachers, parents or guardians of handicapped children, State and local education officials, and administrators of programs for handicapped children, which (A) advises the State educational agency of unmet needs within the State in the education of handicapped children, (B) comments publicly on any rules or regulations proposed for issuance by the State regarding the education of handicapped children and the procedures for distribution of funds under this part, and (C) assists the State in developing and reporting such data and evaluations as may assist the Commissioner in the performance of his responsibilities under section 618.

"(b) Whenever a State educational agency provides free appropriate public education for handicapped children, or provides direct services to such children, such State educational agency shall include, as part of the State plan required by subsection (a) of this section, such additional assurances not specified in such subsection (a) as are contained in section 614(a), except that funds available for the provision of such education or services may be expended without regard to the provisions relating to excess costs in section 614(a).

"(c) The Commissioner shall approve any State plan and any modification thereof which—

"(1) is submitted by a State eligible in accordance with section 612; and

"(2) meets the requirements of subsection (a) and subsection (b).

Notice, The Commissioner shall disapprove any State plan which does not **hearings.** meet the requirements of the preceding sentence, but shall not finally disapprove a State plan except after reasonable notice and opportunity for a hearing to the State.

"APPLICATION

20 USC 1414.

"SEC. 614. (a) A local educational agency or an intermediate educational unit which desires to receive payments under section 611(d) for any fiscal year shall submit an application to the appropriate State educational agency. Such application shall—

"(1) provide satisfactory assurance that payments under this part will be used for excess costs directly attributable to programs which—

"(A) provide that all children residing within the jurisdiction of the local educational agency or the intermediate educational unit who are handicapped, regardless of the severity of their handicap, and are in need of special education and related services will be identified, located, and evaluated, and provide for the inclusion of a practical method of determining which children are currently receiving needed special education and related services and which children are not currently receiving such education and services;

"(B) establish policies and procedures in accordance with detailed criteria prescribed under section 617(c);

"(C) establish a goal of providing full educational opportunities to all handicapped children, including—

"(i) procedures for the implementation and use of the comprehensive system of personnel development established by the State educational agency under section 613(a)(3);

"(ii) the provision of, and the establishment of priorities for providing, a free appropriate public education to all handicapped children, first with respect to handicapped children who are not receiving an education, and second with respect to handicapped children, within each disability, with the most severe handicaps who are receiving an inadequate education;

"(iii) the participation and consultation of the parents or guardian of such children; and

"(iv) to the maximum extent practicable and consistent with the provisions of section 612(5)(B), the provision of special services to enable such children to participate in regular educational programs;

"(D) establish a detailed timetable for accomplishing the goal described in subclause (C); and

"(E) provide a description of the kind and number of facilities, personnel, and services necessary to meet the goal described in subclause (C);

"(2) provide satisfactory assurance that (A) the control of funds provided under this part, and title to property derived from such funds, shall be in a public agency for the uses and purposes provided in this part, and that a public agency will administer such funds and property, (B) Federal funds expended by local educational agencies and intermediate educational units for programs under this part (i) shall be used to pay only the excess costs directly attributable to the education of handicapped children, and (ii) shall be used to supplement and, to the extent practicable, increase the level of State and local funds expended for the education of handicapped children, and in no case to supplant such State and local funds, and (C) State and local funds will be used in the jurisdiction of the local educational agency or intermediate educational unit to provide services in program areas which, taken as a whole, are at least comparable to services being provided in areas of such jurisdiction which are not receiving funds under this part;

"(3)(A) provide for furnishing such information (which, in the case of reports relating to performance, is in accordance with specific performance criteria related to program objectives), as may be necessary to enable the State educational agency to perform its duties under this part, including information relating to the educational achievement of handicapped children participating in programs carried out under this part; and

"(B) provide for keeping such records, and provide for affording such access to such records, as the State educational agency may find necessary to assure the correctness and verification of

Recordkeeping.

such information furnished under subclause (A);

"(4) provide for making the application and all pertinent documents related to such application available to parents, guardians, and other members of the general public, and provide that all evaluations and reports required under clause (3) shall be public information;

Public information, availability.

"(5) provide assurances that the local educational agency or intermediate educational unit will establish, or revise, whichever is appropriate, an individualized education program for each handicapped child at the beginning of each school year and will then review and, if appropriate revise, its provisions periodically, but not less than annually;

"(6) provide satisfactory assurance that policies and programs established and administered by the local educational agency or intermediate educational unit shall be consistent with the provisions of paragraph (1) through paragraph (7) of section 612 and section 613(a); and

"(7) provide satisfactory assurance that the local educational agency or intermediate educational unit will establish and maintain procedural safeguards in accordance with the provisions of sections 612(5)(B), 612(5)(C), and 615.

Application approval.

"(b)(1) A State educational agency shall approve any application submitted by a local educational agency or an intermediate educational unit under subsection (a) if the State educational agency determines that such application meets the requirements of subsection (a), except that no such application may be approved until the State plan submitted by such State educational agency under subsection (a) is approved by the Commissioner under section 613(c). A State educational agency shall disapprove any application submitted by a local educational agency or an intermediate educational unit under subsection (a) if the State educational agency determines that such application does not meet the requirements of subsection (a).

Notice, hearing.

"(2)(A) Whenever a State educational agency, after reasonable notice and opportunity for a hearing, finds that a local educational agency or an intermediate educational unit, in the administration of an application approved by the State educational agency under paragraph (1), has failed to comply with any requirement set forth in such application, the State educational agency, after giving appropriate notice to the local educational agency or the intermediate educational unit, shall—

"(i) make no further payments to such local educational agency or such intermediate educational unit under section 620 until the State educational agency is satisfied that there is no longer any failure to comply with the requirement involved; or

"(ii) take such finding into account in its review of any application made by such local educational agency or such intermediate educational unit under subsection (a).

"(B) The provisions of the last sentence of section 616(a) shall apply to any local educational agency or any intermediate educational unit receiving any notification from a State educational agency under this paragraph.

"(3) In carrying out its functions under paragraph (1), each State educational agency shall consider any decision made pursuant to a hearing held under section 615 which is adverse to the local educational agency or intermediate educational unit involved in such decision.

"(c)(1) A State educational agency may, for purposes of the consideration and approval of applications under this section, require local educational agencies to submit a consolidated application for payments if such State educational agency determines that any individual application submitted by any such local educational agency will be disapproved because such local educational agency is ineligible to receive payments because of the application of section 611(c)(4)(A)(i) or such local educational agency would be unable to establish and maintain programs of sufficient size and scope to effectively meet the educational needs of handicapped children.

"(2)(A) In any case in which a consolidated application of local educational agencies is approved by a State educational agency under paragraph (1), the payments which such local educational agencies may receive shall be equal to the sum of payments to which each such local educational agency would be entitled under section 611(d) if an individual application of any such local educational agency had been approved.

"(B) The State educational agency shall prescribe rules and regula- Rules and
tions with respect to consolidated applications submitted under this regulations.
subsection which are consistent with the provisions of paragraph (1)
through paragraph (7) of section 612 and section 613(a) and which
provide participating local educational agencies with joint responsibilities for implementing programs receiving payments under this
part.

"(C) In any case in which an intermediate educational unit is
required pursuant to State law to carry out the provisions of this part,
the joint responsibilities given to local educational agencies under subparagraph (B) shall not apply to the administration and disbursement of any payments received by such intermediate educational unit.
Such responsibilities shall be carried out exclusively by such intermediate educational unit.

"(d) Whenever a State educational agency determines that a local
educational agency—

"(1) is unable or unwilling to establish and maintain programs
of free appropriate public education which meet the requirements
established in subsection (a);

"(2) is unable or unwilling to be consolidated with other local
educational agencies in order to establish and maintain such programs; or

"(3) has one or more handicapped children who can best be
served by a regional or State center designed to meet the needs of
such children;

the State educational agency shall use the payments which would
have been available to such local educational agency to provide special
education and related services directly to handicapped children residing in the area served by such local educational agency. The State
educational agency may provide such education and services in such
manner, and at such locations (including regional or State centers),
as it considers appropriate, except that the manner in which such
education and services are provided shall be consistent with the requirements of this part.

"(e) Whenever a State educational agency determines that a local Funds,
educational agency is adequately providing a free appropriate public reallocation.
education to all handicapped children residing in the area served by
such agency with State and local funds otherwise available to such
agency, the State educational agency may reallocate funds (or such
portion of those funds as may not be required to provide such education and services) made available to such agency, pursuant to section
611(d), to such other local educational agencies within the State as
are not adequately providing special education and related services
to all handicapped children residing in the areas served by such other
local educational agencies.

"(f) Notwithstanding the provisions of subsection (a)(2)(B)(ii),
any local educational agency which is required to carry out any program for the education of handicapped children pursuant to a State
law shall be entitled to receive payments under section 611(d) for
use in carrying out such program, except that such payments may
not be used to reduce the level of expenditures for such program made
by such local educational agency from State or local funds below
the level of such expenditures for the fiscal year prior to the fiscal
year for which such local educational agency seeks such payments.

"PROCEDURAL SAFEGUARDS"

20 USC 1415.   "SEC. 615. (a) Any State educational agency, any local educational
agency, and any intermediate educational unit which receives assistance under this part shall establish and maintain procedures in
accordance with subsection (b) through subsection (e) of this section
to assure that handicapped children and their parents or guardians are
guaranteed procedural safeguards with respect to the provision of
free appropriate public education by such agencies and units.

"(b)(1) The procedures required by this section shall include, but
shall not be limited to—

"(A) an opportunity for the parents or guardian of a handicapped child to examine all relevant records with respect to the
identification, evaluation, and educational placement of the child,
and the provision of a free appropriate public education to such
child, and to obtain an independent educational evaluation of the

child;

"(B) procedures to protect the rights of the child whenever the parents or guardian of the child are not known, unavailable, or the child is a ward of the State, including the assignment of an individual (who shall not be an employee of the State educational agency, local educational agency, or intermediate educational unit involved in the education or care of the child) to act as a surrogate for the parents or guardian;

"(C) written prior notice to the parents or guardian of the child whenever such agency or unit—

"(i) proposes to initiate or change, or

"(ii) refuses to initiate or change,

the identification, evaluation, or educational placement of the child or the provision of a free appropriate public education to the child;

"(D) procedures designed to assure that the notice required by clause (C) fully inform the parents or guardian, in the parents' or guardian's native language, unless it clearly is not feasible to do so, of all procedures available pursuant to this section; and

"(E) an opportunity to present complaints with respect to any matter relating to the identification, evaluation, or educational placement of the child, or the provision of a free appropriate public education to such child.

Hearing.
"(2) Whenever a complaint has been received under paragraph (1) of this subsection, the parents or guardian shall have an opportunity for an impartial due process hearing which shall be conducted by the State educational agency or by the local educational agency or intermediate educational unit, as determined by State law or by the State educational agency. No hearing conducted pursuant to the requirements of this paragraph shall be conducted by an employee of such agency or unit involved in the education or care of the child.

"(c) If the hearing required in paragraph (2) of subsection (b) of this section is conducted by a local educational agency or an intermediate educational unit, any party aggrieved by the findings and decision rendered in such a hearing may appeal to the State educational agency which shall conduct an impartial review of such hearing. The officer conducting such review shall make an independent decision upon completion of such review.

"(d) Any party to any hearing conducted pursuant to subsections (b) and (c) shall be accorded (1) the right to be accompanied and advised by counsel and by individuals with special knowledge or training with respect to the problems of handicapped children, (2) the right to present evidence and confront, cross-examine, and compel the attendance of witnesses, (3) the right to a written or electronic verbatim record of such hearing, and (4) the right to written findings of fact and decisions (which findings and decisions shall also be transmitted to the advisory panel established pursuant to section 613(a)(12)).

"(e)(1) A decision made in a hearing conducted pursuant to paragraph (2) of subsection (b) shall be final, except that any party involved in such hearing may appeal such decision under the provisions of subsection (c) and paragraph (2) of this subsection. A decision made under subsection (c) shall be final, except that any party may bring an action under paragraph (2) of this subsection.

"(2) Any party aggrieved by the findings and decision made   Civil
under subsection (b) who does not have the right to an appeal under   action.
subsection (c), and any party aggrieved by the findings and decision
under subsection (c), shall have the right to bring a civil action with respect to the complaint presented pursuant to this section, which action may be brought in any State court of competent jurisdiction or in a district court of the United States without regard to the amount in controversy. In any action brought under this paragraph the court shall receive the records of the administrative proceedings, shall hear additional evidence at the request of a party, and, basing its decision on the preponderance of the evidence, shall grant such relief as the court determines is appropriate.

"(3) During the pendency of any proceedings conducted pursuant to this section, unless the State or local educational agency and the parents or guardian otherwise agree, the child shall remain in the then current educational placement of such child, or, if applying for initial admission to a public school, shall, with the consent of the parents or guardian, be placed in the public school program until all such proceedings have been completed.

"(4) The district courts of the United States shall have jurisdiction of actions brought under this subsection without regard to the amount in controversy.

District courts jurisdiction.

"WITHHOLDING AND JUDICIAL REVIEW

"SEC. 616. (a) Whenever the Commissioner, after reasonable notice and opportunity for hearing to the State educational agency involved (and to any local educational agency or intermediate educational unit affected by any failure described in clause (2)), finds—

Notice, hearing.
20 USC 1416.

"(1) that there has been a failure to comply substantially with any provision of section 612 or section 613, or

"(2) that in the administration of the State plan there is a failure to comply with any provision of this part or with any requirements set forth in the application of a local educational agency or intermediate educational unit approved by the State educational agency pursuant to the State plan,

the Commissioner (A) shall, after notifying the State educational agency, withhold any further payments to the State under this part, and (B) may, after notifying the State educational agency, withhold further payments to the State under the Federal programs specified in section 613(a)(2) within his jurisdiction, to the extent that funds under such programs are available for the provision of assistance for the education of handicapped children. If the Commissioner withholds further payments under clause (A) or clause (B) he may determine that such withholding will be limited to programs or projects under the State plan, or portions thereof, affected by the failure, or that the State educational agency shall not make further payments under this part to specified local educational agencies or intermediate educational units affected by the failure. Until the Commissioner is satisfied that there is no longer any failure to comply with the provisions of this part, as specified in clause (1) or clause (2), no further payments shall be made to the State under this part or under the Federal programs specified in section 613(a)(2) within his jurisdiction to the extent that funds under such programs are available for the provision of assistance for the education of handicapped children, or payments by the State educational agency under this part shall be limited to local educational agencies and intermediate educational units whose actions did not cause or were not involved in the failure, as the case may be. Any State educational agency, local educational agency, or intermediate educational unit in receipt of a notice pursuant to the first sentence of this subsection shall, by means of a public notice, take such measures as may be necessary to bring the pendency of an action pursuant to this subsection to the attention of the public within the jurisdiction of such agency or unit.

Petition for review.

"(b)(1) If any State is dissatisfied with the Commissioner's final action with respect to its State plan submitted under section 613, such State may, within sixty days after notice of such action, file with the United States court of appeals for the circuit in which such State is located a petition for review of that action. A copy of the petition shall be forthwith transmitted by the clerk of the court to the Commissioner. The Commissioner thereupon shall file in the court the record of the proceedings on which he based his action, as provided in section 2112 of title 28, United States Code.

"(2) The findings of fact by the Commissioner, if supported by substantial evidence, shall be conclusive; but the court, for good cause shown, may remand the case to the Commissioner to take further evidence, and the Commissioner may thereupon make new or modified findings of fact and may modify his previous action, and shall file in the court the record of the further proceedings. Such new or modified findings of fact shall likewise be conclusive if supported by substantial evidence.

"(3) Upon the filing of such petition, the court shall have jurisdiction to affirm the action of the Commissioner or to set it aside, in whole or in part. The judgment of the court shall be subject to review by the Supreme Court of the United States upon certiorari or certification as provided in section 1254 of title 28, United States Code.

"ADMINISTRATION

"SEC. 617. (a)(1) In carrying out his duties under this part, the

20 USC 1417.

Commissioner shall—

"(A) cooperate with, and furnish all technical assistance necessary, directly or by grant or contract, to the States in matters relating to the education of handicapped children and the execution of the provisions of this part;

"(B) provide such short-term training programs and institutes as are necessary;

"(C) disseminate information, and otherwise promote the education of all handicapped children within the States; and

"(D) assure that each State shall, within one year after the date of the enactment of the Education for All Handicapped Children Act of 1975, provide certification of the actual number of handicapped children receiving special education and related services in such State.

"(2) As soon as practicable after the date of the enactment of the Education for All Handicapped Children Act of 1975, the Commissioner shall, by regulation, prescribe a uniform financial report to be utilized by State educational agencies in submitting State plans under this part in order to assure equity among the States.

Regulations.

"(b) In carrying out the provisions of this part, the Commissioner (and the Secretary, in carrying out the provisions of subsection (c)) shall issue, not later than January 1, 1977, amend, and revoke such rules and regulations as may be necessary. No other less formal method of implementing such provisions is authorized.

"(c) The Secretary shall take appropriate action, in accordance with the provisions of section 438 of the General Education Provisions Act, to assure the protection of the confidentiality of any personally identifiable data, information, and records collected or maintained by the Commissioner and by State and local educational agencies pursuant to the provisions of this part.

20 USC 1232g.

"(d) The Commissioner is authorized to hire qualified personnel necessary to conduct data collection and evaluation activities required by subsections (b), (c) and (d) of section 618 and to carry out his duties under subsection (a) (1) of this subsection without regard to the provisions of title 5, United States Code, relating to appointments in the competitive service and without regard to chapter 51 and subchapter III of chapter 53 of such title relating to classification and general schedule pay rates except that no more than twenty such personnel shall be employed at any time.

5 USC 5101, 5331.

"EVALUATION

"Sec. 618. (a) The Commissioner shall measure and evaluate the impact of the program authorized under this part and the effectiveness of State efforts to assure the free appropriate public education of all handicapped children.

20 USC 1418.

"(b) The Commissioner shall conduct, directly or by grant or contract, such studies, investigations, and evaluations as are necessary to assure effective implementation of this part. In carrying out his responsibilities under this section, the Commissioner shall—

"(1) through the National Center for Education Statistics, provide to the appropriate committees of each House of the Congress and to the general public at least annually, and shall update at least annually, programmatic information concerning programs and projects assisted under this part and other Federal programs supporting the education of handicapped children, and such information from State and local educational agencies and other appropriate sources necessary for the implementation of this part, including—

"(A) the number of handicapped children in each State, within each disability, who require special education and related services;

"(B) the number of handicapped children in each State, within each disability, receiving a free appropriate public education and the number of handicapped children who need and are not receiving a free appropriate public education in each such State;

"(C) the number of handicapped children in each State, within each disability, who are participating in regular educational programs, consistent with the requirements of section 612(5)(B) and section 614(a)(1)(C)(iv), and the number of handicapped children who have been placed in separate classes or separate school facilities, or who have been otherwise removed from the regular education environment;

"(D) the number of handicapped children who are enrolled in public or private institutions in each State and who are receiving a free appropriate public education, and the number of handicapped children who are in such institutions and who are not receiving a free appropriate public education;

"(E) the amount of Federal, State, and local expenditures in each State specifically available for special education and related services; and

"(F) the number of personnel, by disability category, employed in the education of handicapped children, and the estimated number of additional personnel needed to adequately carry out the policy established by this Act; and

"(2) provide for the evaluation of programs and projects assisted under this part through—

"(A) the development of effective methods and procedures for evaluation;

"(B) the testing and validation of such evaluation methods and procedures; and

"(C) conducting actual evaluation studies designed to test the effectiveness of such programs and projects.

"(c) In developing and furnishing information under subclause (E) of clause (1) of subsection (b), the Commissioner may base such information upon a sampling of data available from State agencies, including the State educational agencies, and local educational agencies.

Report, transmittal to congressional committees.

"(d)(1) Not later than one hundred twenty days after the close of each fiscal year, the Commissioner shall transmit to the appropriate committees of each House of the Congress a report on the progress being made toward the provision of free appropriate public education to all handicapped children, including a detailed description of all evaluation activities conducted under subsection (b).

Contents.

"(2) The Commissioner shall include in each such report—

"(A) an analysis and evaluation of the effectiveness of procedures undertaken by each State educational agency, local educational agency, and intermediate educational unit to assure that handicapped children receive special education and related services in the least restrictive environment commensurate with their needs and to improve programs of instruction for handicapped children in day or residential facilities;

"(B) any recommendations for change in the provisions of this part, or any other Federal law providing support for the education of handicapped children; and

"(C) an evaluation of the effectiveness of the procedures undertaken by each such agency or unit to prevent erroneous classification of children as eligible to be counted under section 611, including actions undertaken by the Commissioner to carry out provisions of this Act relating to such erroneous classification.

In order to carry out such analyses and evaluations, the Commissioner shall conduct a statistically valid survey for assessing the effectiveness of individualized educational programs.

"(e) There are authorized to be appropriated for each fiscal year such sums as may be necessary to carry out the provisions of this section.

Appropriation authorization.

"INCENTIVE GRANTS

"Sec. 619. (a) The Commissioner shall make a grant to any State which—

20 USC 1419.

"(1) has met the eligibility requirements of section 612;

"(2) has a State plan approved under section 613; and

"(3) provides special education and related services to handicapped children aged three to five, inclusive, who are counted for the purposes of section 611 (a) (1) (A).

The maximum amount of the grant for each fiscal year which a State may receive under this section shall be $300 for each such child in that State.

"(b) Each State which—

"(1) has met the eligibility requirements of section 612,

"(2) has a State plan approved under section 613, and

"(3) desires to receive a grant under this section,

shall make an application to the Commissioner at such time, in such manner, and containing or accompanied by such information, as the Commissioner may reasonably require.

"(c) The Commissioner shall pay to each State having an application approved under subsection (b) of this section the amount to which the State is entitled under this section, which amount shall be used for the purpose of providing the services specified in clause (3) of subsection (a) of this section.

"(d) If the sums appropriated for any fiscal year for making payments to States under this section are not sufficient to pay in full the maximum amounts which all States may receive under this part for such fiscal year, the maximum amounts which all States may receive under this part for such fiscal year shall be ratably reduced. In case additional funds become available for making such payments for any fiscal year during which the preceding sentence is applicable, such reduced amounts shall be increased on the same basis as they were reduced.

"(e) In addition to the sums necessary to pay the entitlements under section 611, there are authorized to be appropriated for each fiscal year such sums as may be necessary to carry out the provisions of this section.

Appropriation authorization.

"PAYMENTS

"SEC. 620. (a) The Commissioner shall make payments to each State in amounts which the State educational agency of such State is eligible to receive under this part. Any State educational agency receiving payments under this subsection shall distribute payments to the local educational agencies and intermediate educational units of such State in amounts which such agencies and units are eligible to receive under this part after the State educational agency has approved applications of such agencies or units for payments in accordance with section 614(b).

20 USC 1420.

"(b) Payments under this part may be made in advance or by way of reimbursement and in such installments as the Commissioner may determine necessary.".

Regulations.
20 USC 1411
note.

(b) (1) The Commissioner of Education shall, no later than one year after the effective date of this subsection, prescribe—

(A) regulations which establish specific criteria for determining whether a particular disorder or condition may be considered a specific learning disability for purposes of designating children with specific learning disabilities;

(B) regulations which establish and describe diagnostic procedures which shall be used in determining whether a particular child has a disorder or condition which places such child in the category of children with specific learning disabilities; and

(C) regulations which establish monitoring procedures which will be used to determine if State educational agencies, local educational agencies, and intermediate educational units are complying with the criteria established under clause (A) and clause (B).

Proposed regulation, submittal to congressional committees. Publication in Federal Register.

(2) The Commissioner shall submit any proposed regulation written under paragraph (1) to the Committee on Education and Labor of the House of Representatives and the Committee on Labor and Public Welfare of the Senate, for review and comment by each such committee, at least fifteen days before such regulation is published in the Federal Register.

(3) If the Commissioner determines, as a result of the promulgation of regulations under paragraph (1), that changes are necessary in the definition of the term "children with specific learning disabilities", as such term is defined by section 602(15) of the Act, he shall submit recommendations for legislation with respect to such changes to each House of the Congress.

20 USC 402.

Definitions.

(4) For purposes of this subsection:

(A) The term "children with specific learning disabilities" means those children who have a disorder in one or more of the basic psychological processes involved in understanding or in using language, spoken or written, which disorder may manifest itself in imperfect ability to listen, think, speak, read, write, spell, or do mathematical calculations. Such disorders include such conditions as perceptual handicaps, brain injury, minimal brain dysfunction, dyslexia, and developmental aphasia. Such term does not include children who have learning problems which are primarily the result of visual, hearing, or motor handicaps, of mental retardation, of emotional disturbance, or environmental, cultural. or economic disadvantage.

(B) The term "Commissioner" means the Commissioner of Education.

20 USC 1411.

(c) Effective on the date upon which final regulations prescribed by the Commissioner of Education under subsection (b) take effect, the amendment made by subsection (a) is amended, in subparagraph (A) of section 611(a)(5) (as such subparagraph would take effect on the effective date of subsection (a)), by adding "and" at the end of clause (i), by striking out clause (ii), and by redesignating clause (iii) as clause (ii).

AMENDMENTS WITH RESPECT TO EMPLOYMENT OF HANDICAPPED INDIVID-UALS, REMOVAL OF ARCHITECTURAL BARRIERS, AND MEDIA CENTERS

SEC. 6. (a) Part A of the Act is amended by inserting after section 605 thereof the following new sections:

20 USC 1404.

"EMPLOYMENT OF HANDICAPPED INDIVIDUALS

"SEC. 606. The Secretary shall assure that each recipient of assistance under this Act shall make positive efforts to employ and advance in employment qualified handicapped individuals in programs assisted under this Act.

20 USC 1405.

"GRANTS FOR THE REMOVAL OF ARCHITECTURAL BARRIERS

"SEC. 607. (a) Upon application by any State or local educational agency or intermediate educational unit the Commissioner is authorized to make grants to pay part or all of the cost of altering existing buildings and equipment in the same manner and to the same extent as authorized by the Act approved August 12, 1968 (Public Law 90–480), relating to architectural barriers.

20 USC 1406.

"(b) For the purpose of carrying out the provisions of this section, there are authorized to be appropriated such sums as may be necessary.".

Appropriation authorization.

(b) Section 653 of the Act (20 U.S.C. 1453) is amended to read as follows:

"CENTERS ON EDUCATIONAL MEDIA AND MATERIALS FOR THE HANDICAPPED

"SEC. 653. (a) The Secretary is authorized to enter into agreements with institutions of higher education, State and local educational agencies, or other appropriate nonprofit agencies, for the establishment and operation of centers on educational media and materials for the handicapped, which together will provide a comprehensive program of activities to facilitate the use of new educational technology in education programs for handicapped persons, including designing, developing, and adapting instructional materials, and such other activities consistent with the purposes of this part as the Secretary may prescribe in such agreements. Any such agreement shall—

"(1) provide that Federal funds paid to a center will be used solely for such purposes as are set forth in the agreement; and

"(2) authorize the center involved, subject to prior approval by the Secretary, to contract with public and private agencies and organizations for demonstration projects.

"(b) In considering proposals to enter into agreements under this section, the Secretary shall give preference to institutions and agencies—

"(1) which have demonstrated the capabilities necessary for the development and evaluation of educational media for the handicapped; and

"(2) which can serve the educational technology needs of the Model High School for the Deaf (established under Public Law 89–694).

"(c) The Secretary shall make an annual report on activities carried out under this section which shall be transmitted to the Congress.".

80 Stat. 1027. Report to Congress.

CONGRESSIONAL DISAPPROVAL OF REGULATIONS

SEC. 7. (a)(1) Section 431(d)(1) of the General Education Provisions Act (20 U.S.C. 1232(d)(1)) is amended by inserting "final" immediately before "standard" each place it appears therein.

(2) The third sentence of section 431(d)(2) of such Act (20 U.S.C.

1232(d)(2)) is amended by striking out "proposed" and inserting in lieu thereof "final".

(3) The fourth and last sentences of section 431(d)(2) of such Act (20 U.S.C. 1232(d)(2)) each are amended by inserting "final" immediately before "standard".

(b) Section 431(d)(1) of the General Education Provisions Act (20 U.S.C. 1232(d)(1)) is amended by adding at the end thereof the following new sentence: "Failure of the Congress to adopt such a concurrent resolution with respect to any such final standard, rule, regulation, or requirement prescribed under any such Act, shall not represent, with respect to such final standard, rule, regulation, or requirement, an approval or finding of consistency with the Act from which it derives its authority for any purpose, nor shall such failure to adopt a concurrent resolution be construed as evidence of an approval or finding of consistency necessary to establish a prima facie case, or an inference or presumption, in any judicial proceeding.".

EFFECTIVE DATES

20 USC 1411 note.

SEC. 8. (a) Notwithstanding any other provision of law, the amendments made by sections 2(a), 2(b), and 2(c) shall take effect on July 1, 1975.

(b) The amendments made by sections 2(d), 2(e), 3, 6, and 7 shall take effect on the date of the enactment of this Act.

(c) The amendments made by sections 4 and 5(a) shall take effect on October 1, 1977, except that the provisions of clauses (A), (C), (D), and (E) of paragraph (2) of section 612 of the Act, as amended by this Act, section 617(a)(1)(D) of the Act, as amended by this Act, section 617(b) of the Act, as amended by this Act, and section 618(a) of the Act, as amended by this Act, shall take effect on the date of the enactment of this Act.

(d) The provisions of section 5(b) shall take effect on the date of the enactment of this Act.

Approved November 29, 1975.

LEGISLATIVE HISTORY:

HOUSE REPORTS: No. 94-332 accompanying H.R. 7217 (Comm. on Education and Labor) and 94-664 (Comm. of Conference).
SENATE REPORTS: No. 94-168 (Comm. on Labor and Public Welfare) and No. 94-455 (Comm. of Conference).
CONGRESSIONAL RECORD, Vol. 121 (1975):
    June 18, considered and passed Senate.
    July 21, 29, considered and passed House, amended, in lieu of H.R. 7217.
    Nov. 18, House agreed to conference report.
    Nov. 19, Senate agreed to conference report.
WEEKLY COMPILATION OF PRESIDENTIAL DOCUMENTS, Vol. 11, No. 49: Dec. 2, Presidential statement.

resources for teachers

appendix C

PROFESSIONAL BOOKS AND BULLETINS

Berry, Keith, E., *Models for Mainstreaming*. San Rafael, Calif.: Dimensions, 1972.

Birch, Jack W. *Mainstreaming: Educable Mentally Retarded Children in Regular Classes*. Reston, Va.: Council for Exceptional Children, 1974.

Bloom, Lois and Margaret Lehey, *Language Development and Language Disorders*. New York: John Wiley and Sons, 1978.

Busch and Giles, *Aid to Psycho Linguistic Teaching*. Columbus, Ohio: Charles E. Merrill Publishing Co., 1978.

Donahue, Gregory and Arthur Rainear, *Resource Room Approach to Mainstreaming*. *Complete Set*. Pitman, N.J.: Educational Improvement Center-South, n.d.

Fairchild, Thomas N. (series editor), *Mainstreaming Series*. Austin, Texas: Learning Concepts, 1975–1977.
Series Titles:
Behavior Disorders: Helping with Behavioral Problems, 1976.
The Communicatively Disordered Child: Management Procedures for the Classroom, 1977.
Counseling Exceptional Children: The Teacher's Role, 1977.
Education of the Severely/Profoundly Handicapped: What Is the Least Restrictive Alternative? 1977.
Individualized Educational Programming (IEP): *A Child Study Team Process*, 1977.
Keeping in Touch with Parents: The Teacher's Best Friends, 1977.
Mainstreaming Children with Learning Disabilities, 1976.
Mainstreaming Exceptional Children, 1976.
Mainstreaming the Gifted, 1976.
Mainstreaming the Hearing Impaired Child: An Educational Alternative, 1977.
Mainstreaming the Mentally Retarded Child, 1976.
Mainstreaming the Visually Impaired Child: Blind and Partially Sighted Students in the Regular Classroom, 1977.
Managing the Hyperactive Child in the Classroom, 1975.
The Physically Handicapped Child: Facilitating Regular Classroom Adjustment, 1977.
The Public Law Supporting Mainstreaming: A Guide for Teachers and Parents, 1977.

Fountain Valley Teacher Support System in Reading. Fountain Valley, California, 1972. Reference which lists commercial reading series and programs.

Frankly Speaking, free publication from NICSEM.

Gaddis, Edwin A. *Teaching the Slow Learner in the Regular Classroom*. Belmont, Calif.: Learn Siegler, 1971.

Glasser, Joyce Fern, *The Elementary School: Learning Center for Independent Study*. Parker, 1971.

Hammill, Donald D. and N. Bartel, *Teaching Children with Learning and Behavior Problems*. Boston: Allyn & Bacon, Inc., 1975.

Hammill, Donald and Wiederholdt Lee, *The Resource Room: Rationale and Implementation*. Philadelphia, Pa.: Buttonwood Farms, Inc., 1972.

Handbook I: *A Mainstream Approach to Identification, Assessment and Amelioration of Learning Disabilities*. Sioux Falls, S. D.: Adapt Press, 1973.

Hawisher, Margaret and Mary Calhoun, *The Resource Room: An Educational Asset for Children with Special Needs.* Columbus, Ohio: Charles E. Merrill Publishing Co., 1978.

Incentive Publications. *Kids Stuff.* Nashville, Tenn.
Series Titles:

Forte, Imogene. *Center Stuff for Nooks, Crannies and Corners.*

Collier, Mary Jo, Imogene Forte, Joy MacKenzie, *Kids Stuff Kindergarten and Nursery School.*

Frank, Marjorie. *Kids Stuff Math.*

Forte, Imogene, Marjorie Frank, and Joy McKenzie, *Kids Stuff, Reading and Language Experiences: Intermediate–Junior High.*

Forte, Imogene, and Joy McKenzie, *Kids Stuff, Reading and Language Experiences: Primary Level.*

Farnette, Cherrie, Imogene Forte, Barbara Loss, *Kids Stuff Reading and Writing Readiness.*

Forte Imogene and Mary Anne Pangle, *More Center Stuff for Nooks, Crannies and Corners.*

Farnette, Cherrie, Imogene Forte, Barbara Lass, *Special Kids Stuff.*

Forte, Imogene, Mary Ann Pangle, *Spelling Magic.*

Jahn, A. and J. Ysseldyke, *Assessment in Special Remedial Education,* Boston: Houghton Mifflin Co., 1976.

Johnson, R. and P. Magrah, *Developmental Disorders: Assessment Treatment and Education,* Baltimore: University Park Press, 1978.

Kahl, David H. and Barbara J. Gast, *Learning Centers in the Open Classroom.* Encino, Calif.: International Center for Educational Development, 1974.

Kaplan, Sandra Nina, *Change for Children: Ideas and Activities for Individualizing Learning.* Pacific Palisades, Calif.: Goodyear, 1973.

Karlin, Muriel Schoenbrun, *Individualizing Instruction: A Complete Guide for Diagnosis, Planning, Teaching and Evaluation.* West Nyack, N.Y.: Parker, 1974.

Kephart, Newll C., *The Slow Learner in the Classroom.* Columbus, Ohio: Charles E. Merrill Publishing Co., 1960.

Kreinberg, Nancy and Stanley H., L. Chou, (eds.) *Configurations of Change: The Integration of Mildly Handicapped Children into the Regular Classroom.* Sioux Falls, S. Dak. Adapt Press, n.d.

Lloyd, Dorothy M., *Seventy Activities for Classroom Learning Centers.* Dansville, N.Y.: Instructor Publications, 1974.

Mann, Philip, *Mainstream Special Education: Issues and Prespectives in Urban Centers.* Reston, Va. Council for Exceptional Children.

NICSEM, *Frankly Speaking.* University of Southern California, Los Angeles, Calif.

Parents Campaign. *Closer Look.* Washington D.C.: Parents Campaign for Handicapped Children and Youth.

Petreshene, Susan S., *Complete Guide to Learning Centers.* Palo Alto, Calif.: Pendragon House, Inc., 1978.

———, *Complete Guide to Learning Centers Supplement.* Palo Alto, Calif.: Pendragon House, Inc., 1978.

Ryan, Kevin and James Cooper, *Those Who Can Teach.* Boston: Houghton Mifflin Co., 1975.

Reynolds, Maynard C. and Malcolm D. Davis (eds.), *Exceptional Children in Regular Classrooms*. Minneapolis, Minn. Dept. of Audio-Visual Extension, 1971.

Selecting Instructional Materials for Purchase: Procedural Guidelines. Washington, D.C.: National Education Association, 1972.

Siegel, Ernest, *Special Education in the Regular Classroom.* New York: Harper & Row Publishers, Inc.

Special Learning Corp. *Mainstreaming Library.* Guilford, Conn.
    Series Titles
    Special Education
    Learning Disabilities
    Mental Retardation
    Autism
    Behavior Modification
    Speech and Hearing
    Deaf Education
    Emotional and Behavioral Disorders
    Diagnosis and Placement
    Dyslexia
    Visually Handicapped Education
    Physically Handicapped Education
    Gifted and Talented Education
    Mainstreaming
    Psychology of Exceptional Children

Swift, Marshall S. and George Spivak, *Alternative Teaching Strategies.* Champaign, Ill.: Research Press, 1977.

Turnbull Ann B. and Jane B. Shultz, *Mainstreaming Handicapped Students.* Boston: Allyn & Bacon, Inc., Longwood Division, 1978.

Wallace, Gerald and Stephen C. Larsen, *Educational Assessment of Learning Problems: Testing for Teaching.* Boston: Allyn & Bacon, Inc., 1978.

Watson, Marjorie, *Mainstreaming the Educable Mentally Retarded.* Washington, D.C.: National Education Association, 1975.

ADDITIONAL REFERENCES

The following list (compiled by the Northeast Regional Resource Center, Hightstown, New Jersey) contains items helpful to the resource room teacher which can be ordered by mail.

The Assessment of Children with Sensory Impairments: A Selected Bibliography
    National Center on Educational Media & Materials for the Handicapped
    The Ohio State University
    220 West 12th Avenue
    Columbus, OH 43210

Behavior Modification Techniques for Special Education
    MSS Information Corporation
    655 Madison Avenue
    New York, NY 10021

    Contact–Stanley A. Winters, Editor
            Eunice Cox, Editor

    Presented is a collection of 32 articles concerned with the techniques and
    effectiveness of behavior modification programs in a variety of educational
    settings and used with children of many different categories—severely re-
    tarded, austistic, emotionally disturbed, delinquent, nonreading.

Bibliography of Literature Pertaining to the Trainable Mentally Handicapped
    Instructional Materials Center
    1020 South Spring Street
    Springfield, IL 62706

    Presented is a bibliography of articles and texts concerned with the trainable
    mentally retarded regarding arts and crafts, curriculum, parents, speech,
    vocational rehabilitation.

A Bibliography of Resource in Sex Education for the Mentally Retarded
    Behavioral Publications
    72 Fifth Avenue
    New York, NY 10011

CEC Information Center on Exceptional Children
    (ERIC Clearinghouse)
    1920 Association Drive
    Reston, VA 22091

    Provides many relevant bibliographies including:
    1. A Selected Guide to Public Agencies Concerned with Exceptional Children
    2. Directory of Services and Facilities
    3. Learning Disabilities—Early Identification
    4. Learning Disabilities—Elementary Level
    5. Competency Based Teacher Education and Evaluation
    6. Early Childhood Intervention—Exceptionalities

*Compendium of Noncommercially Prepared Nonprint Resources on Educational Personnel
    Preparation* by Wesley C. Meirhenry. ERIC Document Reproduction Service,
    P.O. Box 190, Arlington, VA 22210. 1974. Write for cost information.

    A handy annotated source for selecting mediated teacher training materials
    produced by institutional or nonprofit agencies. Materials are listed alphabet-
    ically by title according to format. Information about production date, cost,
    and suitability for use is included.

Curriculum Materials for Vocational Technical Career Education
    Rutgers University
    Graduate School of Education
    Vocational-Technical Department
    New Brunswick, NJ 08903

    1975 List of vocational technical instructional materials.

Descriptive Materials List
    Lois Davis
    Clifford W. Beers Clinic
    One State Street
    New Haven, CT 06510

Developmental screens, behavior evaluation tools, parent inventories, developmental guidelines, preschool curriculum bibliographies, and videotapes. Useful for both teachers and parents. Free.

Directory of Facilities for the Learning Disabled and Handicapped. C. Ellingson and James Cass, Harper & Row, New York, NY 1972. Descriptions of diagnostic, remedial, therapeutic, and developmental programs listed by state.

A Directory of Selected Resources in Special Education. Compiled by Merrimack Education Center, 101 Mill Road, Chelmsford, MA 01824. 1975. Free.

Useful, up-to-date resources for program administrators, teacher trainers, and parents. Described are programs, projects, classroom techniques, testing/evaluation/assessment tools, child use media and materials, and teacher training materials. Bibliography and ERIC references are included.

Early Childhood Assessment List. Compiled by the Northeast Regional Resource Center, 168 Bank Street, Hightstown, NJ 08520.

Describes a variety of carefully selected assessment tools designed for preschool and early childhood use.

Early Childhood Education for the Handicapped
The American Association for the Education of the
Severely/Profoundly Handicapped
College of Education
Experimental Education Unit
University of Washington
Seattle, WA

Presented is a bibliography of early childhood articles and texts concerned with special education, social factors, paraprofessions, communications development, parents and curriculum.

Educational Technology for the Severely Handicapped–A Comprehensive Bibliography
Personnel Training Program for the Education of the Severely Handicapped
Kansas Neurological Institute
3107 West 21st Street
Topeka, KS 66604

Presented is a bibliography of articles and texts concerned with the severely handicapped and regarding behavior, curriculum, parent training, vocational skills, self-help skills, and speech.

Handicapped Children in Head Start Series: Directory of Selected Instructional Materials. Council for Exceptional Children (CEC). Head Start Information Project, 1920 Association Drive, Reston, VA 22091. 1974. Free.

An annotated listing of commercial materials designed to be used by Head Start teachers serving handicapped children. Materials are listed by areas of instruction and by instructional objectives. Visual Discrimination. Publisher, item description, price, and some use suggestions are given.

Help for the Handicapped Child. Florence Weiner, McGraw-Hill, New York, NY, 1973.

An introduction to public and private services which may be used by the parents of the handicapped.

Home Stimulation and *Exploring Materials.* Two manuals for parents and others working with young children with special needs. Commonwealth Mental Health Foundation, 4 Marlboro Road, Lexington, MA 02173. Payment must accompany orders.

Manual Communication. Dean A. Christopher, University Park Press, 1976.

Contains forty-eight lessons that clearly illustrate, with step-by-step written instructions, more than 800 signs and letters. These are presented in a sophisticated professional format intended for specialists and career-minded students and include encoding and decoding practice exercises with each lesson.

The book first introduces the American Manual Alphabet and basic number concepts, then develops the basic vocabulary of traditional (American Sign Language) signs that are the building blocks needed to communicate in sign language. The lessons form self-contained teaching units covering twenty signs each (suitable for normal class sessions) covering both function and content words so students quickly learn to formulate and communicate in sentences. Signs for morphemic elements are also presented early in the text to encourage students to master the skill of communicating in the Simultaneous Method.

The final four lessons of the book apply manual communication to hearing, speech, and language evaluation in clinical practice. These cover children's case histories, hearing aid evaluation, and related topics.

Medical Problems in the Classroom. Robert Haslam and Peter Valletutti (eds.). Baltimore: University Park Press, 1976.

Multimedia Materials for Teaching Young Children: A Bibliography of Multicultural Resources by Harry A. Johnson. National Leadership Institute/Teacher Education, University of Connecticut, Storrs, CT 06268.

Describes films, filmstrips, recordings, study prints, multimedia kits, and books for teachers and parents.

NICSEM (National Information Center for Special Education Materials)
National Center on Educational Media & Materials for the Handicapped–U.S.C.University Park (RAN) 2nd Floor
Los Angeles, CA 90007

NICSEM is a computer-based on-line interactive retrieval system to aid persons in locating information in the area of special education. Will conduct searches in specific content areas. Now available is information on child use instructional materials and teacher training materials. The system will also contain information about measurement and evaluation materials and prototype materials.

New Haven Preschool Program for Handicapped Children
Lois Davis
Clifford W. Beers Clinic
One State St.
New Haven, CT 06510
Provide preschool screening survey.

Nonvocal Communication Techniques and Aids for the Severly Physically Handicapped.
Gregg C. Vanderheiden and Kate Girilley (eds.). Baltimore: University Park Press, 1976.

The first section of the book reviews the problem of communication for the severely handicapped, discusses the development of alternate communication systems, and introduces nonvocal communication techniques and aids including scanning, encoding, and direct selection. The second section deals with the tools with detailed training sections on each technique. Section three reviews results as seen in four actual programs while the fourth and final section covers what is needed now in terms of the present state of the art and future requirements for progress in nonvocal communication.

A Parent Kit
A. G. Bell Association for the Deaf
3417 Volta Place N.W.
Washington, DC 20007
Introductory materials for parents of deaf and hard of hearing children.

The Preschool Multiply Handicapped—A Selected Bibliography
Instructional Materials Center
1020 South Spring Street
Springfield, IL 62706
Contact: G. F. Wolinsky

Presented is a bibliography of articles and texts concerned with multiply handicapped children of preschool age regarding language development, curriculum, and assessment.

Publisher Source Directory
National Center on Educational Media & Materials for the Handicapped
The Ohio State University
220 West 12th Avenue
Columbus, OH 43210
Pub. # NC-75.302

Contains listings of 1,686 commercial producers of instructional materials and organizations for the handicapped. References each listing as to the primary population dealt with and services or materials provided.

Reintegrating Mentally Retarded People Into the Community (Annotated Bibliography)
Contact: Publications
            The Council for Exceptional Children
            1920 Association Drive
            Reston, VA 22091

A Resource Guide in Sex Education for the Mentally Retarded, American Association for Health, Physical Education & Recreation, 1201 16th Street, N.W., Washington, DC, 1971.

Selected Bibliography Related to Parents as Behavior Modifiers
Experimental Education Unit
Child Development & Mental Retardation Center
University of Washington
Seattle, WA 98195

Contact: American Association for the Education of the Severely/Profoundly
            Handicapped

The bibliography was compiled by Robert York of the Badge School in Madison, Wisconsin which is a Bureau of Education for the Handicapped funded project. The bibliography includes journal articles and texts. The references are not all necessarily for parents, but for professionals who work with parents.

A Selected Bibliography Related to the Vocational Training of Severely Handicapped Persons
American Association for the Education of the Severely/Profoundly Handicapped
Experimental Education Unit
University of Washington
Seattle, WA 98195

Presented is an annotated bibliography of articles and texts concerned with the vocational training of severely handicapped persons.

Special People Behind the Eight Ball: An Annotated Bibliography of Literature Classified by Handicapping Conditions
  Source: MAFAX Associates, Inc.
      90 Cherry Street
      Johnstown, PA 15902

Suggested Program Assessment Checklist
  State University of New York, Albany
  State Education Department
  Albany, NY

  This instructional binder gives teachers specific activities which address the weaknesses and utilize the strengths of the individual child in providing educational instruction. Appropriate to a broad range of handicapping conditions, the programming is integrative and does not seek to train specific abilities in isolation or to utilize isolated abilities as compensatory behaviors.

Teaching the MR Child: A Family Care Approach, K. Bernard & M.L. Powell, St. Louis, Mo.: The C.V. Mosby Company, 1972.
  Emphasis on self-help skills.

University Park Press
  Chamber of Commerce Building
  Baltimore, MD 21202

  Publishes primarily in the area of speech, hearing, language and audiology. Many publications deal with recent research into particular content areas. Useful for teachers and professionals.

Vocational Instructional Materials for Students with Special Needs
  Northwest Regional Educational Laboratory
  700 Lindsay Building
  710 S.W. Second Avenue
  Portland, OR 97204

  Contains list of publications and materials for use in prevocational and vocational training, with many items abstracted. Areas covered include language skills, health occupations, trade and industrial occupations, and public service occupations, 1972.

ANNOTATION OF SELECTED COMPANIES

Academic Therapy Publicatons
  1539 Fourth Street
  San Rafael, CA 94901

  Publishes a *Directory of Educational Facilities for the Learning Disabled.* Also provides materials in the area of teacher training, instructional manuals, etc.

Bowmar
  622 Rodier Drive
  Glendale, CA 91201

  Provides instructional materials in many areas including visual perception and motor skills development. Aids are available in the area of affective development including body image and emotion.

Childcraft Education Corp.
>20 Kilmer Road
>Edison, NJ 08817
>
>Produces instructional materials for large scope of problem areas including: motor skills, eye-hand coordination, visual and auditory perception and discrimination, and articulation and language development. Also available, special items for the blind and the hearing impaired or deaf.
>
>The company stresses the adaptability of its materials for assessment purposes.

Developmental Learning Materials
>7440 North Natchez Avenue
>Niles, IL 60648
>
>Produces instructional materials primarily dealing with motor and perceptual skills. Also other manipulative materials which can be adapted for more specific handicapping conditions.

Edmark Association
>13249 Northrup Way
>Bellevue, WA 98005
>
>Provides instructional materials, many specifically for the handicapped. Many materials to aid in teaching self-help skills for both parents and teachers.

Perceptual Development Laboratories
>P.O. Box 1911
>Big Spring, TX 79720
>
>Produces tests which may be used for assessment purposes, linguistic materials, programmed materials, and projection equipment.

Remediation Associates, Inc.
>Box 318
>Linden, NJ 07036
>
>Produces professional reference materials for staff use as well as materials for preservice and in-service training of staff.

University of Utah
>Educational Media Center
>297 Bennion Hall
>Salt Lake City, UT 84109
>
>Many instructional materials in the training of self-help skills to be used by both parents and teachers.

in-service materials

appendix D

IN-SERVICE MATERIALS

Accepting Individual Differences
Developmental Learning Materials, 1977, $25.00
Four flip books, cassette, five guides.

The kit contains discussion-stimulating color photographs and narratives, dealing with visual impairments, hearing impairments, and mental retardation/learning disabilities.

Approaches to Mainstreaming: Teaching the Special Child in the Regular Classroom. Units One and Two.
Teaching Resources, 1976 and 1977, $76.00 each unit
Filmstrips and cassettes.

These units are useful for in-serivce workshops, college courses, paraprofessional training, and individual teacher study. They focus on specific day-to-day considerations and problems that classroom teachers commonly encounter.

Classroom Management Through Behavior Modification.
Media Informational Systems (available from Media Educational Materials) $12.00
Record

Dr. Kyle gives three management steps to assist teachers in handling disruptive behavior within the classroom.

Coming Back . . . Or Never Leaving: Instructional Programming for Handicapped Students in the Mainstream.
Charles E. Merrill Publishing Co. (Also available from Media Fair), 1977, $145.00 Five filmstrips, five cassettes, book, guide.

The program is designed to assist local education agencies in developing and implementing comprehensive plans for special education, especially for mainstreaming mildly handicapped students, K–12.

DLM Teaching and Learning Series.
For teachers, parents and aids. Video tapes.
I-Sequencing memory and language.
II-Coordination and readiness activities.

The Dyslexic Child: A Teaching View Point.
Media Productions
A recording for teacher training and awareness.

EBSCO IEP-2 (Instructional Exceptional Prescriptions): *A Program on Behavioral, Attitudinal and Pre-Academic Competencies.*
EBSCO Curriculum Materials, 1977, $89.00

IEP-2 provides instructional method cards for teachers of the behaviorally disordered and mildly impaired. Some of the competencies covered are handwriting, reasoning, auditory and sensory perception, listening, self-control, attention span, honesty, task completion.

Educational Aspects of Learning Disabilities.
Media Informational Systems (available from Media Educational Materials), $10.00
Record

This recording deals with a specialized aspect of caring for a child with a learning disability.

Even Love Is Not Enough: Children with Handicaps.
> Parents Magazine Films, 1975, $65.00 per unit
> Four units, each unit has five filmstrips, three cassettes, five scripts, one guide.
> Unit 1: Behavioral and Emotional Disabilities.
> Unit 2: Physical Disabilities.
> Unit 3: Intellectual Disabilities.
> Unit 4: Educational and Language Disabilities.

Exceptional Teaching.
> Charles E. Merrill Publishing Co., 1976.
> Filmstrips and cassettes designed to help the participant develop basic teaching skills and techniques for monitoring student progress.

Goalguide: A Minicourse in Writing Goal and Behavioral Objectives for Special Education.
> Fearon, 1975, $5.00
> Participant manual and workbook, instructor's manual.
> Goalguide is an instructional package for teachers, therapists, and administrators who work with the developmentally disabled. It contains nine hours of in-service or individual study.

"Hello everybody . . ." about Handicapped Kids . . . for Kids.
> James Stanfield Film Associates, 1977, $175.00
> Six filmstrips, six cassettes, teacher's guide, pamphlets.
> This program deals with hearing and speech impairment, visual impairment, orthopedic handicaps, developmental disabilities, learning disabilities and behavior disorders. The program may be found effective with students, teachers, and parents.

How Can Tests Be Unfair? A workshop on nondiscriminatory testing. Council for Exceptional Children, 1975, $35.00
> Cassette and print materials.
> Six stimulation activities allow participants to experience test biases encountered by children with different language or cultural backgrounds, perceptual or motor problems.

I'll Promise You a Tomorrow
> Hallmark Films and Recording Inc., 1974
> The child is prepared for the special class setting. Twenty minutes.
> 16 mm film.

Individualized Education Program Kit.
> MESA Publications, 1977, $14.95
> The materials (process flow sheet, IEP planning folder, and forms for documenting the process) provide a framework and format for systematically administering a special education program.

Individualized Educational Programming (IEP): A Child Study Team Process.
> Learning Concepts, 1977, $49.95
> One filmstrip, one cassette, one guide, one textbook.
> The kit assists in the acquisition of knowledge, skills, and attitudes necessary for the successful implementation of the IEP requirement of Public Law 94–142.

Inside the Resource Room
F.A.M.E. Filming Corp., 20 Mountainside Dr., Chatham, NJ, 1979 ½ inch video VHS format or ¾ inch videotape.

Actual scenes from *The Resource Room Primer* model program.

In-service and Pre-Service Program on Specific Learning Disabilities.
Paul S. Amidon, 1973, $175.00

Guide, ten cassettes, eighty-two transparencies, sixteen hand-out sheets.

This program may be used by regular classroom teachers, school psychologists, speech and language therapists, and learning disabilities specialists. It provides a view of learning and language disorders and offers practical suggestions for dealing with them.

Keeping in Touch with Parents: The Teacher's Best Friends.
Learning Concepts, 1977, $49.95
One filmstrip, one cassette, one guide, one textbook.

The kit assists in the acquisition of knowledge, skills, and attitudes necessary to successfully involve parents in the education of their children.

A New Look at the Retarded Child
Edmark, 1976, $85.00
Five filmstrips, five cassettes, guide.

This material may be used with adult community groups, in-service groups and in regular classrooms to correct misimpressions about the retarded.

Nobody Like Jimmy.
Jab Press, 1975, $29.00
Filmstrip and cassette, 17 minutes.

The role of the speech and language specialist is shown through a specific case history.

The Public Law Supporting Mainstreaming: A Guide for Teachers and Parents.
Learning Concepts, 1977, $49.95.
One filmstrip, one cassette, one guide, one textbook.

The kit assists in the acquisition of knowledge, skills, and attitudes necessary for the successful implementation of the requirements of Public Law 94–142, particularly the due process procedures and procedural safeguards that need to be implemented consistently in local school districts.

Resource Teachers Simulation Training Packet
Charles E. Merrill Publishing Co., 1978

Four sound filmstrips, instructor's manual, text. Illustrates steps to set up a resource room. Ten minutes.

Search and Teach
Walker Educational Book Corp., 1976, $64.90

Search is a test to locate vulnerable children, and *Teach* is a resource book of instructional tasks designed to mesh with *Search*. *Search and Teach* detects learning difficulties in five and six-year-old children and helps prevent later school failure.

Social Learning Curriculum.
Charles E. Merrill Publishing Co., $195.00
Multimedia format.

Emphasis is placed on the day-to-day functioning processes of thinking clearly and acting independently.

The Special Needs Child in the Regular Classroom.
Media Informational Systems (available from Media Educational Materials), $48.00

Teacher Training Program: Mainstreaming Mildly Handicapped Students in the Regular Classroom.
Education Service Center, Region XIII, Austin, TX
Program Titles:

Instructional Management Data Bank.
1975, $108.00 Kit
The materials are to aid in the efficient management of an individualized instructional program. Six instructional formats (IEPs, contracts, learning stations, job sheets, activity cards, programmed instruction) are presented.

Mainstreaming Data Bank.
1975, $60.00 Kit
The program focuses on the major concepts and issues related to mainstream education, and proposes that special students can be successfully mainstreamed into the regular classroom if individualized instructional techniques and processes are used.

Learning Styles Data Bank.
1975, $37.00 Kit
The program focuses on learning and teaching styles and on suiting instructional strategies to the assessed learning style of the student.

Influencing Behavior Data Bank.
1975, $44.00
The material focuses on concepts and skills for positively influencing student behavior and describes two effective ways of avoiding or changing inappropriate behavior: environmental changes and contingency management.

Curriculum Data Bank.
1975, $23.00
The kit examines some of the curriculum problems evident in the classroom and some ways to deal with those problems.

They Can Learn
Real Time Media (also available from McGraw-Hill Films), 1975, $99.50.
Six filmstrips, six cassettes, guide.

The kit is designed to help the regular classroom teacher understand the nature of learning disabilities and the importance of evaluation, and to develop specific techniques for educational management and remediation.

A Walk in Another Pair of Shoes
California Association for Neurologically Handicapped Children, 1972, $6.90.

Eighteen minute color-filmstrip with cassette. A good introduction to difficulties faced by a neurologically handicapped student.

What Is a Handicap?
BFA Educational Media, 1975, $76.50, grades 4–6.
Four filmstrips, four cassettes, twenty-four spirit masters, open-ended fs.

Mark cannot walk; Rosa has difficulty hearing; Cindy cries easily; Tony learns slowly.

Whatever Happened to Prince Planet.
Media Informational Systems (available from Media Educational Materials), $10.00.
Record.
This report tells the story of one boy identified as being emotionally disturbed and highly intelligent.

Who Is the Gifted Child?
Ventura County Superintendent of Schools, $20.00
Filmstrip, cassette, guide, script; nine minutes.

The filmstrip assists parents, educators and teachers discover the basic nature underlying the four types of giftedness and talent development: academic, creative, kinesthetic, psychosocial.

Why Am I Different?
Barr Films, 1978, $90.00.
Four filmstrips, four cassettes, teacher's guide.

The series examines children with mobility handicaps, hearing impairment, visual loss and mental retardation. The program is designed to show how exceptional children think and feel, what they can and cannot do, how to treat them fairly, why everyone should learn to understand their hopes, fears, capabilities and limitations.

IN-SERVICE PRODUCERS

Paul S. Amidon Assoc. Inc.
1966 Benson Ave.
St. Paul, MN 55116

Barr Films
3490 East Foothill Blvd.
Pasadena, CA 91107

BFA Educational Media
2211 Michigan Ave.
P.O. 1795
Santa Monica, CA 90406

California Assoc. for Neurologically
Handicapped Children
Literature Distribution Office
P.O. Box 4088
Los Angeles, CA 90051

Council for Exceptional Children
(CEC)
1920 Association Drive
Reston, VA 22091

Developmental Learning Materials
7440 Natchez Ave.
Niles, IL 60648

EBSCO Inc.
First Ave No. & Thirteenth Street
Birmingham, AL 35203

Edmark Associates
655 South Orcas St.
Seattle, WA 98108

Education Service Center
Region # 13
Austin, TX 78701

Fearon Publishing Co.
2165 Park Blvd.
Palo Alto, CA 94306

Hallmark Films
1511 East North Ave.
Baltimore, MD 21213

JAB Press, Inc.
P.O. Box 213
Fairlawn, NJ 07410

Learning Concepts
2501 North Lamar
Austin, TX 78705

Media Educational Materials
2936 Remington Ave.
Baltimore, MD 21211

Charles E. Merrill Publishing Co.
1300 Alum Creek Drive
Columbus, OH 43216

MESA Publications
P.O. Box 3824
Austin, TX 78764

Parents Magazine
52 Vanderbilt Ave.
New York, NY 10017

Real Time Media Films
2200 Nineteenth Street, N.W.
#306
Washington, DC 20009

James Stanfield Film Association
P.O. Box 851
Pasadena, CA 91102

Teaching Resources
100 Boylston St.
Boston, MA 02116

Ventura County Superintendent of
Schools
Ventura, CA

Walker Educational Book Corp.
720 Fifth Avenue
New York, NY 10019

national
special education
agencies
and addresses

appendix E

AUTISM

National Society for Autistic
Children
169 Tampa Avenue
Albany, NY 12208

BLIND

American Council for the Blind
1211 Connecticut Avenue, N.W.
Washington, DC 20036

American Foundation for the Blind
15 West 16 Street
New York, NY 10011

National Association for Visually
Handicapped
305 East 24th Street
New York, NY 10010

National Federation for the Blind
1346 Connecticut Avenue, N.W.
Dupont Circle Bldg., Suite 212
Washington, DC 20036

CEREBRAL PALSY

United Cerebral Palsy Association
66 East 34th Street
New York, NY 10016

DEAF

Alexander Graham Bell Association
for the Deaf
3417 Volta Place, N.W.
Washington, DC 20007

National Association of the Deaf
814 Thayer Avenue
Silver Spring, MD 20910

DEAF-BLIND

American Association of Workers
for the Blind
1511 K Street N.W.
Washington, DC 20005

American Printing House for the
Blind
1839 Frankfort Avenue
Louisville, KY 40206

National Braille Asociation
85 Godwin Avenue
Midland Park, NJ 07432

National Deaf-Blind Program
Bureau of Education for the
Handicapped
Room 4046, Donohoe Building
400 6th Street, S.W.
Washington, DC 20202

Science for the Blind
221 Rock Hill Road
Bala-Cynwyd, PA 19004

EMOTIONALLY DISTURBED

Mental Health Association,
National Headquarters
1800 North Kent Street
Arlington, VA 22209

EPILEPSY

Epilepsy Foundation of America
1828 L Street, N.W.
Washington, DC 20036

HEALTH IMPAIRMENTS

Allergy Foundation of America
801 Second Avenue
New York, NY 10017

American Cancer Society
777 Third Avenue
New York, NY 10017

American Heart Association
7320 Greenville Avenue
Dallas, TX 75231

Cystic Fibrosis Foundation
3379 Peachtree Road, N.E.
Atlanta, GA 30326

Juvenile Diabetes Foundation
23 East 26th Street
New York, NY 10010

National Hemophilia Foundation
25 West 39th Street
New York, NY 10018

National Kidney Foundation
Two Park Avenue
New York, NY 10016

National Tay-Sachs Foundation and
Allied Diseases Association
122 East 42nd. Street
New York, NY 10017

LEARNING DISABILITIES

American Association of Special
Educators
Box 168
Fryeburg, ME 04037

Association for Children with
Learning Disabilities
4156 Library Road
Pittsburgh, PA 15234

Learning Research and Development
Center
160 North Craig Street
Pittsburgh, PA 15213

Perceptual Development Laboratories
P.O. Box 1911
Big Spring, TX 79720

MENTAL RETARDATION

American Association for the
Education of the Severely/
Profoundly Handicapped
Experiment Education Unit
Child Development and Mental
Retardation Center
University of Washington
Seattle, WA 98195

American Association on Mental
Deficiency
5201 Connecticut Avenue, N.W.
Washington, DC 20015

National Association for Down's
Syndrome
P.O. Box 63
Oak Park, IL 60303

National Association for Retarded
Citizens
2709 Avenue E East
P.O. Box 6109
Arlington, TX 76011

National Down's Syndrome Congress
528 Ashland Avenue
River Forest, IL 60305

PHYSICALLY HANDICAPPED

American Medical Association
535 North Dearborn Street
Chicago, IL 60610

Arthritis Foundation
3400 Peachtree Road, N.E.
Atlanta, Ga 30326

Muscular Dystrophy Association, Inc.
810 Seventh Avenue
New York, NY 10019

National Multiple Sclerosis Society
205 East 42nd Street
New York, NY 10017

National Paraplegia Foundation
333 North Michigan Avenue
Chicago, IL 60601

Spina Bifida Association of America
343 South Dearborn Street
Room 319
Chicago, IL 60604

SPEECH IMPAIRMENTS

American Speech and Hearing
Association
10801 Rockville Pike
Rockville, MD 20852

Language Research Associates
175 East Delaware Place
Chicago, IL 60611

Speech and Language Materials, Inc.
P.O. Box 721
Tulsa, OK 74101

ALL DISABILITIES

American Institute for Research
in the Behavioral Sciences
P.O. Box 1113
1791 Arastraden Road
Palo Alto, CA 94302

American Coalition for Citizens
with Disabilities
1346 Connecticut Avenue, N.W.
Suite 1124
Washington, DC 20036

Center for the Study of
Evaluation
UCLA Graduate School of Education
Los Angeles, CA 90024

National Easter Seal Society for
Crippled Children and Adults
2023 W. Ogden Avenue
Chicago, IL 60612

National Foundation–March of Dimes
1275 Mamaroneck Avenue
White Plains, NY 10606

Northwest Regional Educational Lab.
710 S.W. Second Avenue
500 Lindsay Building
Portland, OR 79204

Remediation Association, Inc.
Box 318
Linden, NJ 07036

Special Education Materials
Development Center (SEMDC)
5401 Westbard Avenue
Washington, DC 20016

Council for Exceptional Children
1920 Association Drive
Reston, VA 22091

MISCELLANEOUS

American Alliance for Health,
Physical Education & Recreation
1201 16th Street, N.W.
Washington, DC 20036

Bibliographic Retrieval Services, Inc.
Corporation Park
Building 702
Scotia, NY 12302

Lockheed Information Systems
Building 201
3251 Hanover Street
Palo Alto, CA 94304

National Association of State
Boards of Education
444 North Capitol Street, N.W.
Washington, DC 20001

National Association of State
Directors of Special Education
NEA Building
1201 16th Street, N.W.
Washington, DC 20036

Northwestern University Press
1735 Benson Avenue
Evanston, IL 60201

University of Utah Educational
Media Center
207 Bennion Hall
Salt Lake City, UT 84109

index